# Iconoclast

# Iconoclast

*A Neuroscientist
Reveals How to
Think Differently*

Gregory Berns, MD, PhD

Harvard Business Press
Boston, Massachusetts

Library of Congress Cataloging-in-Publication Data

Berns, Gregory.
  Iconoclast : a neuroscientist reveals how to think differently / Gregory Berns.
    p. cm.
  ISBN 978-1-4221-3330-9 (pbk. : alk. paper)  1.   Neuropsychology.  2.
Iconoclasm.  3.   Psychology, Industrial.  4.   Creative ability. I. Title.
  QP360.B52 2010
  612.8—dc22

                                                                2009047178

The paper used in this publication meets the requirements of the American National Standard for Permanence of Paper for Publications and Documents in Libraries and Archives Z39.48-1992.

*For Helen and Madeline.*

*Nobody can tell you what can't be done.*

# CONTENTS

# ACKNOWLEDGMENTS

As much as writing is a solitary affair, the ideas in this book came from my interactions with a remarkable group of friends and colleagues. Within the field of neuroeconomics, I cherish the exchanges I've had with Dan Ariely, Peter Bossaerts, Colin Camerer, Ernst Fehr, Dan Houser, Scott Huettel, Brian Knutson, David Laibson, George Loewenstein, Kevin McCabe, Read Montague, John O'Doherty, Elizabeth Phelps, Michael Platt, and Antonio Rangel. In the real world—that is, nonacademia—I am particularly grateful for the time and wisdom that these people have given to me: Reda Anderson, Dale Chihuly, David Dreman, Jim Lavoie, Joe Marino, and Michael Mauboussin. I am very lucky to have a wonderful group of colleagues at Emory University who encourage and stimulate unusual ways of thinking: Monica Capra, Clint Kilts, Helen Mayberg, Andrew Miller, Charles Nemeroff, Charles Noussair, Mike Owens, Giuseppe Pagnoni, and Charles Raison. All of the research that has been done in my lab would not have occurred without an extremely talented and inspirational group to whom I am eternally grateful: Pammi Chandrasekhar, Jonathan Chappelow, Jan Engelmann, Whitney Herron, Sara Moore, Allison Turner, and Cary Zink. Without my agent, Susan Arellano, and my editor, Jacqueline Murphy, none of this would have made it onto the page.

I owe special thanks to my daughters, Helen and Madeline, for their patience (even if they didn't know it) with my writing time. This book is for you. And finally, to my wife, Kathleen: thanks and love for tolerating this writing expedition and for reading it before anyone should have been forced to read it!

# Doing What Can't Be Done

JANUARY 31, 1954, WAS TO be a special day for Howard Armstrong. It marked the fortieth anniversary of sharing the results of his first great invention with his longtime friend, and president of RCA, David Sarnoff. More than any other person, Armstrong was responsible for the three basic technologies that make radio and television possible. In addition to his first discovery, called *regeneration*, which is the technique that allows radio signals to be amplified, Armstrong invented the *superheterodyne receiver*, which transforms high-frequency radio waves into audible sound waves. But his crowning achievement, and his ultimate undoing, was the creation of FM radio—a technology that the entire radio industry had dismissed as inferior.[1]

Although Armstrong and Sarnoff had once been close friends, their relationship had turned acrimonious through years of fighting over patent rights. The legal battles took a steep emotional and financial toll on Armstrong. Since he was never one to accept the opinions of the majority, his colleagues were therefore puzzled when Armstrong removed the air conditioner from the window of his thirteenth-floor apartment overlooking the East River and stepped into the freezing wind of that bleak January night. Edwin Howard Armstrong, the most iconoclastic and influential engineer of radio technology, died as he had lived his life: iconoclastically and, ultimately, alone.

Much of what Armstrong did ran counter to accepted wisdom. Armstrong thumbed his nose at authority, taking nothing for granted except what he could see with his own eyes. As he liked to say, "It's the things people know, that ain't so."[2] Ultimately, he was proved right. His invention of FM radio exemplified the benefits of the rugged individualist who shatters dogmatic thinking. And his suicide underscored the costs. But rather than deal with vague ideas of innovation or psychological constructs like nonconformity or personality traits, I will take an unorthodox view of iconoclasts like Armstrong. In this book, I will dig into the biological basis for iconoclastic thinking—the brain—and how this bit of biology sabotages creative thinking for most ordinary people.

Ever since Guglielmo Marconi had unveiled his wireless telegraph in 1896, the basic technology of radio used amplitude modulation (AM). AM's main advantage was simplicity. Take a radio wave oscillating at a high frequency and change—modulate—it by whatever signal you wish to transmit. AM works quite well as long as the modulating signal is much lower in frequency than the carrier wave. In fact, it worked so well that the radio industry mushroomed around the idea of bringing broadcasts into people's homes. Having installed the first transmitter on the Empire State Building when it was completed in 1931, RCA was at the vanguard of this industry. But anyone who has listened to AM radio knows its limitations. It is noisy; stations interfere with each other; and it is low fidelity.

All this was well known in the 1930s. Radio engineers had discussed the possibility of a different technology based on frequency modulation (FM), but a prominent mathematician who worked for AT&T published a mathematical proof of why FM would be no better than AM radio. The proof was accepted wholesale by virtually every radio engineer. Except Armstrong.

Armstrong had a particular disdain for egghead types who made pronouncements by mathematical chicanery. Armstrong took these theoretical conclusions as a challenge to show not only that the legions of radio engineers were wrong but that he could create something superior. The technical challenges to create an FM receiver were formidable. It took Armstrong nearly eight years to solve the fundamental problem. But by 1934, when he demonstrated it to Sarnoff, the results were startling. For the first time ever, transmitting between RCA's antenna on the Empire State Building and a receiver on Long Island, they could hear with clarity the sounds of someone pouring a glass of water or crumpling a piece of paper. Music was as clear as if you were sitting in a concert hall. Gone was the hiss of AM. In its place was high fidelity.

Sarnoff, as president of RCA, was heavily invested in AM technology. He reacted as would anyone who had to protect the status quo. Perhaps out of fear, but certainly out of necessity, Sarnoff put his best engineers on the problem of discrediting the superiority of his friend's discovery. The strategy worked for a while. He forced Armstrong to remove his transmitter from the Empire State Building. But Armstrong was tenacious. He countered by building his own transmitter across the Hudson River in New Jersey. Compared with RCA's, Armstrong's transmitter was tiny, but the fact that he could broadcast with such high fidelity with low power only made his case for FM stronger. Although Armstrong did eventually license FM technology to General Electric and AT&T, RCA held out, refusing to make deals on the same terms as the others. In the end, Armstrong's widow settled with RCA for $1 million—the same amount RCA had offered Armstrong a year before his death.

Armstrong's story is a cautionary tale. He invented so many of the basic technologies that ushered in the age of communication that it is hard to imagine what the world would have looked like without them. Armstrong's insights occurred at pivotal points in history. His invention of regeneration and the superheterodyne receiver played key roles in both World Wars. But what is most interesting about Armstrong is the extent of his iconoclasm. His extreme iconoclasm, which ultimately advanced radio technology but cost him his life, can be understood by differences in the way his brain functioned.

## The Brain, Neuroeconomics, and the Science of Iconoclasm

You may wonder what the brain has to do with iconoclasts. Indeed, until a few years ago, I really wouldn't have given any thought to an iconoclastic brain either. As a neuroscientist, I had spent the last decade studying which parts of the human brain responded to reward and were responsible for motivation. During this period of time, a revolution had occurred in the way that scientists thought about the biological basis of reward and pleasure. This revolution swept away the idea that there was a pleasure center in the brain that somehow acted as an accelerator to the engine of human behavior. The picture of reward and motivation that emerged from this revolution was a sophisticated mix of computational algorithms and pharmacology. It was a picture in which chemicals like dopamine shuttled between neurons in ways that looked remarkably like the calculations that modern robots perform. And unlike in the antiquated, Freudian notion of the id driving human behavior, we now know that the decisions that humans make can be traced to the firing patterns of neurons in specific parts of the brain. These discoveries gave birth to the field known as *neuroeconomics*.

Running a research laboratory to make these discoveries, however, is a job unto itself. Many labs, like mine, are housed within universities and academic medical centers, but they operate like a business. Funds go in, and knowledge and discovery come out. Since I am the director of such a laboratory, the things I do look very much like what a CEO of a small business does. On a day-to-day level, decisions must be made about how to direct resources and personnel within budgetary constraints. My lab, which is considered modest in size by academic standards, has an annual operating budget of about $1 million. As the head of this operation, I am responsible for growing the business by finding new sources of funding to remain productive.

The laboratory's primary function, of course, is research and development. We have tangible measures of success in the form of publications, and sometimes patents and licensing deals. In the biomedical field, the value of publications is easily gauged by the impact factor of the journal that they are published in. The impact factor measures how many times articles in a particular journal are cited by other people. It is extremely competitive to publish in high-impact journals, but the rewards for doing so are great: promotions, publicity, and more funding. It is a classic trade-off of risk and reward. Risky because so few papers get published in the best journals. Consequently, one of the critical decisions a laboratory head makes is how to allocate resources between high-risk, potentially high-impact projects, and low-risk, low-payoff ones.

Unlike other types of business, however, the business of running a research laboratory is continually driven by the tenuous dance between advancing science within existing frameworks of thought and the headline-grabbing paradigm shifts that all scientists dream about. Every young PhD student fantasizes about winning the Nobel Prize someday—the crown jewel of paradigm-shifting, iconoclastic thinking. Science can be as competitive, and cutthroat, as any business endeavor. In addition to the constraint of resource allocation, the laboratory head must make strategic decisions about whom to collaborate with and when to bring products (discoveries) to market (i.e., publish them). And so, it was within this type of environment that I began to realize that the very thing I was studying, the human brain, also contained the secrets to success in an environment that demanded innovation and being able to do things differently than competitors.

## Different Brains, Different Ways of Thinking

To be clear, I will operationalize the definition of an *iconoclast* as a person who does something that others say can't be done. This definition implies that iconoclasts are different from other people. Indeed, this is true, but more precisely, the iconoclast's brain is different, and it is different in three distinct ways. Each of these three functions maps onto a different circuit in the brain, which will be dissected in short order. For now, it suffices to know that the iconoclastic brain differs in these three functions and the circuits that implement them:

- Perception

- Fear response

- Social intelligence

Naysayers might suggest that the brain is irrelevant for iconoclasm. I have heard this argument many times. It is rooted in a sort of Cartesian mind-body dualism that separates human decision making from the messiness of the physical body, as if the mind somehow existed separately from our imperfect, and sometimes animalistic, bodies. But the fact that we have bodies, that we occupy defined physical spaces, that we need to fuel these bodies and, from time to time, reproduce them, leads to massive constraints on how our minds function. The field of neuroeconomics was born out of the realization that the physical workings of the brain place limitations on the way we make decisions. By understanding these constraints, we begin to understand human behavior and why some people seem to march to a different drumbeat.

The first thing to realize is that the brain is mortal. It is a physical organ that consumes energy and performs feats of astounding complexity that we are just now beginning to understand. But the brain, like any machine, suffers the constraint of limited resources. The brain has a fixed energy budget. It can't demand more power from the energy company when it needs to do something complicated. So it has evolved to do what it does as efficiently as possible. This is where the problem arises for most people and is the biggest impediment to being an iconoclast.

For example, when confronted with information streaming from the eyes, the brain will interpret this information in the quickest and most efficient way possible. Time is energy. The longer the brain spends performing some calculation, the more energy it consumes. Considering that the brain runs on about 40 watts of power (a lightbulb!), it doesn't have a lot of energy to spare. So it must be efficient. This means that it will draw on both past experience and any other source of information, such as what other people say, to make sense of what it is seeing. This happens all the time. The brain takes shortcuts in the interest of efficiency. It works so well that we are hardly ever aware of this process. What eventually bubbles to the surface of consciousness is an image in the "mind's eye." We take for granted that our perceptions of the world are real, but they are really specters of our imagination, nothing more than biological and electrical rumblings that we believe to be real.

How you perceive something is not simply a product of what your eyes or ears transmit to your brain. More than the physical reality of photons or sound waves, perception is a product of the brain. Perception lies at the heart of iconoclasm. Iconoclasts see things differently than other people. Literally. They see things differently because their brains do not fall into efficiency traps as much as the average person's brain. Iconoclasts, either because they were born that way or because they learned how to do it, have found ways to work around the perceptual shortcuts that plague most people. By looking at how the brain transforms perception into action, we can see exactly where these physical differences emerge, and where most people's brains fall into the trap of unoriginal thinking, and how the iconoclast's brain is different.

Although the key process for iconoclasm is perception, this is only the beginning. As I shall explain, perception is not something that is immutably hardwired into the brain. It is a process that is learned through experience, which is both a curse and an opportunity for change. The brain faces the fundamental problem of interpreting physical stimuli that originate from the senses. Everything that the brain sees or hears or touches has multiple interpretations. The one that is ultimately chosen—the thing that is perceived—is simply the brain's best guess at interpreting what flows into it. In technical terms, these guesses have their basis in the statistical likelihood of one interpretation over another. These guesses are heavily influenced by past experience and, importantly for potential iconoclasts, what other people say.

Fortunately, there are ways to limit the effect on perception of past experience and other people's opinions. To see things differently than other people, the most effective solution is to bombard the brain with things it has never encountered before. Novelty releases the perceptual process from the shackles of past experience and forces the brain to make new judgments. As we shall see in the following chapters, there are many ways to accomplish this. Iconoclasts, at least successful ones, have a preternatural affinity for new experiences. Where most people shy away from things that are different, the iconoclast embraces novelty.

The problem with novelty, however, is that, for most people, novelty triggers the fear system of the brain. Fear is the second major impediment to thinking like an iconoclast and stops the average person dead in his tracks. There are many types of fear, but the two that inhibit iconoclastic thinking are *fear of uncertainty* and *fear of public ridicule*. These may seem like trivial phobias, and some people might say, "Just deal with it." Fear of public speaking, which everyone must do from time to time, afflicts one-third of the population. This is too common to be considered a disorder or mental illness. It is simply a common variant of human nature, but it is one that gets in the way of many potential iconoclasts. The true iconoclast, although he may still experience these fears, does not let them inhibit his actions.

Finally (assuming one has conquered perception and fear), to make the transition to successful iconoclast, the individual must sell his ideas to other people. This is where *social intelligence* comes in, and it is where Howard Armstrong ultimately failed. His inability to sell RCA on the superiority of FM radio led to a spiral of depression and his demise. Although Armstrong was an iconoclast, he couldn't persuade the masses to his point of view, and he died without the royalties that he ultimately deserved. But rather than simply dismissing Armstrong as an unfortunate casualty of business, we can learn from his mistakes by looking at social intelligence from a biological point of view.

In the last decade, there has been an explosion of knowledge about the social brain. One of the subfields that has emerged out of the neuro-economic movement is how the brain works to coordinate decision making in groups. If you think about it, almost every decision we make must be considered in the context of how it might affect the other people in our lives. The true iconoclast does not live in a cabin in the woods. Like Armstrong, the modern iconoclast navigates a dynamic social network and elicits change that begins with altered perception and ends with effecting change in other people (or dying a failure). Recent neuro-science experiments have revealed which circuits in the brain are responsible for functions like understanding what other people think, empathy, fairness, and social identity. These brain regions play key roles in whether an individual convinces other people of her ideas. Perception plays an important role in social cognition as well. The perception of someone's enthusiasm, or reputation, can make or break a deal. Under-standing how perception becomes intertwined with social decision making shows why successful iconoclasts are so rare: social intelligence depends on perception, but perception itself is subject to social forces. We see things like other people, and the cycle is difficult to break.

## Doing What Others Say Can't Be Done

Iconoclasts have existed throughout history. A name was given to this type of person when Leo III, emperor of Constantinople, destroyed the golden icon of Christ over his palace gates in AD 725. Leo's act of defiance against the church was to consolidate his power, but the word *iconoclast*, which means literally "destroyer of icons," stuck. In the same vein, the modern iconoclast, whether consciously or not, acknowledges the fact that creation is also an act of destruction. To create something new, you also have to tear down conventional ways of thinking. But whether someone is successful in this enterprise depends largely on the three key circuits in the brain. When Armstrong invented FM radio, he created something that everyone else assumed couldn't be done. Although his iconoclastic views were eventually successful in destroying the dogma of AM's superiority, he died convinced he was a failure. But really, the only thing that failed was the social circuit in Armstrong's brain.

So why write a book about iconoclasts? Because this is the type of person who creates new opportunities in every area from artistic expression to technology to business. The iconoclast embodies traits of creativity and innovation that are not easily accomplished by committee. He eschews authority and convention. He thumbs his nose at rules. But given the proper environment, the iconoclast can be a major asset to any organization. So whether you want to be an iconoclast or not, it is crucial for success in any field to understand how the iconoclastic mind works.

It is, of course, not easy to be an iconoclast. The iconoclast risks social and professional ostracism, frequently alienates colleagues, and must face a daily reckoning with a high likelihood of failure. He walks a tough road. And although there is a certain romantic notion to the image of the rugged individualist, who, against all odds, triumphs over conformity, the simple fact is that most people don't want to be an iconoclast. This book won't make you an iconoclast, but you can learn to think a bit more iconoclastically by understanding how the three key brain circuits work. And the iconoclast can be a real asset in an organization. Even if most people don't want to be an iconoclast, understanding how their brains work can help manage teams with iconoclastic members.

In this book, you will meet modern iconoclasts. Some are well known; others are not. Each of them, however, has accomplished something in their field of endeavor that makes them stand out as unique individuals. Most importantly, they are iconoclasts because they had to buck conventional wisdom, sometimes in the face of overwhelming criticism, and remain steadfast in their beliefs for what they perceived to be the right and true path. While inspiring in their own right, these stories serve as jumping-off points for understanding what happens in the brains of iconoclasts. For this is where the action is.

The overarching theme of this book is that iconoclasts are able to do things that others say can't be done, because iconoclasts perceive things differently than other people. This difference in perception plays out in the initial stages of an idea. It plays out in how they manage their fears, and it manifests in how they pitch their ideas to the masses of noniconoclasts. It is an exceedingly rare individual who possesses all three of these traits. In the following chapters, the stories of iconoclasts provide lessons in how their brains, to varying degrees, implement the three key functions. Each story was chosen to exemplify one of these functions. Roll them all together, and you would have the ultimate iconoclast's brain.

# ONE

# Through the Eye of an Iconoclast

The real voyage of discovery lies not in seeking
new landscapes but in seeing with new eyes.

—Marcel Proust

GLASS DEFIES DEFINITION. At room temperature, glass takes the form of a solid, hard enough to hold its own weight, and when appropriately shaped into a container, strong enough to support other substances. But this is an illusion. It is not really solid. Chemists say that glass is a liquid but with a viscosity so high that it behaves like a solid. Raise the temperature a little bit, and its liquid nature reasserts itself. And that is where the art comes in . . .

Stepping into the hotshop is like entering a carnival funhouse. Completely disorienting. Before you even see what's going on, the roar of the furnaces sounds like a jet engine on full throttle in the moments before takeoff. The noise reverberates off the corrugated steel walls and reflects back to a skylight and bounces around the concrete floor, reaching your ears from all directions. Voices emerge from around a corner, but it's difficult to make out what they are saying. Rising above the din, a bit of laughter here, a snatch of postmodern grunge rock there. Something smells of burning. A clean, industrial burn, not sweet like wood, or paper, or leaves.

Then comes the visual assault. Like falling down Alice's rabbit hole, nothing seems straight. Tubes of color, in the form of glass bars, poke out from cubbyholes stuck to the wall. Every color of the rainbow imaginable is here, neatly organized into a cryptic cataloging scheme. On another wall hang enumerable organic shapes. Curlicues of glass in chartreuse, azure, vermilion, ebony flecked with gold, and colors for which there aren't even names. The roaring furnaces are revealed to be gigantic boxes that are opened and closed by assistants wielding long poles that are gimballed to the furnace doors. When the doors are open, the heat pushes everyone back six feet. You cannot even look at the source of the heat, for it is as bright as the sun, and a brilliant orange light that emerges from one of the glory holes burns a circular blue afterimage on your retina.

This is the Boathouse—the working studio and creative epicenter for the world's preeminent and most iconoclastic glass artist, Dale Chihuly.

At age sixty-six, Chihuly has become synonymous with the studio glass art movement. His glass sculptures and large-scale installations, which have included the garden of the Metropolitan Museum of Art in New York and a permanent installation in the ceiling of the Bellagio in Las Vegas, have become so popular that they verge on ubiquity. Millions of people have seen his work through television shows on PBS as well as the hundreds of exhibits that have occurred throughout the United States and the rest of the world. His studio continues to churn out thousands of pieces a year, and yet, they continue to fetch prices ranging from a few thousand dollars for a modest bowl, to $25,000 for a vase, to well over $1 million for an installation like the one in the lobby of the Bellagio. In 1986, Chihuly became one of the few American artists to have a solo show at the Louvre. Not since Louis Tiffany has there been a force in glass like Chihuly.

Far from a starving artist, Chihuly has also mastered the business of art. Although the Chihuly operation has varied in size, it currently hovers around one hundred people. And with no limit to the prices the market has been willing to pay for Chihuly's work, the artist has done well by all conventional standards of success. Indeed, few artists have achieved a level of financial success like Chihuly. Those inviting immediate comparison include Picasso, Warhol, and Hockney.

For all practical purposes, Chihuly invented the forms of glass sculpture that he is now associated with. His work has become iconic, even to the extent that he has copyrighted some of the forms. There have been lawsuits, of course, with the public airing of gripes from former collaborators and associates, and not all of the media attention has been favorable, but the public's enthusiasm remains unflagging. Chihuly remains the prototypical example of the iconoclast: an individual who single-handedly tears down conventional notions of glass art and creates something entirely new in its place.

He also illustrates the first rule of iconoclasm: *he sees differently than other people*.

Literally. For the first thing you notice about Chihuly is the prominent black patch over his left eye. It is anachronistic. Who wears an eye patch in the twenty-first century? Not since Moshe Dayan, the controversial chief of the Israeli Defense Forces and perhaps the last public figure to wear an eye patch, has anyone made it stylish. The most renowned eye patch wearers remain fictional characters: Bazooka Joe, Rooster Cogburn, Snake Plissken. But there it is, stuck to Chihuly's fleshy face, like a badge of honor. He adjusts it with surprising frequency, seemingly uncomfortable with it even after thirty years. Maybe it's all for show. It makes no difference. The loss of sight in his eye was a defining moment for Chihuly in terms of both his art and his career. Certainly, it changed his perception. It also made him into an iconoclast.

## A Different Perspective

Chihuly does not spend much time in the hotshop. Sometimes he goes in to direct his team, but mostly he conveys his visions through paintings splashed on large pieces of butcher paper. Several paintings, each of which fetches several thousand dollars for an original, are tacked to the walls above the furnaces. Some paintings are simply splashes of color in an unusual shape. Spirals and other organic forms are in abundance. Other paintings clearly convey a particular piece. One painting of a black vase is similar in form and color to the one being blown, but instead of gold feathers, it sprouts a psychedelic version of the Medusa's head, with tangerine-colored snakes.

Although the team approach to glassblowing has been known to the Europeans for centuries, Chihuly didn't really put it into full-blown action until an accident gave him no choice. While he was touring Great Britain in 1976, Chihuly's car crashed, sending the artist through the windshield. The damage to his left eye was irreparable, and he has not had vision out of it ever since. Even while recovering from the accident, he continued to blow glass, at least until another accident sidelined him more or less for good.

"I always felt handicapped after I had my accident. I didn't have any peripheral vision, which was kind of hard because you are close together. And I didn't have any depth perception," Chihuly says:

> About a year after the accident, I went to see a friend in La Jolla for a couple of days, and I dislocated my right arm in the surf. That made it impossible to work in the hotshop. During all that time, while I was recovering, I still worked, but it was the other guy, Billy

Morris, who took over as the main guy, the gaffer. From that point on I could see the advantages of not being the gaffer. Because if you have 10 people out there, and sometimes we have 15, you can watch everything that's going on. You can talk to the guy doing the coloring, and somebody else if you want to make it bigger or speed it up. A lot of those decisions are made on the other side of the shop, not where the gaffer is. I think that made me a lot more creative and perhaps do a lot more work than other people could. It's very tiring to be the gaffer.[1]

Chihuly's story is striking because he did not become an iconoclast until he lost his eye. Although he was not consciously aware of it at the time, in retrospect even a casual observer of Chihuly's work can see a marked change after the accident. In 1975, Chihuly was working and teaching at the Rhode Island School of Design (RISD). He had established the glass department at RISD five years earlier and, in collaboration with James Carpenter, created some of the first glass installations. Chihuly spent his summers back in Washington teaching at the eco-hippie glass school that he founded in Pilchuck. But at RISD, Chihuly was attempting to merge designs from Navajo blankets into glass sculpture. The glass forms were rather unremarkable, cylinders that looked like candle holders. Chihuly, however, had just learned a technique for transferring drawings into glass. He made small paintings that incorporated Navajo designs, and laid them flat on the marvering table. Taking the molten glass cylinders, he would roll the cylinders on top of the paintings until the glass picked up the design. Nor did he limit himself to Navajo paintings but included all sorts of drawings and whimsical doodles, such as French flags and caricatures of James Joyce.

After the accident, however, Chihuly's work took on a decidedly asymmetric form. Working at Pilchuck in the summer of 1977 and learning to deal with the loss of depth perception, Chihuly describes his inspiration after seeing a Northwest Indian basket: "I wasn't really working on anything. And I saw these baskets, and I thought, *I want to make these baskets out of glass*."

He tried a few different methods taken from standard glassblowing techniques, but none gave him the form he was looking for. "It didn't take me too long to figure out that I could have the heat and gravity work for me to make these shapes."

The baskets, although similar to the cylinders in their earthen tones, looked nothing like candle holders. Despite their name, they didn't look much like baskets either. More like dinosaur eggs that had hatched and mutated into some organic form that seemed almost alive. It is no coincidence that Chihuly's work departed from symmetry following the loss of vision in one eye.

For many people, the loss of vision in one eye devastates both the body and the psyche. After Sammy Davis Jr. lost his left eye in an automobile accident, he thought his vision would be half of what it used to be, but after the bandages were removed, he found that it was less than half, describing the sensation of having a wall built over his nose.[2] But the brain adapts quickly, and Chihuly, like Davis, was soon able to work again. Although the brain does a surprisingly good job at compensating for the loss of vision in one eye, it is never quite the same. A great deal of depth perception returns, and slight movements of the head allow one eye to serve the function of two. The greater effect of losing an eye is the way in which the individual sees himself.

In glasswork, symmetry is prized above all else. Ever since the Venetians invented the craft in the thirteenth century, symmetry has been a measure of the skill of the glassblower and has served as a sort of status symbol. Even in the 1970s, when Chihuly was blowing, the worth of a glassblower was measured by the symmetry of his work. It was unthinkable to show work that departed from this standard. Asymmetric vases were the mark of rank beginners. So when Chihuly foisted his deformed baskets on the glass world, he thumbed his nose at centuries of glassmaking dogma.

For artists like Chihuly, the work is very much an extension of the body. Glass sculpture is a physical medium. The requirement of constant motion traditionally ensured that symmetric objects were the most highly prized. And yet, the one-eyed artist is a case study in asymmetry that he must confront in the mirror every morning. Humans do not like asymmetry as a general rule. When we look at someone's face, we judge their beauty in large part according to how symmetric they are.[3] For an artist, beauty reigns above all else. So even though Chihuly adapted to monocular vision, what makes him an iconoclast is his departure from traditional glassblowing into the realm of asymmetry. He found ways to make the asymmetric beautiful—a feat that most glassblowers of the time thought impossible. In Chihuly's case, it took a physical change to see differently. Although it may not be necessary to resort to such drastic means, his story provides the first lesson for iconoclasts. The iconoclast sees differently than everyone else.

## Seeing Differently

We are visual animals. When we imagine something, it is most often a visual image that comes to mind. Where do these images come from? The eyes transmit raw information, but by the time you become aware of it, your brain has processed the information in so many ways that if a neuroscientist were to listen in on the neural signals propagating through your brain, she would have a hard time picking up anything resembling a picture. The first thing to realize is that vision is not the same as perception. Vision is the process by which photons enter the eye and are transformed into neural signals in the brain. Perception, on the other hand, is the much more complex process by which the brain interprets these signals. The end result is a mental image that reaches consciousness. The eye is not much more than an optical lens and an image detector (the retina). After that, what people's brains do with the image is a rather individualistic process.

## The Anatomy of Vision

Vision begins in the eye.[4] The human eye is divided into two components: a lens system and a detector system. The outermost part of the eye, the cornea, collects incoming light rays and passes them through the lens. The lens takes the incoming light rays and focuses them onto the retina, which covers the inner surface of the rear of the eyeball. The lens functions in the same way as a camera lens, but unlike a camera lens, which is made from glass or plastic, the human lens is living tissue made up of cells that have elongated into very thin fibers. These fibers attach to muscles that surround the periphery of the lens. When the muscles contract, the lens flattens out, changing the focus point.

Light entering the eye is projected onto the retina, and it is here that the first transformation from physical image to mental image occurs. The light strikes a specialized type of nerve cell called a *photoreceptor*. These cells contain special pigments that absorb energy from incoming photons and convert this energy into an electrical impulse. There are two types of photoreceptors: *rods* and *cones*, which are named for their shapes under a microscope. The rods have a larger surface area and can detect a few photons at a time, which makes them ideally suited for night vision. The tip of a cone is much smaller and is less sensitive, but the cones are packed close together in the center of the retina. This tight packing makes them ideal for picking up fine details. The cones also contain three different pigments, and the relative concentration of these pigments in a particular cone determines the range of colors it responds to.

Until this point, the eye functions much like a digital camera. But unlike a camera's detector, the photoreceptors in the retina are not spaced uniformly on a grid. Because the cones are packed densely near the center of the retina, and the rod spacing is sparse near the periphery, our ability to make out details of objects declines with distance from the center of vision. So even before the photoreceptors transmit electrical signals to the brain, the image has been fractionated in a way that gives premium bandwidth to things that are in the center of the visual field. By constantly moving your eyes, however, you're able to construct a mental image of your surroundings. Your brain can keep track of this mental image and fill in the gaps in vision by making guesses that are generally pretty good. There are circumstances, however, in which these guesses fail, and it is under these conditions that the brain makes incorrect assumptions about what it is seeing. It turns out that the ways in which the brain makes these assumptions are the same ways it makes it difficult to think like an iconoclast.

For example, there is the blind spot. Cats and dogs don't have blind spots. The phenomenon is unique to humans and other primates. In humans, the photoreceptors are covered by a thin sheet of neurons that make connections (synapses) with the photoreceptors. This sheet of neurons performs basic image processing and then passes the signals on to the brain through the optic nerve. The optic nerve is a cordlike structure that contains the fibers from all the retinal neurons. Because they are collected into one place and pass through a hole in the retina, no photoreceptors can occupy that space, and a blind spot results. But even though you have a hole in the retina, you don't see a black hole in your visual field. The brain mentally fills it in with its best guess of what should be there.

The photoreceptors transmit electrical signals to a thin sheet of neurons that immediately begins to transform the pristine image that has fallen on the retina. Even before these signals leave the eye, they have already been changed in a way that is no longer an exact representation of the world. These neurons, which are called *retinal ganglion cells*, serve two primary purposes: to collect the visual information from the photoreceptors and transmit it to the brain; and to perform "gain" control. The retinal ganglion cells sense the intensity of light that hits the retina and adjust their output to stay within a constant range. These cells turn up the gain for night vision and turn it down in daylight. The retinal ganglion cells also place a limit on how fast visual information can reach the brain. By measuring how frequently the ganglion cells fire and by estimating how many ganglion cells cover the retina, we can estimate the bandwidth of the human eye. One estimate put the bandwidth at about 1 MB per second, which is about the speed of a cable modem.[5]

After traveling down the optic nerve, the electrical impulses make a single synapse in a lime-sized structure called the thalamus and are then transmitted to the cortex, where the real transformations take place and where the mental image is constructed. Interestingly enough, the cortical visual system is laid out in a well-defined topography. The initial site of visual processing is in the part of the brain called the *occipital cortex*, which lies at the very back of the head. This rather large swath of territory is devoted exclusively to the initial processing of visual signals and is called, not surprisingly, *area V1*. If you electrically stimulate the neurons in V1, the person will "see" visual phosphenes. For the same reason, if you get hit in the back of the head, the stars you see result from the electrical discharge of these neurons. There is an almost exact representation of the retina here, with each location in the retina being mapped onto a grid in V1. The neurons here process the incoming information and extract basic features from the image such as the location of edges, their orientation relative to horizontal, and the image disparity between the two eyes, which is one element of depth perception.

## The Anatomy of Perception

Until V1, the visual system behaves like a video camera. Although the neurons perform low-level processing of the visual signals, this type of processing does not yet constitute perception. In fact, we are not even aware of what our brains are doing at this point. After V1, however, the information flows from the back of the head in a generally forward direction toward the frontal lobes. The information takes two paths: the high road and the low road (see figure 1-1). The high road, which is a route of information flowing over the top of the brain, extracts information about where objects are located in space relative to the body. The low road, which is a pathway flowing through the temporal lobes above the ears, processes the visual information in a way that categorizes what a person sees. These two routes, the "where" and the "what" pathways, coordinate with each other so that the end result is a seamless perception of what the eyes transmit. For example, although you move your head and eyes constantly, your brain does not lose track of the objects surrounding you. This is a complicated process, and the only way in which it can be done efficiently is through a process called *predictive coding*. So that it is not overwhelmed with information processing, the brain makes predictions about what it is seeing and changes these predictions only when it makes an error. As we delve deeper into how this occurs, we shall see the points at which it becomes difficult to see things in ways different than you expect. And yet, the ability to do this is absolutely essential for iconoclastic thinking.

**FIGURE 1-1**

**The "what" and the "where" pathways flowing forward from the primary visual area of the brain**

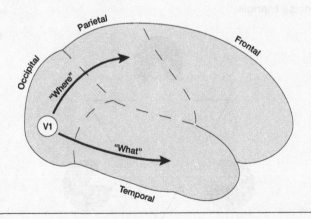

In the early stages of visual processing, such as V1, the brain performs its functions on a local scale. Neurons here do not have information about what other neurons are doing. As the information flows forward through the "what" and the "where" pathways, the information from other parts of the retina becomes increasingly integrated, to the point where the information ceases to be based on retinal location at all. By the time we become aware of what we are seeing, we perceive the visual stream not as a rectangular grid of light and dark spots, but as a landscape of stationary and moving objects, each with its own identity.

To appreciate the transformation from local to global information processing, examine figure 1-2. The figure consists of only three Pac-Man shapes and three pairs of lines, but you perceive a white triangle floating above the background.[6] There is no triangle, but your brain, using its global processing mode, perceives one anyway. You can force yourself to drop down from global processing by staring at one of the individual elements, but this is generally a temporary state as your brain wants to make sense of what it is seeing. A flick of the eyes, and you are back to seeing the floating triangle.

**FIGURE 1-2**

**The Kanizsa triangle**

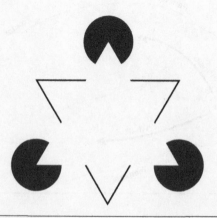

Which is the true perception: Pac-Man or triangle? Regardless of which you see, the information coming from the eyes remains constant. Perception, then, is a product of the mind and brain, not the eyes. Unless you grew up in the '70s, glued to an Atari console, the relative dominance of the triangle perception illustrates the brain's tendency to perceive things as it expects them to be. Triangles are more common than Pac-Men. The perception of a floating triangle also provides a unified interpretation of the entire figure. At a global level, this makes more sense to the brain than the alternative perception of three Pac-Men clustering around an empty space.

The triangle illusion demonstrates a key rule of perception: the most likely way that you perceive something will be in a manner consistent with your past experience. Commonplace perceptions feel comfortable and cost little energy to process. Conversely, uncommon perceptions force the brain into a different mode of processing in which it must figure out what exactly it is seeing, and this costs energy.

The issue of how the brain creates perceptions from raw visual inputs is of critical importance to being an iconoclast. The iconoclast doesn't literally see things differently than other people. More precisely, he *perceives* things differently. There are several different routes to forcing the brain out of its lazy mode of perception, but the theme linking these methods depends on the element of surprise. The brain must be provided with something that it has never before processed to force it out of predictable perceptions. When Chihuly lost an eye, his brain was forced to reinterpret visual stimuli in a new way.

## The Iconoclast Who Discovered MRI

It is easy to take for granted the remarkable advances that medical technology has showered upon us. In an age of CAT scans and MRIs, the image of a human brain doesn't carry quite the same awe-inspiring reaction that it used to. But this is a recent phenomenon. MRI is only thirty years old. The brain is the central player in iconoclasm, and much of what we know about the human brain comes from MRI.

The story of MRI—magnetic resonance imaging—is itself a story of iconoclasm. The basic physical principle behind MRI was actually discovered in the 1940s. When an atom is placed in a magnetic field, the atom will start vibrating. This is called *nuclear magnetic resonance* (NMR). The rate at which the atom vibrates is determined by what kind of atom it is and the strength of the magnetic field. If you put enough atoms in a magnetic field, they will all vibrate in synchrony, and you can actually listen to this vibration with a radio antenna. Until the 1970s, this was all standard technology for chemists, who used NMR as part of their toolkit to analyze chemicals, at least until Paul Lauterbur's revolutionary insight. Lauterbur was a chemist by training who had specialized in the study of NMR spectra of naturally occurring proteins. Because of his expertise, he had maintained informal consulting roles with some of the companies that manufactured NMR equipment. While Lauterbur was consulting with one of these companies, based in a Pittsburgh warehouse, a visiting researcher from Johns Hopkins University was experimenting with the NMR spectra of cancer tissue. He wanted to see whether NMR could distinguish normal tissues from cancerous ones.

Indeed, NMR could tell the difference between healthy and cancerous tissue, but there was a big problem. It couldn't tell you where the differences were. Because NMR came out of chemistry, which had traditionally focused on the analysis of test-tube samples, no one had really thought about using NMR to locate differences inside the samples themselves. Conventional wisdom said it shouldn't matter, reasoning that you could always put a tissue sample into the NMR spectrometer.

Lauterbur thought differently and believed that NMR could be used to find the locations of differences in a tissue sample. One of the big limitations with the technology was constructing a magnet that had a uniform magnetic field. These magnetic nonuniformities resulted in "blurry" chemical signals. Most chemists dismissed this as noise. But Lauterbur started to wonder whether the noise actually couldn't be turned to an advantage. His insight came at a Big Boy restaurant and was scribbled on the back of a napkin. Lauterbur later recalled that "on the second bite of a Big Boy hamburger," he was struck by an idea. Maybe that "blurring" contained embedded information that he could decipher. "Heck," he said, "you could make pictures with this thing!"[7]

Lauterbur's epiphany led him to the idea of purposely making the magnetic field nonuniform. In NMR, this was heretical. But Lauterbur realized that if this inhomogeneity was applied in a predictable way, such as left to right, then the atoms in those different locations would vibrate at slightly different frequencies. These frequency differences could then be assembled into a crude image. Lauterbur tested his idea in the simplest way possible. He embedded a test tube filled with one kind of water inside a test tube filled with another kind of water. Applying an altered magnetic field, he produced the first cross-sectional magnetic resonance image.

He wrote up the results and submitted them to the top scientific journal, which promptly rejected it. As Lauterbur recalled, "Many said it couldn't be done, even when I was doing it!" Of course, the scientific establishment eventually came around, and Lauterbur's insight changed medicine forever. He received the Noble Prize in Medicine in 2003, thirty years after his discovery.

What is interesting about Lauterbur's discovery is that we can trace the moment at which he broke out of conventional thinking. There are striking similarities to Chihuly's story, and the visual nature of their insights is remarkable. What others had written off as noise in the NMR signal, Lauterbur saw as something else. He saw the potential of hidden information.

Over and over again, iconoclasts like Lauterbur and Chihuly point to the visual nature of their insights. And so visual perception is where the hunt for the iconoclastic brain begins.

## Persons, Places, and Things

After V1, the visual information splits into the high road and the low road, to meet up eventually in the frontal cortex. Along these two roads, the brain transitions from local processing mode to global processing and makes judgments of object identities and their locations in space. As you might imagine, it is an incredibly complex feat to perform. Only the most powerful computers can perform the task of identifying objects and cross-reference them with a catalog of labels and images from memory. Although it is a trivial task for you to distinguish an auto-mobile from a bicycle, no matter from which direction you see them, a computer would have a great deal of difficulty doing this. Both objects have wheels, yet they may not be visible when the objects are viewed from behind. Imagine the even more complex task of how we distin-guish different people from one another. Everyone has the same basic anatomy, and yet we are able to identify people, sometimes from extreme angles in which we don't even see their face full on.

The ability to perform such complicated perceptual functions comes with a price. Evolution has resulted in a human brain that can accomplish amazing perceptual tasks, all the while saving energy. The need to distinguish friend from foe, or predator from prey, and to do it quickly enough to decide whether to run or fight, meant that the brain had to take shortcuts and make assumptions about what it was seeing. From the earliest levels of processing in the visual system, the brain extracts useful pieces of information and discards others. Depending on which road the information takes, the bits retained or discarded may be different. The high road is concerned with extracting where objects are located and throws away the elements related to their identity. The low road, on the other hand, is concerned with identification and catego-rization, and less so with objects' spatial locations.

Although the spatial location of what we see may be important, most of what iconoclasts do differently from other people lies in how they categorize what they see. Whether one person sees ugliness or beauty in asymmetry is entirely a result of categorization. In the same way, whether an NMR spectrum is viewed as noisy or full of extra information doesn't come from the image itself, but in the way the viewer categorizes the image. For this reason, understanding how the low road pigeonholes objects into categories suggests ways out of predictable perception.

As in playing the game 20 Questions, the first, and most salient, decision the brain makes is whether it is viewing a person or something else. People constitute a special category of objects. The high degree of social interaction, both at the level of facial and body expression and in the use of language, dictates that the brain treats people differently than anything else. So specialized is this function, neuroscientists have identified the precise location in the brain that responds to human faces. If we were to examine the brain from its underside, the temporal lobes would fan out like butterfly wings. The innermost portion of the lower wings contains neurons that respond only to faces and is called the *fusiform face area*, or FFA. Some of these neurons perform highly specialized functions and seem to be active only when viewing a face from a particular angle. Many years ago neuroscientists hypothesized that the level of specialization might go so deep that neurons might exist that responded to one thing, and one thing only. These hypothetical neurons were dubbed *grandmother cells*, because you might have neurons that fired only when you saw your grandmother. A great deal of specialization does exist in the FFA, although not to this degree (which is probably a good thing, because if your hypothetical grandmother cell became damaged, then you wouldn't be able to recognize your grandmother anymore). Most aspects of facial processing appear to be carried out by a network of neurons in the FFA.[8] This type of architecture is called *distributed processing* and is yet another example of how the brain efficiently organizes information. Because distributed processing employs a network of neurons that process different aspects of faces, no neuron is critical to the overall function, and the network gains a level of flexibility that lets it deploy resources in different ways under different circumstances. Distributed processing also means that the brain can reprogram its networks to perceive things differently.

Although the ability to reprogram neural networks is a key attribute of the iconoclast's brain, that doesn't mean it works for everyone. Sometimes reprogramming must be approached gradually, or else the iconoclast's ideas will be rejected.

## Before *Pac-Man*, the Iconoclast Who Brought Us *Pong*

I used the example of *Pac-Man* earlier because this game was, for a time, the most popular video game in existence. For those who grew up during that era, the image of those pies chunking around a video screen remains indelibly burned into their brains. It is easy to take those images for granted now, but at the time, video games were revolutionary. And the granddaddy of all video games, *Pong*, was perhaps the most iconoclastic of all. Every modern video game, whether it is played on a computer or an Xbox, derives from the deceptively simple computer version of table tennis.

In 1970, *Pong*'s inventor, Nolan Bushnell, was just another electrical engineer working in Silicon Valley. He was making decent money working for Ampex, a manufacturer of recording equipment, but Bushnell's real love was for games, and he soon found himself designing coin-operated arcade games for a much smaller company, Nutting Associates. The result was a game called *Computer Space*, which was a sort of galactic dogfight between a spaceship and a flying saucer. Although *Computer Space* was a hit with his engineering friends, it didn't go over so well in the usual environment for arcade games: bars. In fact, it was a flop. Although the game was simple by today's standards of video gaming, it required players to control a spaceship using "thrust," "fire," and "rotate" buttons. At that time, Bushnell observed too many players dropping a quarter into the game and just standing there waiting for something to happen. What happened was, the flying saucer flew over and zapped their spaceship. The players did not have a category in their brains for interpreting this type of amusement.

Because of this failure, Bushnell left Nutting and with his friend Ted Dabney and $500, formed his own company, calling it Atari, after a term for the Japanese game of Go. Outside of big mainframes, computers didn't exist, so all these video games had to be created with specialized electronics. They hired Al Alcorn, a young engineer, to carry out the electrical wizardry. As a warm-up exercise, Bushnell gave Alcorn the simple task of creating a video version of Ping-Pong.

Nobody, for a minute, believed that a computer version of Ping-Pong would have any appeal. After all, if you wanted to play Ping-Pong, you might as well just play on a table. The pattern of dogmatic thinking was identical to what chemists said about NMR. But Bushnell eschewed dogma and plowed ahead. Keeping it as simple as possible, Bushnell suggested the screen should show only one ball, two paddles, and the players' scores. It didn't take Alcorn but two weeks to come up with a working prototype. Much to everyone's surprise, the game was remarkably entertaining and addictive. And most important, it didn't require any instructions or reprogramming in the brains of end users, who, if they were playing in a bar, were probably drunk anyway.

*Pong* was field-tested for the first time in 1972 at Andy Capp's Tavern in Sunnyvale. Two weeks later, the bar owner called Bushnell, asking him to come and fix the machine. But *Pong* wasn't broken. The coin box had simply jammed with too many quarters. Bushnell was onto something, and the coin-op arcade business ate it up. *Pong*'s simplicity also threatened to destroy Atari. The game was easily copied, and rivals began selling competing versions to arcades. On the verge of bankruptcy, Bushnell made the bold move into a home version of *Pong* and bucked conventional wisdom that said arcade games were only played in arcades. For a company with no experience in the consumer electronics sector, it was a risky strategy. Advances in silicon chip technology had advanced sufficiently so that, in 1974, a custom chip containing all the circuitry that the arcade game had could fit into a home console. Eventually Sears bought exclusive rights for one year and ordered 150,000 units, enough to save Atari and launch Bushnell into his next venture, Chuck E. Cheese's.

## Seeing Like an Iconoclast

If we can say one thing about the iconoclast's brain, it would be this: it sees differently than other people's brains. When Chihuly lost the vision in one eye, he began to see the world differently. But this is a drastic measure. It does, however, illustrate the importance of new perspectives in the creation of new ideas. The overwhelming importance of the visual system to the human mind means that many of the great innovations began with a change in visual perception. It wasn't until Paul Lauterbur stared at a blurry NMR spectrum of cancer that he realized the potential for creating MRI. In both of these cases, the iconoclasts' key insights were triggered by visual images. For Chihuly, it was a realization that beauty in glass sculpture need not be equated with symmetry, which was a reflection of his own asymmetry. For Lauterbur, it was a realization that blurriness in an NMR spectrum need not be equated with noise. Even Nolan Bushnell's realization that *Computer Space* was too complicated for people came from seeing customers being dumbfounded by the game.

Iconoclasm begins with perception. More specifically, it begins with visual perception, and so the first step to thinking like an iconoclast is to see like one.

At every step in the process of visual perception, the brain throws out pieces of information and assimilates the remaining ones into increasingly abstract components. Experience plays a major role in this process. The human brain sees things in ways that are most familiar to it.

But epiphanies rarely occur in familiar surroundings. The key to seeing like an iconoclast is to look at things that you have never seen before. It seems almost obvious that breakthroughs in perception do not come from simply staring at an object and thinking harder about it. Breakthroughs come from a perceptual system that is confronted with something that it doesn't know how to interpret. Unfamiliarity forces the brain to discard its usual categories of perception and create new ones.

Sometimes the brain needs a kick start. Although Chihuly was already marching down the path of artistic creativity, the loss of vision in one eye jolted his brain in a very literal sense to see differently. Chihuly's brain probably adapted to monocular vision within about six months, but the effect on his art was indelible. He continued to be a visual artist, seeking out inspirations in unlikely places. Although he works in a medium that dictates individual pieces can only be a foot or two tall, he gets ideas from nature and, nowadays, architecture. It stimulates his visual system, and yet, at a different level, architecture is a tactile experience for Chihuly. Unusual spaces force his brain to process inputs in novel ways, sprouting new connections and making synapses where none existed before.

Sometimes a simple change of environment is enough to jog the perceptual system out of familiar categories. This may be one reason why restaurants figure so prominently as sites of perceptual breakthroughs. A more drastic change of environment—traveling to another country, for example—is even more effective. When confronted with places never seen before, the brain must create new categories. It is in this process that the brain jumbles around old ideas with new images to create new syntheses.

New acquaintances can also be a source of new perceptions. Other people will frequently lend their opinion of what they see, and these ideas may be enough to destabilize familiar patterns of perception. A change of vantage point may also be sufficient to yield new perceptions. The floating triangle example illustrated how focusing on details versus standing back and looking at the whole can yield markedly different visual perceptions.

By forcing the visual system to see things in different ways, you can increase the odds of new insights. It sounds remarkably simple. But it is not quite that easy. As we shall see in the next chapter, the brain frequently resists exactly these types of new experiences because they cost energy to process.

# TWO

# From Perception
# to Imagination

Education consists mainly in what we have unlearned.

—Mark Twain

**H**UMANS DEPEND ON VISION, more than any other sense to navigate through the world. Mostly we take the visual process for granted. And rightly so, for if we had to think too much about what we see from moment to moment, scarce brain power would remain for doing anything else. Most of the time, the efficiency of our visual systems works to our advantage. Hitting a major league fastball, for example, requires the precise coordination of eyes and body. A 90-mile-per-hour fastball reaches the plate in about 0.4 seconds, but the batter must decide whether to hit it when it gets about halfway. The limit of human reaction time is about 0.2 seconds, which means that the task of hitting a fastball pushes the vision and motor systems to their limits. There is no time for thought. The connection between eye and body must be seamless. This automaticity lets us accomplish anything that requires hand-eye coordination, but this automaticity comes with a price. In the interests of crafting an efficient visual system, the brain must make guesses about what it is actually seeing. Most of the time this works, but these automatic processes also get in the way of seeing things differently. Automatic thinking destroys the creative process that forms the foundation of iconoclastic thinking.

The brain is fundamentally a lazy piece of meat. It doesn't like to waste energy. This is not too surprising given that all animals must conserve energy, so the brain, like every other organ, has evolved to be as efficient as possible for what it does. There's a myth that we only use 10 or 15 percent of our brains. Although only a fraction of the brain is active at any moment in time, the real truth is that we use all of our brains—just not all at the same time. At any instant, a battle wages between the different parts of the brain. Each piece of the brain serves its own particular set of functions, but in order to carry out these functions, it needs energy. The parts of the brain that accomplish their tasks with the least amount of energy carry the moment. The neuroscientist Gerald Edelman, called this *neural Darwinism*, meaning that the brain has evolved, and continues to evolve, by principles of resource competition and adaptation.[1] Energy is precious; so efficiency reigns above all else.

The efficiency principle has major ramifications for the visual system. It means the brain takes shortcuts whenever it can. In the last chapter, we saw how one shortcut, categorization, streamlines visual perception. In this chapter, we will take a closer look at where these categories come from and how iconoclasts break out of them. Novelty will play a key role.

Another side effect of the efficiency principle is that the brain uses circuits like the visual system for multiple purposes. Visual creativity— imagination—utilizes the same systems in the brain as vision itself. *Imagination comes from the visual system.* Iconoclasm goes hand in hand with imagination. Before one can muster the strength to tear down conventional thinking, one must first imagine the possibility that conventional thinking is wrong. But even this is not enough. The iconoclast goes further and imagines alternative possibilities. But imagination is a fickle process, and most iconoclasts have good days, when the ideas flow freely, and bad days, when their thinking is stale and cliché. The good days hold nuggets of insight into the imaginative process, and in this chapter, I will examine the conditions in the brain that foster imagination and creativity. This is the story of the search for the holy grail of creativity, an almost childlike imagination and willful abandonment to dream crazy thoughts.

Perhaps it is a result of the way we are educated, or perhaps it is simply a reflection of the biological maturation of our brains, but creativity seems to become more difficult for many people as they get older. The efficiency principle, coupled with the consolidation of large amounts of information and experience as we get older, means that the brain needs to categorize. And yet, imagination stems from the ability to break this categorization, to see things not for what one thinks they are, but for what they might be.

## Walt Disney—The Iconoclast of Animation

One of the greatest innovators of the entertainment industry, Walt Disney, was also an iconoclast because he did something that nobody thought could be done. He changed the animated cartoon from being a movie trailer to a main feature. Disney had always been interested in drawing as a child, and Disney became a competent, if enthusiastic, illustrator while he was stationed in France at the end of World War I. He drew sketches for the canteen menu featuring a doughboy character he had invented. He also developed a small business selling caricatures of his fellow soldiers to send back to their families.[2] After returning home to Kansas City, Disney began earning money by drawing advertisements and letterheads. He was a decent illustrator, but because he was so gung ho about drawing, his reputation as a hard worker grew, and business owners liked him. In short order, the Kansas City Slide Company, which produced promotional slides shown in movie theaters, hired the nineteen-year-old to illustrate its ads.

Disney was clearly taken with the idea of combining drawing with movie technology. Disney wasn't working on movies per se, but his work, even though it still consisted of single cartoons, was being projected onto a big screen. These visual images, cartoons that would normally be viewed on a piece of paper, now appeared larger than life. These images had a profound effect on Disney's visual perception. The exposure to film technology gripped Disney's imagination. What if he could turn his cartoons into a movie? In his free time, he set up his own studio in a garage his father had built, even paying him $5 a month for rent. With his earnings as an illustrator, Disney bought an overhead camera stand and some studio lights. He borrowed a glass negative camera and began experimenting with taking pictures of his drawings. Nobody seemed to notice at the time, but Disney's photographic experiments changed his visual perception of his drawings, and even his perception of himself, to the point that he quickly saw himself not as an illustrator, but as an animator.

Disney did not invent animation, but he took it further than anyone thought possible. When he got into the business, animations were only used for the advertisements before the main feature. Disney became an iconoclast when he decided to make his animation the main feature. What is interesting about Disney's story is that although he had drawn since he was a child, the accomplishments that he is best known for had their origin in a change in visual perception. Disney didn't wake up one day suddenly thinking he was going to create animated feature-length films. The ability to imagine this possibility first required a novel visual stimulus in the form of seeing a static cartoon projected on a movie theater screen. These images changed Disney's categorization of drawing from one of static cartoons to that of moving ones—drawings that told stories in a narrative sense.

## The Evolution of Perception

Disney's epiphany had its roots in a perceptual shift, and this change in perception opened the floodgates of his imagination. Perception and imagination are closely linked because the brain uses the same systems for both functions. You can think of imagination as nothing more than running the perceptual machinery in reverse. The reason that it is so difficult to imagine truly novel ideas has to do with how the perceptual system interprets visual signals from the eyes. Whatever limits the brain places on perception naturally limit the imagination. So let's take a closer look at how the perceptual system works.

For over one hundred years, the predominant view of how the brain constructs a mental image has been one of progressively higher-order feature extraction. Indeed, when we follow the flow of visual information through the brain, whether it is through the high road or the low road, we see a gradual transition from local processing based on the retinal grid to global processing where objects and their locations are extracted. The traditional view of this process has been one of progressively greater integration of lower-level features in a sort of pyramid approach vision. Experience was thought to play only a small role in this process. Recent advances in neuroscience, however, have shown just how big a role experience plays in perception.

Dale Purves, a neuroscientist at Duke University, has been the most vocal proponent of what can be termed an evolutionary approach to perception. As Purves points out, the images that strike your retina do not, by themselves, tell you with certainty what you are seeing. As we saw in the last chapter, there are at least two interpretations of the Kanizsa triangle: floating triangle or Pac-Man attack. The historical, bottom-up theory of visual perception would say that you see a triangle because of local interactions of contrast edges in the figure. Purves offers a different explanation: you see a triangle because that is the most likely explanation for what your eyes are transmitting. Purves believes that visual perception is largely a result of statistical expectations. Perception is the brain's way of interpreting ambiguous visual signals in the most likely explanation possible, and the likelihood of these explanations is a direct result of past experience.[3]

This is a radical theory of perception that has major implications for thinking like an iconoclast. If you have never played *Pac-Man*, then the preceding paragraph will make no sense because you will surely see a triangle floating above the background, and so the Pac-Man interpretation will not even enter your consciousness, and you'll have no possibility of perceiving an army of hungry little Atari creatures.

Consider this famous illusion, shown in figure 2-1, devised in 1913 by the Italian psychologist Mario Ponzo. In the illusion, the upper horizontal line is perceived to be longer than the lower one, even though both are actually the same length. The bottom-up theory of perception says this occurs because the lower line has more empty space on either side, which the brain interprets as shorter. The evolutionary theory says that the difference in perceived line lengths comes from your past experience. In the real world, lines that converge toward each other at the top generally mean that the lines are parallel but are receding into the distance. Railroad tracks, roads, and skyscrapers (viewed from street level) all look like this. These views are so commonplace that your brain has become accustomed to transforming lines that look like pyramids into their parallel equivalents. In the Ponzo illusion, this transformation drags along the upper line so that your brain thinks that it is bigger than the lower one. If this were a sketch of a skyscraper, then you would naturally come to the conclusion that the upper line is longer because it stretches close to the edges of the building, while the lower one does not. To prove this, turn the figure upside down. In the real world, you almost never see lines that converge toward each other at the bottom and certainly not lines that recede into the distance. The illusion that the upper and lower lines are different lengths disappears.

If experience plays such a profound role in shaping our perceptions, then it should be possible to test this theory by giving people controlled experiences and seeing how their perceptions change. In a recent neuroimaging experiment, neuroscientists at Georgetown University did exactly this.[4] Instead of converging lines, the researchers presented subjects with pictures of fictitious cars that they had generated on a computer. The cars were designed along a continuum such that at one end of the continuum, the car was deemed type A, while at the other end of the continuum, it was type B. Using computer morphing, the researchers were able to generate versions of the car that were intermediate between A and B. The researchers used functional MRI (fMRI) to measure neural activity while they presented the various versions of the car to their subjects. Following the initial scanning, the researchers trained their subjects, through trial and error, to differentiate type A from type B cars. They then rescanned their brains' responses to the cars, looking specifically for parts of the brain that changed their firing pattern after training. Because of the efficiency principle, they knew to

**FIGURE 2-1**

**The Ponzo illusion**

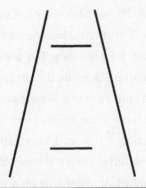

look for regions that had a decreased response to the cars. A decreased response on repeated viewings meant that a particular part of the brain had adapted to that type of information and served as a fingerprint for neural processing along a particular cognitive dimension.

The researchers found that a specific part of the brain's visual system called the lateral occipital (LO) area differentiated the types of cars after training but not before. The LO area is located in the earliest part of the low road. What was interesting was that after training, the LO area had higher activity when two cars of different categories were presented, compared to when two cars of the same category were presented. Before training, the LO area displayed no such changes in activity.

These results are important because they demonstrate two principles. First, the way we perceive something, which is a function of the low road, depends on the way in which we categorize objects. Without categories, we do not have the ability to see features that differentiate objects. In other words, we cannot see that which we don't know to look for. Second, the ability to see these subtle differences depends on experience. And this means that perception can be changed through experience.

## Florence Nightingale and the Perception of Death

Take the horrors of war. The usual perception, fueled by images of bodies mangled by bombs, is that casualties occur from war injuries. That has been the perception for millennia. But until the last century, the reality has been that most soldiers did not die from their wounds. They died from disease. Not until Florence Nightingale came on the scene in the 1850s did this perception change. Her name is synonymous with the art and science of nursing. Also an iconoclastic feminist, she transformed the image of the nurse from a woman of low social status to a professional with technical contributions on a par with doctors of the era. And, to top it off, she was no less a pathbreaker in the emerging field of mathematical statistics. Nightingale was an iconoclast three times over.

On the issue of war casualties, Nightingale learned to change her perception of death by her experiences during the Crimean War. Conventional wisdom said that soldiers died from their wounds, and so their treatment should be aimed at their injuries. Nightingale went against this dogma and showed how it was disease that killed soldiers. During the winter of 1854, Nightingale and a staff of thirty-eight women volunteered to staff the British barracks near Constantinople. Far from being effective, she watched helplessly as the death rate soared. Instead of dying from their wounds, soldiers were dying of highly communicable diseases such as typhoid and cholera. Initially, Nightingale believed these deaths were due to poor nutrition, which was the prevailing explanation. Indeed, the soldiers were malnourished. But because so many men were dying, the military ordered an investigation, during which Nightingale learned to see the deaths in a different light.

In the spring, the makeshift sewers in the barracks were flushed out, and the death rate began to fall. This was a key event for Nightingale that caused her to change her perception of what was killing people. She began to systematically collect information for the investigation on the causes of death and their relationship to injuries, nutrition, and hygiene. It was her mathematical prowess, however, that led to the culminating shift in perception for which she is famous. In a pioneering letter to Queen Victoria, Nightingale used a novel form of data presentation, a polar diagram, similar to a pie chart. Nightingale graphically demonstrated just how many men were dying of diseases stemming from poor hygiene and when they were dying. Iconoclastic in form, this may have been the first practical use of this form of chart that led to a wholesale change in the way that patients were cared for. The graph also illustrates how simply taking information and presenting it in a new visual configuration is an effective way to change one's perception of cause and effect.

Prior to this graph, the military assumed that its soldiers were dying from battle-related complications. This was a natural result of military leaders' experience in battle. But they had little experience with medical care. Nightingale shattered this dogma by taking her experience, which was fundamentally different from the generals', and instantly conveyed it in a visual form. Because of her experience, she learned to see medical care differently and, in turn, was able to teach others to see the way she did.

## How the Brain Learns to See

Entire books have been written about learning, but the important elements for iconoclasts can be boiled down to this: experience modifies the connections between neurons such that they become more efficient at processing information. Traditionally, psychologists and neuroscientists have divided learning into two broad categories. The first category was discovered by Pavlov in his famous dog experiments, and this is known as *classical conditioning*, also called *associative learning*. When a dog sees its owner reaching for the bag of food, it becomes excited and starts wagging its tail. The dog does this not necessarily because it is happy, but because it has learned to associate the bag of food with what will follow. To the owner's eyes, the dog may appear happy, but this is really just a projection of a human emotion onto his pet. We have no way of knowing the subjective experience of the dog itself. Interestingly, the dog's behavior causes associative learning to occur in its owner's brain too. When he reaches for the bag of food, the owner knows exactly how the dog is going to behave, and because humans find canine attention so enjoyable, the dog reinforces feeding behavior in its owner without even knowing it.

When we look in the brain to see what happens to neurons during classical conditioning, we find analogous changes at the neuronal level. In a now classic experiment, Wolfram Schultz, a Swiss neuroscientist, measured the firing rates of monkeys' dopamine neurons while they underwent classical conditioning. We will go into dopamine more deeply when talking about risk, but for now, it is important to note that dopamine is a neurotransmitter synthesized by a very small group of neurons in the brain stem (less than 1 percent of all the neurons in the brain). From about 1950, when dopamine was discovered, until about 1990, scientists thought that dopamine served as the pleasure chemical of the brain. This was a natural conclusion because dopamine is released to all the things that people and animals find pleasurable, including food, water, sex, and drugs. Schultz, however, was interested in how dopamine facilitated associative learning like the type that Pavlov did with his dogs. Schultz trained rhesus monkeys to observe a light. When the light turned on, they received a small drop of juice on their tongues. Before the monkeys learned the association between the light and the juice, Schultz observed that the dopamine neurons fired in response to the juice itself—a finding consistent with the pleasure hypothesis of dopamine. After a brief period of training, however, the monkeys quickly learned to associate the light with the juice, and, interestingly, Schultz observed that the dopamine neurons stopped firing to the juice and began firing to the light. These findings illustrated that like every other neural system in the brain, the dopamine system adapted to environmental contingencies and essentially learned the correlation between arbitrary events such as lights flashing and behaviorally salient outcomes such as fruit juice.[5]

The same learning process occurs in the perceptual system. When the brain is repeatedly presented with the same visual stimuli, the neurons in the visual system continue to respond, but with decreasing vigor. The phenomenon has been called *repetition suppression*, and it has been observed both at the local processing level in V1 and at the object processing level in both the high and the low roads. In the Georgetown experiment, the researchers took advantage of this adaptation to identify which brain regions distinguish car types before and after training. But repetition suppression is important in its own right because it demonstrates the brain's efficiency principle in action. As a rough rule, the brain responds in a linearly decreasing fashion to subsequent observations of an object such that after six to eight observations, the normal response is about one-half of its original level. Of course, a variety of factors mediate this effect, including the time between repetitions and what other intervening events occur, but the general observation holds: repetition leads to smaller neural responses.

There are three competing theories for repetition suppression. The first possibility is that neurons become fatigued like muscles and do not respond as strongly. The second possibility is that neurons become primed to stimuli and respond faster with repetition, which might appear as decreased activity, depending on how one makes the measurement. The final, and most likely, explanation for repetition suppression is the *sharpening hypothesis*. Because the brain does not generally rely on grandmother cells, the vast majority of cognitive and perceptual functions are carried out by networks of neurons. When these networks repeatedly process the same stimulus, neuroscientists have observed that neurons within these networks become more specialized in their activity. So while on initial presentation, the entire network might process a stimulus, by about the sixth presentation, the heavy lifting is being performed by only a subset of neurons within this network. Because fewer neurons are being used, the network becomes more energy efficient in carrying out its function, and we observe this as a decrease in neural activity.[6]

Looking deeper into the process of repetition suppression, we find changes occurring at the molecular level of synapses themselves. These changes occur on different timescales, ranging from milliseconds to days or even years. At the very shortest timescales, neurons that repeatedly fire will eventually deplete critical ions such as potassium and calcium. On a slightly longer timescale of a few seconds, neurons might run out of neurotransmitters, such as dopamine, leading to a phenomenon called *synaptic depression*. But what is really interesting is what happens over the long haul. These temporary depletions of ions and neurotransmitters are believed to lead to an adaptation within neurons themselves called *long-term potentiation* and *long-term depression*. The end result is that neurons adapt by turning on and off genes that control their function. These genes might lead to sprouting of new synapses and pruning of old ones that are nonfunctional.

## From Visual Imagery to Imagination

The brain's reliance on distributed processing goes well beyond simple fail-safe features that prevent you from forgetting your grandmother. Distributed processing means that the brain can also construct images when no information is coming from the eyes. This is a process called *mental imagery*, and it has a close relationship to imagination.

The link between perception, imagery, and imagination has been debated for decades, but only in the last decade has neuroscience revealed where imagination comes from in the brain. The old view of these functions was that visual perception was a one-way street toward the frontal cortex, where the heavy lifting of imagination and cognition was performed. Recent experiments, however, have shown that the visual cortex and its immediate neighbors in the parietal and temporal lobes play integral roles in mental imagery.

The process of mentally visualizing an image is much like running the perceptual process in reverse.[7] The structures used to visualize something are the same as those that process something when you actually see it. Even more amazing, the strength of activity in the visual cortex correlates with the intensity and vividness of what the person visualizes.[8] The stronger the activity, the more vivid the scene a person imagines.

Unfortunately the efficiency principle works against imagination. As an example, close your eyes and visualize the sun setting over a beach.

How detailed was your image? Did you envision a bland orb sinking below calm waters, or did you call up an image filled with activity—palm trees swaying gently, waves lapping at your feet, perhaps a loved one holding your hand? How different was your imaginary beach from a postcard image? The problem is that the sun setting over a beach is an iconic image itself, and most people imagine exactly that. Whether it is through personal experience or simply seeing the sun set over enough Pacific oceans courtesy of Hollywood, there is a striking lack of imagination in this sort of visualization task. The brain simply takes the path of least resistance and reactivates neurons that have been optimized to process this sort of scene.

If you imagine something less common, perhaps something that you have never actually seen, the possibilities for creative thinking become much greater because the brain can no longer rely on connections that have already been shaped by past experience. For example, instead of imagining the sun setting over a beach, imagine you are standing on the surface of Pluto. What would a sunset look like from there? Notice how hard you have to work to imagine this scene. Do you picture a feature-less ball of ice with the sun a speck of light barely brighter than a star glimmering along the horizon? Do you envision frozen lakes of exotic chemicals, or do you picture fjords of ice glimmering in the starlight? The possibilities seem much more open than with its terrestrial coun-terpart. In large part, this is because nobody has ever seen a sunset on Pluto, and you really have to work new neural pathways to imagine it.

These imagery tasks also reveal a key psychological factor in imagi-nation. To imagine something in detail, you must devote a significant amount of mental energy to the task. More precisely, mental energy refers to the ability to direct and sustain attention for the job at hand. The issue of attention has captivated psychologists and neuroscientists for centuries, in large part because of its ineffable quality and the close association of the human sense of self with attention. We feel that we own attention; that it is a matter of free will and individual choice to direct our attention when, and where, we please. Sometimes attention feels like the conductor in the brain, orchestrating the disparate circuits to play their parts at the right times and be quiet when not needed. The modern, neurobiological view tells us something quite a bit different about attention than this Wizard of Oz fantasy, and it also tells us about perception and imagination.

William James, the nineteenth-century psychologist, said this about attention: "Everyone knows what attention is. It is the taking possession by the mind in clear and vivid form, of one out of what seem several simultaneously possible objects or trains of thought . . . It implies withdrawal from some things in order to deal effectively with others, and is a condition which has a real opposite in the confused, dazed, scatter-brained state."[9]

Quite right. Everyone does know what attention is, but that doesn't mean it has been easy to pin down scientifically. To sort through this field, it is helpful to divide attention into two broad categories based on how long the process operates. *Sustained attention*, as the name suggests, acts over extended periods of time and is closely related to drive and motivation, a topic to which I will return later. *Selective attention* is transient and detail oriented. This is the form of attention to which James referred, and because of its transient nature, has been the preferred form to study scientifically.

Details, which on casual observation go unnoticed, become revealed only under the powers of selective attention. And because of this, *attention changes perception*. But where in the brain does attention come from? In one of the first brain imaging experiments to try to answer the question of where attention comes from, researchers at University College, London, presented subjects with visual cues that directed their attention to either the left or the right side of a computer screen.[10] When they compared this with the condition in which no cue was presented, the researchers found attention was associated with increased activity in both prefrontal and parietal areas. Subsequent studies narrowed down this result and distinguished between attention that is directed by external cues, as in the computer experiment, and attention that is directed internally by the person herself. Internal attention seems to depend critically on a subregion of the prefrontal cortex called the dorsolateral prefrontal cortex (DLPFC). When it comes to directing attention to locations in space, the right DLPFC plays a greater role than the left.

But whether externally or internally guided, the parietal cortex plays the crucial role of integrating the effects of attention. Recall that the visual cortex maintains representations of the world on a local, grid-based system, which is a direct result of being closest to the retina. As we move toward the front of the brain on both the high and the low roads, the neural systems switch over to more global and object-based representation systems. By the time the information gets to the frontal lobes, the representations are quite abstract and bear no resemblance to the retinal grid. But we immediately see the problem when it comes to attention. If we wish to direct our attention to something, we need to know where to look. And this is where the parietal cortex comes in. The parietal cortex serves as the crucial intermediary between local representations in the visual cortex and global representations in the frontal cortex. The parietal cortex allows for the seamless transition between these two very different representations. It performs this function from the bottom up, and it also performs it from the top down. It can enhance activity in the visual cortex under the direction of the frontal cortex.[11]

Although attention enhances activity in the visual cortex and other visual areas, the exact nature of this enhancement is not known. There are some clues in the nature of the distributed processing that occurs in these neural networks. Because the brain does not rely on grandmother cells, it uses networks of neurons to perform several different functions and represent many different objects. These networks, then, must be reconfigured every time you look at something different. Although this is highly efficient from an energy perspective, it also means that there are limitations on how many things you can process at once. Attention, under the direction of the frontal cortex and the parietal cortex, switches the nature of the representations in these distributed networks. This reconfiguration of neural networks is also where imagination comes from. Sometimes the reconfiguration can occur under internal guidance, but most of the time, a novel external stimulus is required to jump-start the process.

## Branch Rickey—The Iconoclast Who Hired Jackie Robinson

In 1942, the baseball commissioner, Kenesaw Mountain Landis, famously remarked, "There is no rule, formal or informal, or any understanding—unwritten, subterranean, or sub-anything—against the hiring of Negro players by the teams of organized ball."[12] It was, of course, a lie. The owners of the Major League Baseball teams adhered to the rigid segregation of blacks and whites, despite the fact that the vast majority of players themselves would have welcomed the opportunity to play with members of the Negro League. Many already did in barnstorming exhibitions.

Enter Branch Rickey. Even before entering the debate on racial segregation, Rickey had distinguished himself among baseball managers. His Midwestern roots led to a work ethic that became legendary in his career. He had put himself through law school at the University of Michigan by coaching college baseball. But rather than heading into the law profession, he allowed his passion for baseball to ultimately carry the day, and in 1913, he started working for the St. Louis Browns. After the Browns were sold, Rickey shifted to the St. Louis Cardinals as a field manager. On the field, Rickey created some remarkable innovations, including sliding pits and batting tees, both of which are standard fare today. Although he was innovative on the field, his real talent lay in the front office. In 1925, he was hired as general manager of the Cardinals.

During his time with the Cardinals, Rickey's greatest innovation was the creation of the minor league farm system. It was Rickey who devised the system by which the owners controlled a chain of minor league teams that were used to groom the best players for promotion to the majors. As a side effect, those players who weren't good enough for the majors were sold, at a profit, to other teams. Rickey had a long run with the Cardinals, but by 1941, Rickey had come to irreconcilable differences with the owners. As luck would have it, the Brooklyn Dodgers were in the market for a new general manager.

The Brooklyn fans did not receive Rickey well. The Dodgers fell to seventh place in 1944, and the rising chorus of calls to fire Rickey was fueled by a hostile local press. Rickey began to trade away some popular but aging players in an attempt to build up his team. But the uncertainties of the war were making it difficult. He couldn't count on a young player making it through a season without being drafted into the army.

It was the war itself that prompted Rickey to change his perception of blacks. Although much later he remarked, "I couldn't face my God much longer knowing that His black creatures are held separate and distinct from His white creatures in the game that has given me all I own," Rickey's motives were also economic.[13] He needed talent, and the Negro League was the last source. As the historian, Jules Tygiel, wrote, "Rickey clearly perceived that being the first to sign blacks would propel the Dodgers to pennants."[14] Maybe it was more than that. Rickey, known as "the Mahatma" among sportswriters, also aspired to be an agent of social change. Here was an opportunity to really change the social landscape of America.

Despite the commissioner's statement, the unwritten rule was that blacks could not play for a major league team. The dogma was that the fans would rebel. Rickey became a true iconoclast the moment he set plans in motion to topple this dogma. But Rickey didn't get to be the head of a baseball team without knowing something about owners. The year after arriving in Brooklyn, he started planting seeds in the owners' minds about recruiting black players. The timing was right. Despite the unwritten rule of segregation, they responded favorably and swore each other to secrecy. Keeping a secret like that wasn't going to be easy. Rickey knew that whoever he recruited would have to be a special type of person. Yes, he would have to have the talent to play with the whites, but he would also need something more. Rickey needed someone who could play at a high level for a long period of time while simultaneously being subjected to intense public abuse. By May 1945, Rickey's scouts had focused his attention on the twenty-six-year-old shortstop for the Kansas City Monarchs, Jackie Robinson. But that is a story for later chapters.

Years later, Rickey remarked, "The utter injustice of it always was in my mind—in St. Louis a negro was not permitted to buy his way into the Grandstand—and it has only been in recent years that he has been permitted to go into the Grandstand and of course there was no negro player in baseball—I felt very deeply about that thing all my life and within a month after I went to Brooklyn I went to Mr. George McLaughlin [one of the owners] and had a talk with him about it and found he was sympathetic with my views about it."[15]

Although Rickey had always had a talent for management, it is the Robinson story that propels him into the ranks of iconoclasts. Here, we see the iconoclast's imagination in action. In fact, it was the war itself that triggered Rickey's perception of blacks to run in reverse and imagine the possibility of a black playing for the Dodgers. No doubt, part of this was motivated by the desire for a pennant. Rickey also had deep-seated feelings about integration that he traced to his Midwestern upbringing. It simply took the catalyst of the war and the need to recruit talent to unleash his perceptual system from the shackles of segregation in baseball and imagine how to do it.

## Breaking Out of Categories

The relationship between perception, insight, and imagination goes well beyond basic psychology or historical debates. To recap the neuroscience view, imagination comes from using the same neural circuits used to perceive natural objects. In this way, imagination is like reverse perception. Perception, however, is constrained by the categories that an individual brings to the table. Although categories may not be absolute, they are learned from past experience, and because of this relationship, experience shapes both perception and imagination. In order to think creatively, and imagine possibilities that only iconoclasts do, one must break out of the cycle of experience-dependent categorization—or what Mark Twain called "education." For most people, this does not come naturally. Often the harder one tries to think differently, the more rigid the categories become. There is a better way, a path that jolts the brain out of preconceived notions of what it is seeing: bombard the brain with new experiences. Only then will it be forced out of efficiency mode and reconfigure its neural networks.

One of the most important scientific discoveries in the last thirty years had its origins in exactly these types of novel circumstances. Kary Mullis came up with the basic principle of the *polymerase chain reaction*, or PCR, while driving up the northern California coast in 1983. PCR is the fundamental technology that allows any type of genetic test to be performed. PCR is used in genetic fingerprinting, crime scene investigations, paternity testing, and detection of hereditary diseases and cancer. PCR is also used widely in cloning and genetically engineered products such as vaccines. Mullis won the Nobel Prize in chemistry in 1993 for his discovery, and the circumstances of his discovery also make him an iconoclast.

A chemist by training, Mullis had been conducting experiments on small fragments of DNA for Cetus Corporation, a biotech start-up in the Bay Area. DNA is composed of only four types of nucleotides, and they are strung together in long double chains. These chains may contain thousands of nucleotides, and the specific sequences contain the code for producing all the proteins that make up an organism. Although the code had been cracked decades before, DNA existed in only minute quantities in the body, which made it difficult to purify and study, even in the 1980s.

Cetus and several other biotech companies had developed technology to make short sequences of DNA, called *oligonucleotides*, but these were only ten base pairs long. Nothing close to human genome length. Conventional wisdom said there was no way to synthesize DNA strands anywhere near the length of what exists in nature. And although the machines at Cetus were efficient at cranking out oligonucleotides, they still weren't very long and were not useful for much. With the machines making buckets of oligonucleotides, Mullis turned his attention to denaturing natural DNA. Although DNA strands will separate at 95°, they will also come together again if the temperature is dropped back down. Mullis began to play around with programming computers that could control the denaturing and annealing processes, and realized he could automate much of it.

The breakthrough idea came to Mullis not in the Cetus laboratory, but on a spring evening while he was driving up the northern California coast.

As I drove through the mountains that night, the stalks of the California buckeyes heavily in blossom leaned over into the road. The air was moist and cool and filled with their heady aroma.

How about this, I thought? What if I mix the DNA sample with the oligonucleotides, drop in the [DNA] polymerase and wait? After this was complete I could heat the mixture, causing the extended oligonucleotides to be removed from the target, then cool the mixture allowing new, unextended oligonucleotides to hybridize.

EUREKA!!!! The result would be exactly the same only the signal strength [DNA] would be doubled.

And again, EUREKA!!!! I could do it over and over again. Every time I did it I would double the signal. For those of you who got lost, we're back! I stopped the car at mile marker 46.7 on Highway 128. In the glove compartment I found some paper and a pen. I confirmed that two to the tenth power was about a thousand and that two to the twentieth power was about a million, and that two to the thirtieth power was around a billion, close to the number of base pairs in the human genome.[16]

Mullis realized that he could amplify a piece of DNA exponentially by simply repeating the cycle of denaturing DNA, adding an oligo-nucleotide to get the process started, and dumping in a bunch of naked nucleotides with some DNA polymerase. After only twenty cycles, he would have amplified a single piece of DNA a million times. Although it took him about six months of trial and error back in the laboratory, ultimately he was successful and proved wrong every other biochemist about synthesizing DNA.

The interesting part of the story, however, is how Mullis came to the crucial insight. All the pieces of the puzzle had been known for several years, and so he didn't discover a new process per se, but instead figured out how to link several existing technologies in a way that would have far-reaching ramifications. The insight did not occur as he was hunched over his laboratory bench. Instead, the eureka moment came at mile marker 46.7 on Highway 128. As with Lauterbur in the Big Boy restaurant, or Disney in the movie theater, the insight came in a novel environment.

## Novelty as a Trigger for Running the Perceptual System in Reverse

In the previous chapter, we saw how novel experiences trigger new ways of seeing the world. Because imagination comes from the perceptual system, the same principle applies to imagination. Imagination is like running perception in reverse.

The wrinkle, however, is that the brain operates under the efficiency principle, which means that it will do its job in a way that takes the least amount of energy. It is lazy. The efficiency principle dictates that the brain will take shortcuts based on what it already knows. These shortcuts, although they save energy, lead to perception being shaped by past experience. How you categorize objects determines what you see. And because imagination comes from perception, these same categories hobble imagination and make it difficult to think differently.

The brain is extraordinarily efficient in using its resources. Too efficient. While in familiar surroundings, whether Mullis's laboratory or Chihuly's hotshop, the brain perceives things in ways that it has become accustomed to. Only when the brain is confronted with stimuli that it has not seen before, does it start to reorganize perception. This reorganization spills over and influences the internal images that can be held in the mind's eye. So even though Mullis had been thinking about DNA and oligonucleotides for months, something happened in his car that evening that triggered a new perception of the problem that was previously unavailable to him in familiar surroundings.

For the same reason, Disney didn't imagine the possibilities of animation until he saw the novel juxtaposition of projected illustrations with moving pictures. Only then did his perception of drawing change from a static one to a dynamic one that could tell a narrative. And it took the realities of war to trigger the imagination of Florence Nightingale to change the sanitary conditions that were killing soldiers.

Fortunately, the networks that govern both perception and imagination can be reprogrammed. The frontal cortex, which contains rules for decision making, can reconfigure neural networks in the visual pathways so that an individual can see things that she didn't see before simply by deploying her attention differently. But it is difficult to do this under business-as-usual conditions. It typically takes a novel stimulus—either a new piece of information or getting out of the environment in which an individual has become comfortable—to jolt attentional systems awake and reconfigure both perception and imagination. The more radical and novel the change, the greater the likelihood of new insights being generated. To think like an iconoclast, you need novel experiences.

As in the last chapter, the surest way to evoke the imagination is to confront the perceptual system with people, places, and things it hasn't seen before. Categories are death to imagination. So the solution is to seek out environments in which you have no experience. The environments may have nothing to do with the individual's area of expertise. It doesn't matter. Because the same systems in the brain carry out both perception and imagination, there will be crosstalk.

Novel experiences, especially big changes such as relocations, figure prominently in the imagination of an iconoclast. Without losing sight of why novel experiences are so effective at unleashing the imagination (because they force the perceptual system out of categories), the real target is categorization. The tendency of the brain to take shortcuts through categorization means that the iconoclast maintains a state of vigilance over the use of categories.

An effective strategy to fight categorization is to confront categories directly. Whether it is categorizing a person or an idea, write out the categories. Jot down some words that categorize an idea. Use analogies. You will naturally fall back on things that you are familiar with. Allow yourself the freedom to write down gut feelings, such as stupid or hot. Only when you consciously confront your brain's reliance on categories will you be able to imagine outside of its boundaries.

# THREE

# Fear—The Inhibitor of Action

I have learned over the years that when one's
mind is made up, this diminishes fear; knowing
what must be done does away with fear.

—Rosa Parks

IF BRANCH RICKEY WAS AN iconoclast for hiring Jackie
Robinson to play for the Brooklyn Dodgers, Robinson was
equally an iconoclast for having the courage to do so. It is hard to over-
estimate the symbolic importance of Jackie Robinson. Born in Cairo,
Georgia, in 1919, a grandson of a slave, Robinson seemed an unlikely
candidate to become an icon. His father left when he was six months
old, and Robinson's mother picked up the family and moved to Southern
California. Although he grew up in a somewhat more integrated environment in Pasadena, Robinson still knew the pains of discrimination
from an early age. But he didn't let fear get in the way of what he did.

Sports became a respite for Robinson. He had natural athletic ability. Later winning a scholarship to UCLA, he became the university's first four-letter man in basketball, baseball, football, and track. But reality soon began to creep in, and Robinson left UCLA after two years, convinced that "no amount of education would help a black man get a job."[1] After Pearl Harbor, Robinson enlisted in the army, but he had a rough time there. He was outspoken about how blacks were treated, particularly with the seating arrangements on buses. The result was a court-martial. Fortunately, Robinson was acquitted and received an honorable discharge in 1944. But still without any job prospects, he signed up to play black baseball in the Jim Crow leagues.

Robinson knew Branch Rickey's motives weren't entirely altruistic. Rickey was chasing a pennant. But it was Robinson who had to face real fear. He had to disprove the prevailing opinion, at least among the team owners, that blacks were incapable of playing in the majors. And for going against this overwhelming opinion, Robinson deserves the label "iconoclast."

On opening day in 1947, Robinson endured an unending stream of racial epithets emanating from the Philadelphia Phillies' dugout. Robinson later wrote, "Of all the unpleasant days in my life, [this day] brought me nearer to cracking up than I ever had been.[2] It was almost enough to make him question his own ability. He entertained images of pummeling the Phillies' bench.

And then came Robinson's epiphany. As with every iconoclast, there is a point in time that stands crystallized in their memory as the moment when something changed their perception of the world. For Robinson, his fear subsided when he looked over at Rickey and realized, "Rickey had come to a crossroads and made a lonely decision. I was at a crossroads. I would make mine. I would stay."[3]

Of course, that wasn't the end of it. Hotels refused to accommodate Robinson with his teammates. He received bags of hate mail. The lives of his wife and son were threatened. But his persistence paid off. His teammates rallied around him. Not because he was black, but because Robinson was a key player who helped the Dodgers win the pennant that year. As his athletic prowess became apparent, the fans supported him too. "The black and the young were my cheering squads. But also there were people—neither black nor young—people of all races and faiths and in all parts of this country, people who couldn't care less about my race."[4]

So how did Robinson do it? How does an individual squelch the fear of the unknown, the fear of physical harm, and the fear of social isolation? The answer lies in how his brain dealt with the second key function of iconoclasm: the fear response.

## Fear: The Mother of All Stress

Fear feels bad. When you are scared, your body is under stress. Very few human behaviors are as stereotypical as the stress response. The triggers may vary from individual to individual, but the picture of stress is always the same. The blood pressure rises, and the heart starts beating faster. Sweat glands seem to blossom in locations that you didn't even know existed. The moisture emerges in all the wrong places as the mouth dries up and with it the words coming out. Fingers tremble. The voice warbles and cracks, and the stomach flip-flops. Sometimes the body tries to compensate by lowering blood pressure, with the unfortunate result of feeling lightheaded.

The human stress response, although sometimes rearing its head in the most inopportune times, is part and parcel of our evolutionary history. Only the fittest have survived in what has been many times in the past a hostile environment. The world changes. Animals try to eat you. Others compete with you for food and reproductive rights. Yes, growing up as a species on the planet Earth is a stressful process.

But stress is different today. And while humans do not fend off saber-toothed tigers, we sure have our share of other stressors. The social fabric of society is far more complex than any culture that humans evolved in. And still, we carry the burden of millions of years of evolution. We possess a stress response system that evolved in very different circumstances than exist today. In fact, the stress system is so important, and so active, that it can override every other system in the brain. The stress system is not rational. It reacts when provoked, and this reaction is powerful enough to derail many of the most innovative people out there. *The ability to tame the stress response represents the second great hurdle to becoming an iconoclast.*

Let's break down the stress response.[5] There are two distinct components: the neural system and the hormonal system. The neural component of stress is controlled by the autonomic nervous system, which itself is divided into two subparts. One part of the autonomic nervous system, called the *sympathetic* system, becomes activated during stress, and the other part, called the *parasympathetic* system, is turned off during stress. Both parts of the autonomic nervous system connect the brain to the internal organs of the body. The autonomic nervous system can operate quite well without the brain, and so its connection to the brain is a fairly low-bandwidth connection that keeps the big kahuna apprised of system status. Not that the brain can do much about it. For example, you may become aware that something is amiss in your digestive tract, but if your autonomic nervous system decides that its GI contents must be purged, there's no way your brain can stop it.

A vast network of internal nerves makes up the autonomic nervous system. These nerves are completely separate from the spinal cord. The sympathetic nervous system is made up of a network, called *ganglia*, that exists in parallel with the spinal cord. These ganglia can be found in the thorax, in the abdomen, and in the pelvis. They look like a vast disorganized spider web, and you can trace the nerves to organs such as the heart, stomach, and bladder. The sympathetic system sends nerves to salivary glands too, and when active, inhibits the production of saliva. It even dilates the pupils when you're excited. And in an excitement of a different sort, the sympathetic nervous system is responsible for orgasm.

The other half of the autonomic nervous system, the parasympathetic system, is just as important for human life as the sympathetic, but it doesn't get as much attention, because it is responsible for the quiet, restorative aspects of life. The parasympathetic system has its own network too, accomplishing most of its business through a single large nerve branching off of the brain stem, called the *vagus nerve*. The vagus sends branches to all the same organs that the autonomic nervous system does, but its actions are opposite. The vagus, for example, slows down the heart. It stimulates salivary glands and speeds up the digestive process. And although the sympathetic system gets credit for the money shot, it is the parasympathetic system that is responsible for sexual arousal.

As you might have guessed, it is the sympathetic system that presents problems for the iconoclast. The sympathetic system causes all the physical manifestations of stress that are well suited for running away from predators or fighting with other humans. But these are primitive physical systems. None are well suited for, or really have anything to do with, creativity and innovation. If you've ever had a shot of epinephrine, you know that the physical response is so overwhelming that it is impossible to think. Indeed, that is the whole point of the sympathetic system: action without thought.

The other part of the stress response that gets a lot of attention is the hormonal side. Like neurotransmitters, hormones cause physiological responses in target organs. The main difference between a hormone and a neurotransmitter is that a neurotransmitter is released from a nerve ending at a specific location, while hormones are released into the bloodstream and circulate throughout the body. Because hormones course through the entire body, their effects are much more widespread than those of a neurotransmitter. The other big difference, which stems from the mode of release, is how long it takes for these systems to react.

When the sympathetic nervous system fires, you feel the effects instantaneously. Because hormones have to be released into the bloodstream and circulate to their final destination, hormonal responses generally become apparent only after several minutes and sometimes hours.

There are scores of hormones in the human body, but as far as the stress response goes, only one is important: cortisol. *Cortisol* is a steroid and is chemically identical to hydrocortisone—the same stuff you buy in the drugstore as an anti-itch cream. Cortisol is produced in the adrenal glands, which look like a small glob of fat sitting on top of each kidney. How do the adrenal glands know when to release cortisol? When the brain tells them to. Although interestingly, the brain doesn't accomplish this through neuronal connections. When you encounter something stressful, a signal reaches a tiny part of the brain called the *hypothalamus*. The hypothalamus contains several different groups of neurons related to hormonal functions. When the body is stressed the hypothalamus releases a chemical called CRH, which stands for corticotropin releasing hormone. CRH enters the bloodstream right next to the hypothalamus and flows about 1 inch, where it reaches the pituitary gland. The pituitary dangles from the underside of the brain, looking like a pair of mouse testicles. Here, CRH stimulates the release of yet another hormone, called ACTH (adrenocorticotropin releasing hormone). It is ACTH that finally enters the bloodstream, where it flows to the adrenal glands.

The hormonal stress response may seem convoluted, but there is good reason for using hormones in addition to neurotransmitters. While neurotransmitters cause instantaneous reaction in the body, the effect of hormones is more subtle and long lasting. Hormones direct different organs in the body to change their physical configuration, especially in response to stresses that don't go away. Chronic stressors, such as physical injury or starvation, require the body to shift its resources to either repair damage or deal with an ongoing lack of nutrients. The human body is amazingly flexible in this regard. It is well evolved for dealing with the stresses that our ancestors encountered thousands of years ago.

Modern stress is different. If your stress system is activated, it is probably for a reason different from physical injury. Today, the major stressor for most people stems from social reasons. Social stressors come from conflicts with spouses, bosses, and competition with peers. Add on top of that an increasing perception of lack of control over the environment, and you have a recipe for ongoing stress that takes a toll on the body. The toll, of course, is collected in the form of all the major medical ailments, such as heart disease, high blood pressure, and diabetes.

The brain is not immune from the effects of stress either. As the flashpoint for the stress response, the brain is the organ that initiates the cascade. The brain responds to perceived threats and activates the sympathetic nervous system, and the brain initiates the cascade of hormonal responses. On the receiving end, the brain remodels itself in response to stress. Some of the remodeling occurs at the neuronal level through simple learning mechanisms. Other changes occur under the effects of hormones such as cortisol. These physical changes may have wide-ranging effects on behavior. Repeated stressors, for example, cause changes in key parts of the brain related to decision making and even iconoclastic thinking.

## The Accidental Iconoclast: Fear and the Dixie Chicks

Nobody knows the stress response like people who have had their life threatened. Time and again, history has shown how iconoclasts like Jackie Robinson are treated. The truly unpopular have been killed. We would like to believe that such possibilities are a thing of the past, but they are not. Sometimes the iconoclast arises out of the most unlikely circumstances, a sort of accidental iconoclast. Natalie Maines, lead singer of the Dixie Chicks, is exactly this type of iconoclast.

Maines's comment on a London stage in March 2003 was almost an afterthought, an off-the-cuff remark between songs from someone well known for speaking her mind. But when Maines announced, "We're ashamed the President of the United States is from Texas," all hell broke loose. The United States was on the eve of invading Iraq, and support for Bush was at an all-time high. To make matters worse, patriotism and country music had always gone hand in hand, and Maines's remark was taken as a direct insult by large segments of their fan base. Intentionally or not, Maines and the Chicks became iconoclasts when they took a stand against the dogma that said "country music = unflagging patriotism." They were one of the most popular acts in country music, and overnight they plummeted to one of the most reviled targets.

Public destructions of their CDs looked eerily similar to Nazi book burnings. Emily Robison, who plays banjo and guitar in the band, recalled, "A radio station said they had our picture on the side of one of their vans, and they were just driving down the highway when a car pulled up with a shotgun and pointed it at them. Just because our picture was on their van."[6]

The death threats were the worst. Maines received the brunt of them. One, in particular, was quite specific: you will be shot dead at your show in Dallas. Although Maines already had around-the-clock protection, she had to extend it to her family, including her parents. Three years later, Robison still shudders at what the Chicks endured. "It was like the McCarthy days, and it was almost like the country was unrecognizable." Maines's view of the conservative media: "If you don't share their opinions, they label you as a terrorist or a person who doesn't have any family values."[7]

When the Dixie Chicks released their next album, three years after the incident, a curious thing happened. The tide of public opinion about the Iraq war had changed. Much of the United States supported troop withdrawal. The Chicks' ties to country music, however, were damaged. Their single "Not Ready to Make Nice" floundered on *Billboard* charts but, at the same time, was the number-one download on iTunes. Maines understood what was going on with the radio stations that still wouldn't give them any airtime: "When a hundred people e-mail you that they'll never listen to your station again, you get scared of losing your job. They caved."[8]

What is most impressive about Maines and the Dixie Chicks, like Jackie Robinson before them, is how they did not let their fear of public ridicule, or even fear of death, prevent them from standing up for what they believed. Where most people would succumb to these pressures, Maines learned to embrace her now very public role. "I feel a responsibility to do it now. I didn't realize how quiet I was being. But it's exhausting to keep doing it. You feel like you're fighting an uphill battle. But, it's just not in me to shy away from things that I truly believe in. I'm not afraid."[9]

Maines's comment illustrates a common attribute among iconoclasts and how they deal with fear. They transform the emotion into something else. While Jackie Robinson transformed his fear into anger, Maines changed hers into pride. Recognizing that fear can paralyze action, the iconoclast takes the autonomic arousal associated with fear and uses it for something productive. The prefrontal cortex is largely responsible for this override control, but before we get to how it does this, a closer examination of where fear resides in the brain is called for.

## Fear Conditioning

Remember Ivan Pavlov, the good old Russian psychologist who got his dogs to salivate at the sound of a bell? He was the guy who discovered *classical conditioning*, the simplest form of learning. In classical conditioning, a neutral stimulus, such as a light or a bell, is paired with something that evokes a response, such as food. The latter is called an *unconditioned stimulus* (US) because it causes a response, such as salivation, on its own. The neutral stimulus is called a *conditioned stimulus* (CS) because pairing it with the US *conditions* the animal to respond to the neutral thing. In Pavlov's experiments, the US was something desirable—food—so this type of learning is called *appetitive conditioning*. It doesn't have to be that way. Classical conditioning also works for things that animals don't like. Electric shocks, bitter liquids, loud noises, and air puffs to the eyeball are all common "unconditioned stimuli" used in *aversive conditioning*. Such tactics have been used as part of behavior modification therapy for things such as smoking cessation and invisible fences for dogs.

For fear conditioning, one brain structure serves as the critical processing center. About the size and shape of an almond, the *amygdala* lies deep within the temporal lobes just off the midline of the brain. The amygdala is a structure critical for emotional processing, and the bulk of the evidence supports its role as a gateway for fear vis-à-vis the autonomic nervous system.[10]

The amygdala also influences the functioning of cortical regions, including perception itself. In a famous series of experiments in the 1970s, neuroscientists discovered that the amygdala can fine-tune the response of neurons in the auditory cortex. First, the researchers used a technique in which they recorded from neurons in the auditory cortex while playing tones of different frequencies to the animal. Auditory neurons possess a tuning curve in which they respond maximally to a specific range of frequencies. The neuroscientists then picked the frequency that was just off the best frequency for a particular neuron, and paired that tone with an electric shock. After just a few such pairings, they found that the auditory neurons had shifted their preference to match the tone associated with the shock. Moreover, this change persisted for weeks. These results demonstrate the powerful effects of fear conditioning on perception itself. The amygdala, by associating a particular tone with a shock, rewired the cortex so that the brain became more attuned to this frequency. These changes are profound and long lasting.

Many scientists believe that fear conditioning cannot be undone. For an unpleasant stimulus like an electric shock, it doesn't take long for fear conditioning to occur. Typically, it only takes a few pairings of sound and shock. If, however, you began presenting the CS without the shock, the animal will stop responding to the CS. The process is called *extinction*. For many years, scientists believed that the animal actually forgot the association of the CS with the shock. More recent evidence suggests otherwise. Although the responses to the conditioned stimulus diminish over time, it turns out that they are inhibited, not eliminated. This has important implications, because it means that conditioned fear responses can reappear with only the slightest provocation. The key structure for extinction turns out to be the prefrontal cortex. Although the amygdala is still necessary for the expression of fear responses, it is the prefrontal cortex that keeps it in check. Damage to the prefrontal cortex, or conditions in which the prefrontal cortex is occupied with other tasks, may result in the release of the amygdala brake and the reemergence of a fear response.

So while it is true that time heals all wounds, as far as the brain goes, scars remain.

## Computer Associates and the Fear of Failure

The fear of public ridicule figures prominently for many people, but the fear of failure deserves equal billing in terms of its toxic effects to both the individual and the organization. The story of Computer Associates (CA) provides a case study in how both types of fear can tear an organization apart.[11]

Charles Wang, born in Shanghai, immigrated to the United States when he was eight years old. In 1976, with one piece of software for mainframe computers, he founded Computer Associates International. With an aggressive management style, Wang grew his company rapidly.

Computer Associates' expansion was fueled largely through the acquisition of smaller companies and competitors. A favorite tactic of Wang's was the hostile takeover of a competitor, followed by an ultimatum given to the workers of the acquired company: accept a new contract with a pay cut or be fired. All in all, Wang engineered at least fifty such takeovers.

Fueled by his appetite for acquisitions, Wang grew Computer Associates to a company with $1 billion in annual sales by 1989. He seemed to have a magic touch for exceeding Wall Street's expectations for earnings. He ran the company like a family business. He rarely used e-mail or written documents to communicate with his management team, and former employees described a management style based on fear and intimidation.

Wang and his CEO, Sanjay Kumar, ran Computer Associates driven by the overriding fear of not meeting earnings estimates. The company's products, which came largely through external acquisitions instead of internal innovation, derived from the shrinking mainframe market. Computer Associates developed a reputation of playing hardball with its clients, essentially locking its customers into long-term maintenance contracts for outdated equipment and software. In an effort to pump up its earnings, CA evolved a set of questionable accounting practices that ranged from booking revenues from maintenance contracts all at once (instead of the normal practice of distributing those revenues over the length of the contract) to the infamous thirty-five-day month, in which sales after the end of the month were booked retroactively.

Ultimately, the accounting practices were outed under lawsuits from CA's investors. Criminal investigations against senior management were launched by the Justice Department. Kumar pleaded guilty to fraud and was sentenced to twelve years in prison in 2006 and to pay $800 million in restitution. Wang resigned from CA's board in 2002, and the board subsequently launched its own investigation against him. He has never been indicted. What is interesting about the investigation's report is the culture of fear prevalent within CA:

> Mr. Wang caused additional harm to CA by creating a "culture of
> fear," which caused CA employees, at all levels, to refrain from
> offering dissenting opinions. He did this by making personnel
> decisions in an arbitrary manner, routinely firing CA personnel
> on a subjective basis. This had the effect of suppressing corporate
> dialogue, by both lower and midlevel employees, as well as in the
> highest ranks of senior management. According to one witness,
> CA employees felt as if they were constantly "hanging on by their
> fingernails." In the SLC's view, this culture was the breeding
> ground in which the 35-Day Month practice originated and later
> flourished. This atmosphere proved particularly toxic at CA, since,
> under Mr. Wang, missing Wall Street estimates was to be avoided
> at all costs.[12]

Computer Associates provides a good example of how to inhibit both innovation and iconoclastic thinking through fear and intimidation. Even Wang's and Kumar's decision making was distorted by their own fears of failing to meet earnings expectations. Although it is possible to run a company this way, it is not possible to foster iconoclastic thinking when fear is pervasive. Such a company can only grow through the acquisition of others' innovations.

## An Alternative to Fear: The Idea Market

Jim Lavoie, age sixty, is the CEO of Rite-Solutions, a software company based in Newport, Rhode Island, that creates novel software solutions for demanding environments. The company makes programs for submarine command and control systems and visualization tools for Coast

Guard helicopter pilots on rescue missions. With his business partner and longtime friend, Joe Marino, fifty-eight, who is the president, the two formed a company whose founding principle is the creation of a culture that fosters fun and innovation. Lavoie is the gregarious one. He exudes energy and enthusiasm and possesses a personality well suited for networking and raising capital. Marino is serious. Down-to-earth, practical, he knows how to run a company and has a good sense for the type of employee who benefits from the culture that they have created. He boasts that Rite-Solutions has a 2 percent annual attrition rate, a feat unheard of in the software industry, in which the norm is 10 to 20 percent. Rite-Solutions is not a big company (about 150 employees), but it has attracted a great deal of attention for its approach to innovation. Lavoie and Marino are not iconoclasts, but they are attempting to coax potential iconoclasts out of their shells. They represent the antithesis of the CA management style.

"Most companies have this funnel," says Lavoie. "Give me all of your ideas and we'll choke them down to two ideas. In my old company, if you had a great idea, we would tell you, 'Okay, we'll make an appointment for you to address the murder board,' because the murder board's job was to make sure the company took no risk. Their job was to shoot down ideas."[13]

Marino explains what would happen. "Some technical guy comes in with a good idea. Of course questions are asked of that person that they don't know. Like, 'How big's the market? What's your marketing approach? What's your business plan for this? What's the product going to cost?' It's embarrassing. Most people can't answer those kind of questions. The people who made it through these boards were not the people with the best ideas. *They were the best presenters.*"

Lavoie confesses, "If you know the game, you can get through the funnel. You make up stuff. I made it to executive VP not by being bright, but by being theatrical. By being passionate. You can fake passion. And the better ideas were being shot down because the other guy didn't do theater as well."

Their approach to coaxing innovation, even iconoclasm, is through the idea market. Everyone, on the day they start work at Rite-Solutions, is given $10,000 in opinion money. This money can be invested in ideas in an internal stock market. The market has a superficial similarity to a real stock market, but it has some crucial differences that allow ideas to evolve. Employees log in to the market and can view an "expectus," which is a brief description of an idea that someone else in the company came up with. It might be a simple idea, such as developing a piece of computer code to perform some new visualization function. At this stage of the game, it is still just an idea. If another employee likes the idea, they can invest part of their opinion money in that idea.

An investment grows in value through the next two components of the market. For an idea to gain traction, other people have to make comments and criticisms within the market about how to improve the idea. This is called "interest" money. Lavoie and Marino operationalize the amount of interest by the number of comments for a particular idea. They have structured the market so that interest money counts for twice as much opinion money. But to realize a profit, employees must put in real time working on an idea. This is called the investment phase, and it is the most valuable of all, because it transitions an idea off the drawing board into reality. It need not be complex. It can be as simple as someone saying, "Here's what needs to be done, and I'm willing to contribute two hours of my own time."

One wonders why someone would spend their own time working on ideas that are not directly related to Rite-Solutions' contract work. Marino believes the answer has to do with trust. "Going in on Day 1, we let our people see anything that anybody is working on. Very few companies do that." Another reason is that the market helps people create their own jobs. "Not only does the originator of an idea benefit financially, but if the idea is successful, then he's going to be the one working on that technology," Lavoie says. This is a nice perk especially if it's a particularly hot technology that people are dying to work on.

Lavoie and Marino came up with a novel solution to the problem of social fear and how this fear stifles innovation. To be sure, it doesn't remove all of the fear of sharing one's ideas publicly, but it attempts to take some of the drama out of it. It also has another, unanticipated benefit in terms of transparency. The market makes it clear to everyone in the company what everyone else is working on, in essence providing a big picture for everyone who wants to know how their work fits into the company as a whole. Lavoie and Marino didn't design the market to address the problem of secrecy in organizations, but the market has turned out to help decrease a third common fear that gets in the way of iconoclasm: the fear of the unknown.

## Fear of the Unknown: A Biological View of Uncertainty

Although fear of the unknown is an entirely different type of phobia from the fear of failure, it is also processed through the amygdala. This is actually good news, because it means that the pathways by which fear inhibits behavior flow through this one structure. We have learned a great deal about the amygdala in the last several years, and this knowledge can be applied to ameliorate this particular roadblock to iconoclasm.

Fear of the unknown, or ambiguity, is a funny thing. It is not a specific event such as an electric shock or the pain experienced from the criticism of an unempathetic supervisor. Ambiguity stems from a lack of knowledge. It looms over the psyche like a dark cloud on the horizon. The brain constantly tries to predict what's going to happen next, and when it can't, a sense of foreboding ensues. Some people are better at dealing with ambiguous situations than others, but when fear of ambiguity bubbles to the surface, it is universally experienced the same way.

Recent advances in neuroeconomics offer clues about heading off this demon before it inhibits behavior. Consider a classic conundrum, known as the Ellsberg paradox.[14] There are two large urns placed in front of you (see figure 3-1). The urns are completely opaque, so you cannot see their contents. The urn on the left contains ten black marbles and ten white ones. The urn on the right contains twenty marbles, but you do not know the proportion of black to white. Now, the game is to draw a black marble from one of the urns. If you are successful, you win $100. You only have one chance, so which urn will you draw from? Keep the answer in your mind.

Let's play again. Now, the game is to draw a white marble. Again, you only have one chance, so which urn will it be?

Most people when confronted with these choices choose the urn on the left—the one with the known proportions of black and white

**FIGURE 3-1**

## The Ellsberg paradox

*The urn on the left contains ten black marbles and ten white marbles. The urn on the right contains twenty marbles of an unknown ratio of black to white. Draw a black marble to win $100. Which urn do you choose to draw from?*

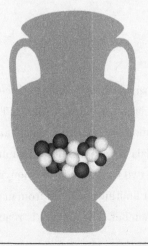

marbles. And therein lies the paradox. If you choose the left-hand urn when trying to pull a black marble, that means you think your chances are better for that urn. But because there are only two colors in both urns, the odds of pulling a white must be complementary to the odds of pulling a black. Logically, if you thought the left-hand urn was the better choice for a black marble, then the right hand urn should be the better choice for a white marble. The fact that most people avoid the right-hand urn altogether suggests that people have an inherent fear of the unknown (also called *ambiguity aversion*).

In 2005, researchers at Caltech performed an important neuroimaging study of the Ellsberg paradox. Although the paradox had been known for decades, the neurobiological reason for ambiguity aversion remained a mystery. Economists had relegated the effect to the growing garbage bin of anomalies from expected utility theory. The Caltech group placed subjects in an MRI scanner while they performed a series of trials based on the Ellsberg paradox. When the researchers examined the brain responses to risky versus ambiguous decisions, they found two regions that were more strongly activated to ambiguity. One region was the underside of the cortex that sits above the eyeballs, called the *orbitofrontal cortex*. The other region was the amygdala.

## Taming the Amygdala Through Reappraisal and Extinction

The amygdala is a twitchy character with a long memory. Once the amygdala encodes an unpleasant association, it doesn't forget. These memories sometimes resurface at the most inopportune times, and in the worst of circumstances, the amygdala is responsible for traumatic flashbacks. But all is not lost. There are two ways to keep the amygdala in check. One is proactive, preventing or limiting the brain from making unpleasant associations that it will remember. The second is reactive, which acknowledges the fact that unpleasantness is unavoidable but need not be paralyzing.

For many people, the types of fears that get in the way of iconoclastic thinking were laid down long ago. Although key brain structures like the amygdala are responsible for the fear response, it is often formative experiences during childhood and adolescence that end up rearing their heads in adult life. Consider the fear of public speaking. Thirty percent of the U.S. population has a fear of public speaking.[15] It is, by far, the most common phobia. Although some fears may be innate and hardwired, such as the fear of snakes and spiders, the fear of public speaking is an acquired phobia. In this sense, the neurobiological mechanisms are no different from the classical conditioning experiments described earlier. The only difference is that instead of an electrical shock, a person experiences the pain of social embarrassment. Typically, this conditioned response is laid down in childhood when children are made to perform in front of classmates, teachers, and parents. From a child's perspective, they are in the position of extreme uncertainty (ambiguity aversion here). They are trying to learn material that everyone else knows, but they themselves do not. Depending on how well this goes for them, they may learn to like speaking in public, or they may learn to fear it. As far as fear conditioning goes, it does not take many negative outcomes to solidify an unpleasant association. And the fact that this never really goes away, but instead may be inhibited by the prefrontal cortex, underscores the deep-seated nature of this type of phobia.

So, instead of trying to eradicate the fear response, a more reasonable approach is to examine the situations that tend to set off the amygdala, and use the prefrontal cortex to inhibit it. Lavoie and Marino exemplified this tactic. They identified one of the critical fears that inhibit people from sharing their ideas: the fear of being rejected. At its core, this fear has its origin in social pressure, which is one of the most common of human phobias. Their solution was novel. By removing as much of the social drama as possible, Lavoie and Marino were able to create an environment in which individuals who tended toward social reticence felt comfortable pitching half-baked ideas. Although their stock market still relies on input from coworkers, the movement into virtual space stripped away some of the social pressure. This works particularly well in an environment in which people spend most of their time in front of a computer. As Lavoie and Marino realized, most of their employees were more comfortable instant messaging each other than walking down the hallway for a face-to-face conversation. Of course, criticism still stings, but the virtual nature of the stock market makes the process a little less painful and a little less personal.

The other triggers of the amygdala, such as uncertainty and fear of failure, require a different approach. While it is impossible to eliminate uncertainty in any competitive environment, it is still possible to keep the amygdala in check through fairly simple psychological approaches. The amygdala has an input and an output stage. The lateral amygdala serves as the input stage and makes the associations between environmental cues and unpleasant events. But it is the central part of the amygdala that is primarily responsible for activating the stress response. Although a conditioned fear may not ever go away, the output, or expression of this fear, can be inhibited. One of the most effective strategies for regulating the expression of fear is through a technique called *cognitive reappraisal*. This simply means reinterpreting emotional information in such a way that the emotional component is diminished. For example, if you saw a woman crying outside a church, your initial reaction might be to interpret the crying as evidence that someone had died. However, as we have seen before, perception is ambiguous. It would be equally possible to reappraise the scene as someone crying for joy, as at a wedding.

There is growing neurobiological evidence that when people reappraise emotional circumstances, the prefrontal cortex comes online and inhibits the amygdala. A recent fMRI study found that when people successfully reappraised emotional scenes, meaning they replaced a negative reaction with a positive one, activity in the left prefrontal cortex increased, in an amount that correlated with the decrease in the amygdala.[16] Even something more concrete, such as the classical fear conditioning to a shock, can be diminished by imagining a soothing scene, which also comes from the left prefrontal cortex.[17]

Reappraisal works well for short-term stressors, such as the fear of public speaking or even the fear of ambiguity. Sometimes it is difficult to implement these cognitive strategies on one's own. Seeking the advice and counsel of a mentor or colleague will often do the trick. Such strategies need not be complicated. Simply relying on a neutral third party, who can reframe the circumstances in nonemotional terms, may be enough.

Much of the problem with acute stressors derives from perception. Because perception is a product of the brain, reappraisal works well to change perception in such a way that the fear system is not activated. As we saw previously, fearful perception is also a statistical process. If someone consistently perceives public speaking as an unpleasant event, the brain will default to this interpretation. To extinguish this perception, the person must experience the conditions that lead to the stress response but without the unpleasantness. Reappraisal can help mitigate the unpleasantness. Sometimes more active measures are required to accelerate the extinction of unpleasant memories. Fear of public speaking, for example, can be effectively attenuated with practice. Programs like Toastmasters have proved time and again that any fear, even public speaking, can be managed through practice.

Fear of the unknown, the other great inhibitor of innovation and iconoclasm, can also be managed through the same techniques of reappraisal and extinction. The Ellsberg paradox comes from the universal aversion to ambiguity. This is quite different from risk aversion. Risk aversion is a value judgment based on known probabilities and outcomes, which I will address in chapter 5. Ambiguity aversion comes straight from the fear of the unknown. This type of fear may be even more deeply entrenched than the fear of public speaking. Every study that has looked at this phenomenon in other animals has found evidence for ambiguity aversion. We are dealing with a deeply ingrained biological tendency. But that does not mean it can't be inhibited. Humans possess a much larger prefrontal cortex than any other animal and therefore possess the brainpower to keep this fear in check.

One technique that may be particularly effective is to convert ambiguity into risk. This is a form of reappraisal. For example, in the Ellsberg experiment, it might be useful to imagine the urn with the unknown ratio of marbles with a known ratio. Without any further information, a reasonable guess would be a 50-50 ratio, as with the left-hand urn. This actually creates an opportunity to hone one's estimate. If you actually chose the right-hand urn, then the marble that you drew would give you a great deal of information about the urn's contents. For example, if you drew a black marble, then the chances of drawing another black marble from that urn would go up. This is called *Bayesian updating*, which is the statistical process of using new information to update probability estimates. It is a mathematically sound principle that has been known for over two hundred years but used rarely in daily decision making. The brain is not wired to think in Bayesian terms, but that does not mean that with some effort it can't be done. The key reappraisal for ambiguous circumstances is to view ambiguity as an opportunity for gaining knowledge. If one has multiple opportunities for knowledge updating, then ambiguity can be converted very quickly into a risk judgment.

Stress is unavoidable, and one cannot live one's life running away from stress. The good news is that stress creates opportunity (think: reappraisal!). If individuals reappraise all sources of stress as an opportunity to discover something new or find a market niche that other people are afraid of, stress may itself decrease. If this is not possible, then the strategy of substituting a short-term stress for a chronic one may be very effective. Paradoxically, physical exercise, which is a short-term stressor, is perhaps the best remedy for chronic stress. Similarly, the individual who feels overwhelmed by uncertainty or social stresses in the workplace may benefit from taking on projects that have defined endings. Although these may increase stress in the short term, their completion may actually decrease overall stress.

So although fear is the great inhibitor of action, its location in the brain is well known. The recent advances in neuroimaging show with increasing precision that cognitive strategies are highly effective at keeping the fear system under control, and these cognitive strategies have their origin in the prefrontal cortex. So rather than people needing to avoid the situations that cause fear or the circumstances that make them stress out, neuroscience is showing how the rational part of the brain can regain control over such toxic emotions like fear.

# FOUR

# How Fear Distorts Perception

The soft-minded man always fears change. He feels security
in the status quo, and he has an almost morbid fear of the
new. For him, the greatest pain is the pain of a new idea.
—Martin Luther King Jr.

I N THE LAST CHAPTER, we saw how fear can inhibit action.
Fear also has another pernicious effect on potential iconoclasts: fear has the potential for interacting with the perceptual system and changing what a person sees (or thinks he sees). This is a far more dangerous scenario than the inhibitory effects of fear. In the last chapter, I focused on how fear prevents people from doing things. But when fear changes perception, the individual is not necessarily inhibited from action. Instead, he might choose the wrong course of action. Sometimes the results are deadly.

When the space shuttle *Challenger* exploded shortly after launch on January 28, 1986, the world witnessed the fatal result of a chain of bad decisions. The independent commission that spearheaded the subsequent investigation laid the blame squarely on NASA for poor management practices and a culture that minimized the risks involved in space travel. Although the failure of an O-ring on the solid rocket booster was the immediate cause of the explosion, the commission came to the damning conclusion that the accident itself was "rooted in history." Specifically: "The Space Shuttle's Solid Rocket Booster problem began with the faulty design of its joint and increased as both NASA and contractor management first failed to recognize it as a problem, then failed to fix it and finally treated it as an acceptable flight risk."[1]

What is amazing about this statement is how it captures the gradual shift in perception about the shuttle's design. Even after Morton Thiokol, the contractor that built the booster, discovered the design flaw in the O-rings, "they did not accept the implication of early tests." NASA engineers, however, raised concerns about the design. One engineer, Leon Ray, submitted a report after a test firing revealed dangerous opening of the O-ring joint, recommending a complete redesign as the best long-term fix. Even so, NASA management minimized this concern in briefings with Thiokol. The commission concluded that costs were the primary concern of the NASA selection board, and that "cost consideration overrode any other objections."

Problems with the O-rings continued to mount. Temperature testing revealed that at 50°F the O-ring became so stiff that its seal was nonfunctional. (The air temperature at the *Challenger*'s launch was 31°F.) Even engineers at Thiokol started becoming afraid that the O-rings could lead to catastrophe: "It is my honest and very real fear that if we do not take immediate action to dedicate a team to solve the problem, . . . then we stand in jeopardy of losing a flight along with all the launch pad facilities."[2]

If so many engineers, within both Thiokol and NASA, were concerned about the O-rings, then one might reasonably ask why nothing was done. NASA had a safety program in place, but as the president's commission found, it was largely ineffective. The unrelenting pressure to meet an accelerated flight schedule meant the safety program had to take a backseat. In fact, it was fear itself that changed the perception of risks within NASA management. Early in the booster development program, the O-rings were flagged as a problem of the highest level (criticality 1—potential for loss of vehicle and life if component fails). But somehow, by the time launches were occurring, this perception had changed.

NASA management was under intense public pressure to maintain a high rate of launches. It had promised almost one a month. It was an unrealistic plan. Afraid of losing congressional funding as well as commercial, paying customers, NASA let this fear change the collective perception of risk.

## When the Emperor Has No Clothes

If there was a single figure who clearly laid the blame for the *Challenger* disaster on NASA's management practices, it was the Nobel Prize–winning physicist from Caltech, Richard Feynman. When Feynman demonstrated for Congress what happens to a piece of O-ring when frozen, he became a public hero for his candor. Feynman, however, was already renowned within physics circles for his iconoclasm.

Unlike many of the other people profiled in this book, Feynman didn't learn to become an iconoclast. He was born that way. At first, when he was growing up on Long Island, it wasn't immediately apparent. But by the time he was in high school, Feynman had surpassed most of his teachers in his mathematical ability. When solving mathematical word problems, while others furiously cranked through algebraic formulas with pencil and paper, Feynman would eschew these mechanical approaches and see the problems differently, often blurting out answers without lifting a pencil.[3] But it was the exciting developments in European physics that really grabbed the teenager. Finally, after centuries of debate, German physicists such as Bohr, Heisenberg, and Schrödinger had proven that matter was really composed of invisible, discrete particles called atoms. To Feynman, this was the single greatest discovery in all of human history. And it shaped his view of the world.

It was a short-lived fascination. By the time Feynman was in graduate school at Princeton, his natural mathematical ability had forced him to abandon reading even the basic papers by Bohr and others. Studying physics at Princeton in the 1930s was a sink-or-swim operation. There were no required courses. You just had to pass a qualifying exam. Most students studied from an outline of basic physics: mechanics, electromagnetism, and atomic physics. Not Feynman. He chose to study things with no answers. In his "Notebook of Things I Don't Know About," he began to deconstruct every branch of physics, cataloging, and analyzing gaps in the standard explanations for basic physical phenomena.[4] Dissatisfied with algebraic explanations for atomic behavior, Feynman created his own graphical way of representing these types of problems. It was an approach that would foreshadow what he would eventually win the Nobel Prize for.

And then came World War II. It was Robert Wilson, one of Feynman's mentors, who let him in on the soon-to-be Manhattan Project. "Feynman's persistent skepticism, his unwillingness to accept any assertion on authority, would be useful."[5] Indeed it was. Because of his mathematical prowess, he was put in charge of teams who had to manually crank through long calculations. He developed a reputation for seeing differently, being able to spot mistakes even when he didn't know what the right answer was. He would look at calculations from unique vantage points, such as approaching from infinity or approaching from the other direction, infinitesimal numbers. Even J. Robert

Oppenheimer took notice: "He is by all odds the most brilliant young physicist here."[6]

One thing about the Manhattan Project that did make a big impression on Feynman was how iconoclasts make decisions. "It was such a shock to me to see that a committee of men could present a whole lot of ideas, each one thinking of a new facet, while remembering what the other fella said, so that, at the end, the decision is made as to which idea was the best—summing it all up—without having to say it three times. These were very great men indeed."[7]

Feynman already had an innate sense of seeing things his way, and he refused to be intimidated by others. His description of the Trinity test was characteristic, refusing to let unfounded fears of blindness get in his way of seeing the first atomic explosion, and it is this refusal to let fear color his perception that makes him the most iconoclastic physicist ever:

> They gave out dark glasses that you could watch it with. Dark glasses! Twenty miles away, you couldn't see a damn thing through dark glasses. So I figured the only thing that could really hurt your eyes is ultraviolet light. I got behind a truck windshield, because the ultraviolet can't go through glass, so that would be safe, and so I could see the damn thing. Everybody else had dark glasses, and the people at 6 miles couldn't see it because they were all told to lie on the floor. I'm probably the only guy who saw it with the human eye.[8]

## A Minority of One

Although Feynman had no problem with his role as perennial iconoclast, for most people the willingness to stand alone for one's opinion does not come easily. Like the fear of public speaking we saw in the last chapter, the fear of social isolation is deeply woven into the human brain. We readily discount our own perceptions for fear of being the odd one out.

All our primate cousins, and even the earliest hominids, have depended on their clans for survival. As a result, a million years of mammalian evolution have produced a human brain that values social contact and communication above all else. The way in which we interact with each other is, in many ways, more important than what our own eyes and ears tell us. So much so, that the human brain takes in information from other people and incorporates it with the information coming from its own senses. Many times, the group's opinion trumps the individual's before he even becomes aware of it. And while we humans readily ascribe our thoughts and feelings to ourselves the truth is that many of our thoughts originate from other people.

There is, of course, great value in belonging to a group. Safety in numbers, for one. But there is also a mathematical explanation for why the brain is so willing to give up its own opinions: a group of people is more likely to be correct about something than any individual. Both of these factors—social value and the statistical wisdom of the crowd— explain why so few people end up being true iconoclasts. Understanding these effects can encourage would-be iconoclasts and foster conditions for innovation within organizations. The story begins in the 1950s . . .

The men dress with conspicuous purpose.[9] They have volunteered for a psychology experiment in visual acuity. Most of the men have never taken a course in psychology, sticking instead to a course of study in history, politics, and economics that is well known to the Wall Street recruiters each spring. At the designated time, a group of eight assemble in an ordinary classroom. Most of the men know each other in some fashion, for the campus is one of the smaller of the Ivies. All have been recruited by a friend, classmate, or fraternity brother, but the recruitment process is strictly *sotto voce*, lending an air of mystery to the whole enterprise.

The professor enters the room. Solomon Asch wears a weathered tweed coat over a matching vest and woolen pants. He is shorter than most of the volunteers and points to the two rows of desks. With an

Eastern European accent, he asks the men to please take their seats. There ensues some jockeying of position, but one subject of particular interest ends up in the middle of the second row.

In fact, he is the only subject. The other seven are acting as stooges to go along with the professor's experiment.

The subject looks up from his desk and sees an artist's easel holding a stack of white pieces of cardboard. He begins to wonder why he volunteered for this exercise. He had heard about the experiment from a fellow who lived in a neighboring suite of his dorm, but this dorm mate isn't someone he would call a friend under most circumstances. The other men in the room seem so at ease with themselves, talking about the recent Dewey-Truman fiasco and smoking cigarettes.

Asch clears his throat and explains the task.

"Before you is a pair of cards. On the left is a card with one line. The card at the right has three lines differing in length." He turns over the first pair of cards to illustrate his point. "They are numbered 1, 2, and 3, in order. One of the three lines at the right is equal to the standard line at the left. You will decide in each case which is the equal line. There will be eighteen such comparisons in all."

Asch pauses and looks around the room to make sure that his audience understands the task. He takes in this particular group and adds, "As the number of comparisons is few and the group small, I will call upon each of you in turn to announce your judgments, which I shall record here on a prepared form." The professor points to the person nearest him in the front row and adds, "Suppose you give me your estimates in order, starting here in the first row, proceeding to the left, and then going to the second row."

The fellow sitting next to the subject plays the part of a wiry, nervous sort. He chain-smokes and fidgets constantly. He raises his hand and asks, "Will there always be a line that matches?"

Asch assures him that there will. "Very well. Let's begin with the card currently showing."

The card on the left has a single line, about ten inches long. The right-hand card has three lines, the middle line being substantially longer than the other two and also clearly of the same length as the target.

The first person says, "Line Two is the correct answer."

Asch marks something down on a clipboard and motions to the second person to answer. The men (actors) proceed around the room until the subject—the only subject—must answer.

The task seems straightforward, and by this point he is somewhat relieved that it isn't difficult. "Two," he says.

The second set of cards contains lines that range in height from one to two inches, but as with the first set, it is not difficult to pick out the ones that match. Everyone gives the correct answer.

The third set looks like what is shown in figure 4-1.

The first person says, "One. It's Line One."

The subject does a double take, and while he regards the lines with renewed intensity, the second person says, "One." So does the third. And the fourth, and everyone in front of him.

**FIGURE 4-1**

## Asch experiment

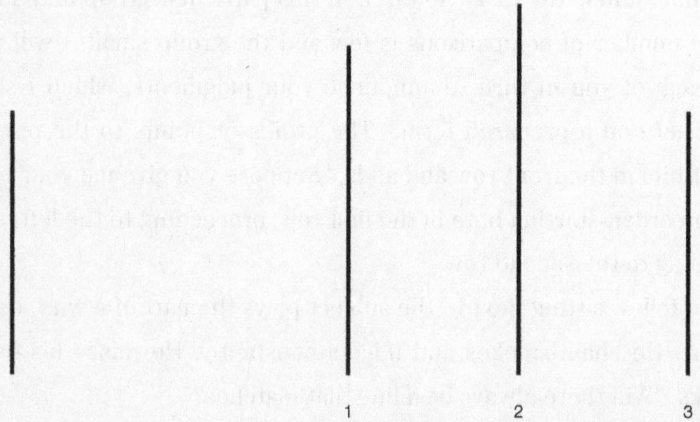

The subject becomes intensely aware that the entire group is await-ing his answer. He thinks, *I don't see how they can answer so quickly. I thought it was Three, but I can see how One might be the same length. My eyes must be going bad.* Feebly, he states, "One." The fidgety guy lights up another cigarette and takes a long drag, getting immense enjoyment from the drama playing out in the seat next to him.

It does not get any better for the subject. Of the eighteen trials, the group is unanimously wrong on twelve. The unwitting subject, despite what his eyes see, goes along with the group 100 percent of the time.

After the experiment, everyone but the true subject is dismissed. Asch pulls him aside and asks, "How often did you answer as the others did, against your own first choice?" This was a standard question asked of all the subjects. Invariably, even the most conformist of subjects underestimated the number of times that he went along with the herd.

The subject replies, "Possibly as many as one-fourth or one-third." The subject thinks about his estimate and continues, "Mostly I wasn't sure, I was undecided. Plus, some of the choices were difficult."

In fact, the choices were not difficult. It was the group pressure to give the wrong answer that made the choices seem difficult.

Although most subjects were not totally conformist like the one just described, the amount of conformity was, nevertheless, shocking. With-out a group giving wrong answers, 95 percent of subjects performed *without a single error*. But with the group, only one-fourth of the sub-jects were able to maintain this perfect performance. Most subjects caved to group pressure about one-third of the time.

Asch's debriefing procedure revealed that most subjects had some awareness of what they were doing, although as just illustrated, most subjects underestimated by a large degree the number of times they went along with the group. Some just accepted the group's judgment as an indication that their own perceptions were wrong. One particularly conformist subject stated, "I just wondered what was wrong with me."

Another said, "There were so many against me that I thought I must be wrong."

Others gave no evidence that they were even aware of the fact that they were wrong.

## See as I Say

Asch was an iconoclast himself, single-handedly creating the field of social psychology. As a Polish Jew conducting experiments in the years following WWII, Asch aimed to understand how millions of Germans could blithely follow the Nazi ideology of extermination. Asch's approach, which stands as one of the most influential psychology experiments of the twentieth century and has been replicated hundreds of times, showed that even when you strip away all the ambiguity of what an individual sees, and there is no possibility of personal gain or reprisal, people will still go along with the group.

The social psychologists who followed Asch favored this explanation of conformity: we know what we see, and we know right from wrong, but with enough social pressure, we cave in to the fear of standing alone. Ironically, this explanation of conformity contains a certain heroic element that accounts for its persistence. If we grant that we are all a bit reticent at times to stand up for our personal opinions, this leaves the door open to act as individuals when we choose. It is a noble grasp for free will. But—and this is the kicker—we must be brave enough. This was Asch's point. Even in a neutral laboratory setting, most people are not that brave.

Now you may think, *Surely, I would be brave enough to stand my ground.* True, not everyone in Asch's experiment went along with the group. But even if some are not that brave, they might think that they could decide, for whatever reason, whether to go along or not. But what if that is wrong, and we do not have as much free will as we'd like to think? What if groups of people change how we see the world? Then we are dealing with a much more pernicious form of conformity: a form of conformity we might not even be aware of and one that dooms the would-be iconoclast before he even knows it.

The extent to which perception can be altered by fear is a question that has lingered over social psychology. It is a difficult question to answer, for if a person's perception were truly altered, he might not even know it. Asch realized that at least two distinct mental processes go into making a perceptual judgment like his line task. The first is perception itself. As we saw in the first chapter, perception is shaped not only by what the eyes transmit but by an individual's expectation of what they are seeing. The second process—judgment—is a type of decision making. In Asch's experiment, the decision was simple: picking the two lines that were the same length. It is important to note that these are distinct cognitive processes and are potentially mediated by different circuits in the brain.

Ever since Asch, most social psychologists have assumed that conformity is exerted at the decision-making stage in a sort of spineless capitulation to the majority. Nevertheless, hints of perceptual shifts can be found throughout the literature on social conformity. Even Asch reported several subjects who marched along with the group and yet seemed blithely unaware that they were wrong. Their unawareness suggested, but by no means proved, that their perception had been altered. The traditional entrée into a person's perception is to ask him or her— either directly, or indirectly through experiments. But no matter the method, perception has never been fully separated from the judgment process. At least until fMRI came along.

Although neuroscientists have been using fMRI to systematically map out the neurobiology of processes such as memory, emotion, attention, and perception, nobody had thought to use fMRI to answer the looming question of whether other people can change what you see. To answer this question, in 2005 my research group tackled the problem of how fear might change perception in a modern variation of Asch's experiment.[10]

The logic of our experiment was simple. If other people change what you see (or what you think you see), then fMRI should detect changes in perceptual regions of the brain. If, on the other hand, conformity occurs at the decision-making level, we should see changes in decision-making regions. As we saw in the first chapter, visual information originating from the eyes first hits the brain in the back of the head in the occipital cortex. The information then flows forward, splitting into two paths—one through the high road in the parietal cortex, the other through the low road in the temporal lobe—and they meet again in the frontal lobes. Because perception occurs largely in the first stages of this process, in the back of the brain, we hoped that we could separate the perceptual side of conformity from the decision-making side.

No matter how it turned out, the answer would have wide-ranging implications for how we, as individuals, make decisions in groups. Take, for example, the democratic institutions that have been erected in the last two centuries. They all depend on self-determination. In the Bill of Rights, we protect the liberties of individuals. In return, there is an implicit contract that requires everyone to participate in the governance of society. This includes voting for representatives, adherence to the rule of law, trial by jury, and the conduct of business according to accepted practices. We allow for differences of opinions, but these differences are resolved through institutions such as voting. Beneath all these institutions lies the assumption that individuals "call it as they see it."

Like Asch, we hired actors to play the roles of experimental subjects. When the real subject arrived for the experiment, he saw that four other people were participating. At least he thought they were participating like him. As a group, everyone was told they would be doing a task of visual perception on a computer. Everyone would have their own computer, and everyone would see the same thing. In addition, each participant would be able to see each of the others' answers.

The task was actually quite simple. Each trial began with two abstract three-dimensional shapes appearing on the screen. The shapes were rotated with respect to each other. As in Asch's experiment, all the subject had to do was decide whether the two shapes were the same or different. The kicker was that, unknown to the real subject, the actors had been given instructions to answer incorrectly. Figure 4-2 shows what the subject saw.

The actors' faces appeared on the right of the screen, along with the answers that each of them registered. In this example, the shapes are actually the same because they can be mentally rotated to match each other. Under these circumstances, many people think their eyes are playing tricks on them.

Of course, nothing was wrong with their eyes. The visual task, although a little harder than Asch's, was not as difficult as most of the participants thought. When doing the mental rotation task by themselves,

**FIGURE 4-2**

### Shape rotation experiment

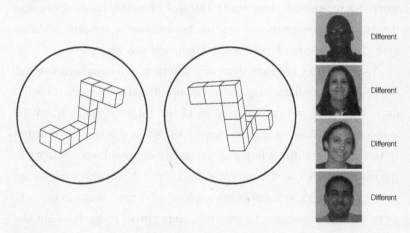

*Source:* Reprinted from Gregory S. Berns et al., "Neurobiological Correlates of Social Conformity and Independence During Mental Rotation," *Biological Psychiatry* 58, no. 3 (2005): 247, with permission from Elsevier.

the participants arrived at the correct answer 86 percent of the time. But when the group gave the wrong judgment, the rate of correct answers dropped to 59 percent—statistically no better than if they had flipped a coin.

We debriefed our subjects, and, like Asch, found a wide range of insight into what had happened. Some of our subjects stuck to their own intuitions and were not swayed by the group. Others went along with them almost 100 percent of the time. Most lay somewhere between these two extremes. Nobody had strong recollections of why they did what they did and just vaguely remembered going with the group sometimes and not others.

The fMRI data told the story.

The mental rotation task by itself caused a network of specific brain regions to come online. Visual processing regions, located in the back of the head, were highly active while the person stared at the screen, examining the myriad facets of the shapes. The visual representations get reassembled in the parietal cortex and the temporal lobe. Within these two regions, the brain decides what it's seeing (the low road) and where it's located (the high road). Our task of mental rotation, because it required all these elements to work in coordination, resulted in strong activation in the visual, parietal, and temporal regions.

You would not normally think of conformity as a visual process, but that is precisely what we found. The group altered the patterns of activity in the visual and parietal regions of the subjects' brains when the subjects went along with them incorrectly. When a subject capitulated to the group, and the group was wrong, we observed more activity in the parietal cortex, as if it were working harder. A plausible explanation is that the group's wrong answers imposed a "virtual" image in the subject's mind. In the case of conformity, this virtual image beat out the image originating from the subject's own eyes, causing the subject to disregard her own perceptions and accept the group's. This didn't happen all the time, but when it did, the shift in patterns in brain activation was striking. Even more interesting was the fact that we didn't find nearly as striking a change the frontal lobes. If anything, there was a slight decrease in activity when the subject conformed, suggesting that the group's answers took some of the load off the decision-making process in the frontal lobe.

Even when the subjects stood their ground and gave the correct answer in the face of a unanimously wrong group we found changes in brain activity. Not in the perceptual regions, in this case. Instead, non-conformity went along with increased activity in an almond-sized region of the brain called the amygdala. Recall from the last chapter that the amygdala has direct connections with the arousal system of the brain, notably the hypothalamus. When the amygdala fires, a cascade of neural events is unleashed that prepares the body for immediate action. It is the first step in the "fight-or-flight" system, but the end result of amygdala activation is a rise in blood pressure and heart rate, more sweating, and rapid breathing. Lots of things trigger the amygdala, but fear is, by far, the most effective. Its activation during nonconformity underscored the unpleasant nature of standing alone—even when the individual had no recollection of it. In many people the brain would rather avoid activating the fear system and just change perception to conform with the social norm.

## A Lesson in Conquering Fear

Martin Luther King Jr., perhaps the greatest iconoclast of the civil rights movement, knew firsthand the damaging effects of fear on perception. By championing the rights of blacks, he immediately incurred the wrath of the Southern whites who surrounded him in Atlanta. King and others were pummeled with intimidation, tactics designed to instill fear in blacks. Consider James Meredith, who in 1962 became the first black to enroll in the University of Mississippi, sparking riots across the state. After graduating, Meredith organized the March Against Fear from

Memphis, Tennessee, to Jackson, Mississippi, only to be shot by a sniper along the way. But in 1963, in the March on Washington, King really laid out his philosophy in his "I have a dream" speech.

Taking cues from Gandhi, King adopted a philosophy of nonviolent civil disobedience. At its heart, the tenet of nonviolence was aimed directly at conquering the damaging effects of fear. It targeted blacks' fear of white retaliation by showing how peaceful protest, in large numbers, provided a relatively safe haven for effecting social change. Rather than standing alone, the strategy of nonviolence played into the safety in numbers that is so deeply wired into the human brain. More important, however, was King's deep-seated conviction that nonviolence was the only way to garner public support from whites. Not all the black leaders agreed with this approach. Notably, Malcolm X advocated for more direct tactics of confrontation.

King's strategy of nonviolence came to a head on March 7, 1965, when five hundred supporters started marching out of Selma, Alabama, to protest the intimidation tactics used by whites to prevent blacks from registering to vote. The governor of Alabama, George Wallace, declared the march a threat to public safety and ordered the police to take action against the marchers. With television cameras rolling, the nation witnessed the police attack with billy clubs and tear gas on the peaceful demonstrators. Several of the marchers were hospitalized, leading the marchers to call it "Bloody Sunday." Two days later, King organized a second march but turned back before crossing the bridge into Montgomery, avoiding another violent confrontation. Eventually, his strategy paid off. A week later, a federal judge ruled that the state of Alabama did not have a right to block the peaceful demonstration. The marchers finally reached the capital on March 24. Several months later, Lyndon Johnson signed into law the Voting Rights Act of 1965, which outlawed any qualification tests to vote.

King well understood how fear was damaging the perception of blacks, both of themselves and by whites. As he said in his Nobel Peace

Prize acceptance speech: "Nonviolence has also meant that my people in the agonizing struggles of recent years have taken suffering upon themselves instead of inflicting it on others. It has meant, as I said, that we are no longer afraid and cowed. But in some substantial degree it has meant that we do not want to instill fear in others or into the society of which we are a part."[11]

King saw nonviolence as the only way to eliminate the damaging effects of fear: "It is the method which seeks to implement the just law by appealing to the conscience of the great decent majority who through blindness, fear, pride, and irrationality have allowed their consciences to sleep."[12]

We begin to see clues about how the individual must invoke conscious, rational thought processes to control fear. It is a theme to which I will return at the end of the chapter. But before we get to these strategies, it helps to understand where the power of intimidation comes from.

## The Law of Large Numbers

It may seem counterintuitive that the human brain is so susceptible to the opinions of others that it is willing to disregard its own visual inputs, but viewed from a statistical perspective, this biological capitulation makes perfect sense. As we saw in the first chapter, the information that the eyes transmit to the brain does not uniquely determine what the individual perceives. The brain must make educated guesses to construct a visual percept based on the context and the individual's past experience. The evolutionary theory of perception, coupled with the efficiency of the brain, means that perception is a statistical process. For any given visual image transmitted by the eyes, the brain must choose one of several possible interpretations. Efficiency dictates that the brain will pick the most likely interpretation for what it is seeing.

The way in which an individual categorizes objects markedly influences his perception. We have considered this process to be a product of experience, but there is another, even more potent source of categorization that affects perception: other people.

In both the Asch experiment and our subsequent version with fMRI, the subjects made perceptual judgments that were seemingly straightforward. The fact that individuals were swayed by group opinion raises the ominous conclusion that they would be even more susceptible to group influence with judgments that were more subjective. What if we are to consider questions in which the answers are unknown, such as who will win the World Series this year, or at what level will the Dow Jones Industrial Average close next month? While everyone may have an opinion about these questions, their confidence in their answer may vary widely from one person to another. In such situations, it makes sense to look toward other individuals to see what they think. It is a fact that other people are more likely be correct than any given individual. The reason comes from the statistics of aggregating information.

The problem has much to do with the Asch effect and is not too different from guessing how many jelly beans are in a jar. In the classic bean jar game, you buy a guess for $1, and the person guessing the closest to the actual amount wins the pot of money and the jar of beans. If you gather up enough people and record their guesses, the distribution of guesses will be similar to a bell-shaped curve.[13] Even more important, if the participants don't share information or disclose their guesses, then the average of the guesses will be very close to the true number of beans in the jar. Typically, the average of the guesses will be better than 95 percent of the participants'. In other words, the average of a group of independent observers is better than any individual, and frequently the average is as good as, or better than, even the best individual in the group. The more diverse the group of participants, the better the group's average. The only thing that matters is that the participants act independently of one another.[14]

Jacob Bernoulli, a Swiss mathematician, proved this mathematically in 1713, and although the proof itself is complex, the idea is simple.

Bernoulli's proof has come to be known as the *law of large numbers*, because the more measurements you make of something, the more accurate the average of these measurements becomes. But we rarely have the opportunity to make as many measurements as the law would require. We take our best shot given the available information. Since we lack the possibility of do-overs, the next best thing is to see what other people do. Because an individual's opinion is more likely to miss the mark than a group of people rendering independent opinions, the strategy of following the crowd can be very efficient.[15] So if you want to know how many jelly beans are in a jar, ask a bunch of people what they think, and average their answers.

The law of large numbers is mathematically rock solid, and the only thing that is really surprising about it is that it took so long to be discovered. But just because we have known about it for only three hundred years doesn't mean that its effects weren't felt long before. Perception is a statistical judgment by the brain. Given the multiple interpretations of visual stimuli, the brain chooses the most likely interpretation. The interpretation may be guided by past experience and how the individual categorizes people and objects, but the law of large numbers comes into play as well. When other individuals render opinions, the brain readily incorporates these opinions and changes its interpretation of visual information. It is far too inefficient for an individual brain to make repeated guesses about what it is seeing, and when offered the opinion of other people as potentially independent observers (whether true or not), the brain will readily assimilate this information into its own interpretation and perception.

Viewed from the perspective of evolution, the law of large numbers will give any animal that uses it a distinct survival advantage. Consider a creature whose life depends on finding food and water. One strategy would be to forage for food in the hopes of stumbling upon something good to eat. If successful, this could pay off handsomely because the animal could horde it and gain an advantage over its competitors. This would be a risky strategy with a relatively low likelihood of success but a high payoff if it worked. The law of large numbers, however, says that such an individual strategy would most likely fail. Another animal, that was perhaps a little more strategic in its thinking, would observe what other animals did before deciding its own course of action. Because a group is statistically superior to an individual, an animal that discovered this strategy would always do better than the loner. In addition to vastly increasing the likelihood of success, the second strategy is much lower in risk and does not cost the animal much energy to observe what other animals do. The power of the group is so much greater than the individual, evolution favored animals that used it, and "groupthink" became the dominant strategy for all animals that could observe each other's behavior.

Although statistically superior to individualistic thinking, the law of large numbers is also the bane of the iconoclast. Millions of years of evolution have resulted in a human brain that has the law of large numbers hardwired into it. When Asch observed individuals capitulating to the group, they were acting in accordance with the law and simply making the statistically sound judgment that the group was more likely correct than they themselves were. When my laboratory repeated the experiment with brain imaging, we saw the law of large numbers operating at multiple levels. The first level was at the perceptual stage, but we observed the fear system kicking in, almost like a fail-safe when the individual went against the group. These are powerful biological mechanisms that make it extremely difficult to think like an iconoclast. Our brains are evolved to make judgments as quickly and efficiently as possible, and when other people's opinions are present, the brain will incorporate them, whether we want it to or not.

## Mitigating the Effects of Fear on Perception

All the strategies outlined in the previous chapter pertaining to the amygdala apply here as well. Cognitive reappraisal, for example, works

to effectively look at a situation that induces fear from a different vantage point. In addition, there are other strategies that work specifically
in situations where the fear of isolation has the potential for changing
perception. Nobody likes to look stupid, but the pain of being the odd
person out often seems worse.

Fortunately, there is a straightforward workaround for the brain's
hardwired propensity to follow the herd. A minority of one is the most
extreme form of iconoclasm, because it means that the individual
stands entirely alone against the crowd. One possibility is to isolate one-
self so that one doesn't have to face others' opinions. The tactic of
avoidance, however, merely postpones the inevitable confrontation of
the individual against the group. Another solution, in the spirit of Feynman, is to develop a tough skin and simply not care what others think.
Although this can work sometimes, it runs the risk of coming off as
being aloof or antisocial. It is best suited to dominant personalities.

For most iconoclasts, change begins on a small scale. When Asch
repeated his experiments, he quickly discovered that only a unanimous
group was effective in getting subjects to conform. One dissenter was
typically enough to break the herd effect. From the iconoclast's perspective, *this means that the most effective strategy for dealing with
a group is to recruit one like-minded individual.* Although two people may not be sufficient to sway the group's opinion, having one ally is
all that is needed to maintain one's own judgment. Groups are, indeed,
superior to individuals, but only when they are diverse and individuals
act as individuals. Statistically, most people in a group will lie along a
spectrum of opinions, but because of the social pressure to belong,
these opinions contract to the social norm. The availability of a minority
position breaks the stranglehold of conformity, and groups that allow
for minority opinions are statistically more likely to make better decisions than groups that require unanimity.

At an institutional level, the implications are clear: *committees
should not be required to arrive at a unanimous decision.* Dissension

must be encouraged. Although it is standard committee practice to go around a table and vote, this often results in an Asch effect because individuals have varying degrees of confidence in their judgments. A more effective strategy is to have individuals provide a numerical rating. This works well for binary decisions, where someone might rate zero for option A and ten for option B. The distance from the midpoint of the scale reflects the strength of their opinion. It also works well for decisions in which options must be ranked. And although not typically the norm for committees, closed balloting alleviates much of the stigma of social isolation.

Managers often do not like to hear these suggestions because they imply a certain reticence on the part of their employees. Individuals are hired and promoted according to their ability to perform a job and act independently. But even a board of directors contains a wide range of personality types. The most effective way for a group to make a decision is by aggregating the opinions of *independent* individuals. It also follows that a group with a lot of diversity among its members is more likely to arrive at a good decision than a group that is composed of members who are alike.

On an individual level, there are several effective strategies for mitigating fear. In addition to cognitive reappraisal, extinction is a useful approach. In general it is impossible to stay fearful of something for a long period of time. The prefrontal cortex can inhibit fear through repeated exposure. This works well when the fear is well defined and can be experienced on a repetitive basis. In committee situations, for example, the individual who is afraid of looking stupid in front of a group must force himself to voice his opinion. It can be painful at times, but it is only through repetition and practice that the fear response becomes attenuated and fear no longer clouds perception.

Finally, there is the strategy advocated by Martin Luther King. In his strategy, which is closely related to cognitive reappraisal, King appealed to the rational part of the brain to make the amygdala shut up.

Realizing that fear is the enemy of civil rights, King made fear itself his target. Safety in numbers helps. But the real change must occur within the individual's mind. Fortunately, fear is easily recognizable. One only needs to listen to the body's responses to know that one is scared. But once fear is recognized the individual must bring online cognitive processes to deconstruct what the fear is. Only when the fear is broken down into its component pieces can it be eliminated. The key is recognizing the fear in the first place and not to make judgments while under the influence of fear.

Think of fear like alcohol. It impairs judgment. You shouldn't make any decisions while under its influence.

# FIVE

# Why the Fear of Failure Makes People Risk Averse

Making money in the stock market is so simple a monkey could do it. Here's the secret: Buy low and sell high.

—David Dreman

IN THE LAST TWO CHAPTERS, we saw how fear affected both perception and decision making. Fear prevents people from taking action, and even worse, fear changes the way they see the world. Fear touches everything that we do on a daily basis, but it is perhaps no more clearly evident than in the stock market. Here, we see fear manifest in all its glory.

Fear can be boiled down to three types. First, fear of the unknown, as in "What's the deal with this Chinese company I've never heard of that my broker is pushing on me?" Second, fear of failure. In finance, this masquerades as "risk," but we all know it as the fear of losing money. And finally, the fear of looking stupid. For many, there is nothing worse than your neighbor making a killing on a stock that you sold too soon. And if you run an investment fund, there really is nothing worse than being outperformed by your competitors or (God forbid) the S&P 500.

Few arenas are more punishing to the iconoclast than the stock market. If you're in the market, you confront head-on the stark reality that when you invest money, you take a risk. I will get to the financial approach to risk shortly, but for now, think of risk simply as the odds of failure. Risky investments have a relatively high likelihood of tanking. Unfortunately, for most people, the emphasis falls on failure, and the fear of failure prevents them from taking risk, even when it can be profitable to do so. As we shall see, there are biological reasons for this behavior that originate in the brain's distortion of perception, especially under the influence of fear. It is so common that simply not behaving this way makes for an iconoclast.

If you're a fund manager, and you fancy yourself an iconoclast, think twice, because the stock market is an ideal setting to weed out the true iconoclasts from the pretenders. The New York Stock Exchange (NYSE) had a collective market capitalization of $21.2 trillion at the end of 2005. In a typical month, about $1 trillion in stocks changed hands. In 2002, 85 million people (42 percent of the U.S. adult population) either were directly invested in the NYSE or owned stocks that were traded on the NYSE through mutual funds and retirement plans. And this represents just the NYSE, not to mention the NASDAQ or foreign exchanges. With so many individuals actively participating in the market, the odds of being an iconoclast are slim, to say the least. Moreover, the public availability of fund performance makes it straightforward to see who the iconoclasts really are. The successful Wall Street iconoclast is the fund manager who beats the market on a consistent basis.

Morningstar reports statistics on over two thousand mutual funds. Despite the required warnings about past performance, the prospectuses of most of these funds paint a rosy picture of that fund's investment strategy. But the dirty secret of Wall Street is that, in fact, hardly any funds consistently do well. According to Standard & Poor's, only 10.8 percent of large-capitalization (large-cap) funds maintained a top-half ranking over five consecutive twelve-month periods.[1] That's top-half—just consistently better than average. The figure was even lower for mid- and small-cap funds. If we look for the real standouts—say, consistently in the top 25 percent of funds over five consecutive years—we find a grand total of three large-cap funds (1.12 percent) that make the grade.

The low percentage of funds that consistently do better than their peers indicates that little consistency exists in the market. These dismal results suggest that the warning that past performance is no guarantee of future results might be interpreted more accurately as this: past performance has *nothing to do with* future performance. If this were the case, then a fund's ranking relative to its peers would be random from one year to the next, and whether a fund was in the top half in a given year would be like flipping a coin. Taking a top-half fund and flipping a hypothetical coin four more times means that 6.25 percent of funds would be expected to have consecutively good performance—by chance alone. The fact that 8–10 percent of funds eke out this feat means that fund performance is only a little better than coin flipping.

But this sets the bar fairly low. Once transaction fees are taken into account, actively managed funds rarely beat the market as a whole. Nothing could be further from iconoclastic investing than putting money in an index fund. Index funds contain stocks in proportion to their relative weight of major market indexes such as the S&P 500, which tracks large-cap companies, or the Russell 2000, which tracks small-cap companies.

The beauty of the market lies in the tenuous balance between buyers and sellers. The very definition of a market means that for every buyer there must be a seller. So for every person buying a stock, there is someone else who wants to get rid of it. Who is right? Who is the iconoclast?

## The Economics of Risk

Returning to the randomness of mutual fund performance, we might ask what a reasonable person would be willing to pay for what amounts to little more than successive coin flips. Consider the following, which is a guaranteed way to make money. You walk into a bar and offer to pay $20 to anyone who is willing to take this bet. The bet goes like this: the person who accepts the bet places $2 on the table. You will flip a coin. If it comes up heads, the other person gets the $20 and the game is over (while you keep the $2, but realizing a net loss of $18). If it comes up tails, the taker of your bet must double the money in the pot, and you flip the coin again. Heads, you take the pot; tails, the taker must double down again. The game continues until the first heads appears.

Think that $20 is too much to pay for such a bet? How much would you be willing to pay?

The issue boils down to how much this game is worth. It's like buying a lottery ticket. The most rational, and mathematically correct, way to calculate the value of a lottery is to multiply the payoff by the odds of its occurrence. On the first round, you've got a $2 payoff on the table, and the odds of winning it are one-half. Two dollars times one-half equals $1, so the *expected value* of the first round is $1. So far, this does not seem like a good bet. If you make it to the second round, the payoff doubles to $4, but the odds of this occurring are one-half times one-half, or one-fourth. The expected value of the second round is $4 times one-fourth, or again $1. The odds of making it to the third round (three tails in a row) drop to one-eighth, and the payoff doubles again, to $8. Thus, the expected value of every round is $1.

The expected value of the entire game is simply the sum of the value of each round. Since there are potentially an infinite number of rounds (albeit increasingly unlikely but with payoffs increasing exponentially), the expected value of the game is infinity. Therefore, a rational person should be willing to pay any amount of money to play this game. But, of course, nobody does.

The fact that people are unwilling to wager anything significant on this game, despite the mathematical rigor of the determination of its value, underscores the fundamentally irrational way that humans deal with risky decisions. This game, known as the St. Petersburg paradox, was articulated by the eighteenth-century Swiss mathematician Daniel Bernoulli, and his explanation of why people are unwilling to play this game forms the basis of the modern economic approach to risk.[2]

Bernoulli proposed an elegant solution to the paradox. He suggested that the reason people are unwilling to play this game stems from the fact that they don't value money in a linear manner. To get around this limit, Bernoulli introduced the idea of *utility*. The value of something, be it a new car or a $100 bill, is governed not by its price, but by the utility it yields. Utility is the subjective benefit that a person experiences. The price, according to Bernoulli, depends only on the thing itself, but the utility it confers to someone depends on the individual. This makes intuitive sense. A $100 bill confers more utility to a pauper than to a rich man. To account for this observation, Bernoulli suggested that money has diminishing marginal utility. The more you have, the less utility each additional dollar adds. An extremely wealthy person would experience very little increase in utility from getting more money. This may seem irrational, and it is, but then again, not playing the St. Petersburg lottery is itself an irrational act.

Bernoulli proposed that the utility of money follows a logarithmic curve, which has the property of flattening out the higher you go. If people make decisions about money according to the utility they get, as opposed to the actual face value, then the mathematical logic assumes a different form. Although the exponentially decreasing odds of successive tail flips are balanced by the exponential doubling of the pot, the utility of the pot does not keep pace with the decrease in odds. The utility of the game is no longer infinite, which means that every person will have some finite price they are willing to pay to play.

It seems like a roundabout way of explaining a quirk of human behavior, but it explained why people seem to have an aversion to risk. There are several definitions of risk, but from an economic point of view, risk is anything where there is a possibility of loss. Playing the St. Petersburg game is a risky decision because someone will lose, either the person placing down the $20 or the person doubling the pot. Bernoulli's solution was elegant because he said that what appeared to be an aversion to risk stemmed from the way the human mind distorted the value of money. The idea could be extended to anything else that conferred utility based on the quantity consumed—food, for example.

To put risk aversion in the context of the previous two chapters, think of it as fear of failure. Bernoulli said that people look at, say, $1,000 but don't treat it as ten times more than $100. In other words, their perception of the value of money is distorted. Why should that be? Because they are afraid of the alternative. The fear of losing money, aka the fear of failure, distorts the functioning of the perceptual system in the brain. The end result is, for lack of a better word, an *irrational* decision. Only the iconoclast resists this type of perceptual distortion.

Suppose that you did not distort utility in the manner Bernoulli suggested. Suppose the utility you obtained from a given amount of money exactly tracked the face value of the money. Your utility function would be a straight line, and you would behave in an objective, risk-neutral manner. This is precisely the characteristic that disciplined money managers have. In fact, it is the only way to invest money rationally. It also goes against deep biological biases to behave the way Bernoulli suggested, and it is why there are so few people who can manage risk objectively. How the brain perceives value and utility suggests why most people (and animals) behave this way. But before getting to the neuro side of the story, we must first get to the twenty-first century in terms of economic theory.

By the twentieth century, it became apparent that Bernoulli's explanation of risk aversion was incomplete. Some argued that people are unwilling to play the St. Petersburg game because to do so would require a belief in unlimited resources available to keep the pot doubling. A dubious assumption in any gambling scenario, especially a bar. But the core idea of utility being the guiding principle behind decision making continued to hold sway. In 1944, the mathematicians John von Neumann and Oskar Morgenstern formalized the idea that *all* decisions could be understood if one assumed that individuals make choices as if they were trying to maximize their utility.[3]

Von Neumann and Morgenstern said that when an individual is faced with a decision and must make a choice between competing alternatives, the person chooses the course of action with the greatest expected utility. The way to calculate expected utility, or EU, is similar to what Bernoulli suggested. You multiply the utility of every possible outcome by the probability that it will actually happen. Then you choose the action with the highest EU. Expected utility theory, or EUT, explains a great deal about decision making from a mathematical perspective. EUT also paints a clear picture of what is the best course of action to take from a rational perspective, and it remains the foundation of almost all economic models of human decisions.

Despite its mathematical elegance, EUT may strike the average person as a completely unreasonable way to go about making decisions. It requires you to accurately gauge how you will feel about every possible outcome, and calculate the odds of each outcome actually occurring. The vast majority of people, in fact, do not consciously make decisions this way, but recent neuroimaging experiments suggest that the brain does perform calculations similar to this, even when the person is unaware of it. As it turns out, the people who actually do make decisions resembling what EUT predicts are probably the true iconoclasts. Everyone else suffers from a host of perceptual distortions that lead to a cornucopia of decision-making maladies.

## The Contrarian: David Dreman

Buy low and sell high. This principle is so obvious, a monkey should be able to make money in the stock market, right? According to David Dreman, a sort of Yoda of contrarian investing, in fact it is this simple. If only you can set aside the fear of failure and the possibility of looking stupid while your peers surpass you.

At age seventy, Dreman has weathered his share of market bubbles and crashes. He has written several best-selling books on contrarian investment, including *Psychology and the Stock Market* and *Contrarian Investment Strategies: The Next Generation*. In addition to his regular columns for *Forbes*, Dreman manages over $6 billion in assets through two mutual funds that adhere to the contrarian principles he espouses. He is the chairman of Dreman Value Management, which, in addition to the mutual funds, manages investments for select institutional and private investors. The Dreman High Equity Return Fund, which is sold through Scudder Funds, has delivered a ten-year annualized return of 11.2 percent, compared with 8.6 percent for the S&P 500 Index. The fund ranks in the top 20 percent of funds with ten-year records.

Dreman's core principle harks back to the father of investment advice, Benjamin Graham. This investment strategy centers on the idea of buying out-of-favor stocks, hence the contrarian label, and in the world of finance amounts to being an iconoclast. An *out-of-favor stock*, by definition, means that the bulk of the market finds the stock relatively unappealing. According to Dreman, these stocks are easily identified by straightforward measures of valuation. The simplest, and one proposed by Graham seventy years ago, is the price-to-earnings, or P/E, ratio. Dreman looks for stocks that are below the market average P/E and will often buy stocks that are in the bottom fifth.

Dreman laughs when questioned about whether his strategy is really contrarian. He freely admits there is no big secret to his approach. "There are many good filtering tools to find stocks with low P/E ratios." But Dreman is quick to add, "But most people don't do this, even though statistically low P/E stocks outperform over time." The problem, he says, is that most people, including professionals, can initiate the approach but have trouble following through with it. "The problem is totally anchored in psychology."[4] Actually, it is anchored in the brain's perceptual systems.

Deceptively simple, the P/E ratio is calculated by dividing the stock price by earnings per share. The P/E ratio represents how much the market values the company relative to what it is currently earning. High P/E ratios imply that the market believes a company will earn more in the future than it is currently earning. In other words, the company is expected to grow. The determination of what constitutes a high P/E ratio depends on several assumptions. If a company is not expected to grow, then it is in steady state. And if it is not growing, a steady-state company can only earn money by carrying on business as usual. The value of a company in this condition is roughly equal to its net operating profit divided by the cost of raising money. If the cost of raising money, through loans and shareholder equity, is 8 percent, then the steady-state valuation is 12.5.[5] Thus, as a very rough benchmark, companies with P/E ratios greater than 12.5 are expected to grow in value by finding new customers and new markets. Less than that, the market expects the company to shrink.

Companies with low P/E ratios, those that Dreman hunts for, may have low ratios for two possible reasons. The first is that the company is fundamentally solid, is growing earnings above the market rate, but for perceptual reasons, is out of favor with investors. These are the bargains Dreman tries to find, and according to him, they outperform the rest of the market over the long haul. But not everyone agrees with this sentiment. The second reason a company could have a low P/E ratio is that it is at the end of its life. According Michael Mauboussin, chief investment officer at Legg Mason Capital Management, "Low multiples [P/E ratios] generally reflect low (and justified) expectations."[6] Thus, a low P/E ratio, rather than being a bargain, as Dreman believes, could signal the imminent death of a company.

Dreman is steadfast in his belief in the low-P/E approach to investment. Eschewing complicated technical analysis, he is also used to wearing the iconoclast label. Raised in Winnipeg, Canada, Dreman had an early exposure to the stock market.[7] "My father was a very good commodities person, but he was actually a contrarian," said Dreman. "So it's very natural for me."

Recounting his early professional experiences, Dreman said, "When I was in my 20's, I was a junior analyst in a Wall Street shop, and I tended to buy favorites. This was really a growth firm, but there was real pressure to buy what everyone else was buying. And this came from the top. I noticed the senior guys would meet their friends at dinners and charities and such, and they all liked the same stocks. It went all the way down the line.

"Now the senior guys," Dreman continued, "they had strong likes and dislikes. But there was also a belief that if you didn't stay with these favorite stocks, you'd lose your accounts." Dreman paused to think about this. "And if you're an analyst, you might lose your job."

Referring to the peak of the Internet bubble, Dreman said, "We had a lot of clients in '99 who moved out of our fund and said, 'Value is all in the past!' Some really good value managers quit, and others experienced *value drift*. There was enormous pressure to switch strategies. Even someone like myself, I stayed with it, but I didn't know if our company would exist. It's very hard to go against the crowd. Even if you've done it most of your life, it still jolts you.

How does someone like Dreman resist the pull of the crowd? How does he resist the fear of standing alone? A calm temperament and self-confidence helps, but what about biological factors? A recent twist in the types of brain imaging studies being conducted has shed some light on the murky area of individual differences. Differences in brain function may explain why some people have the chops to go against the herd, while others fall in line.

## The Iconoclast Who Beats the Market: Bill Miller's Approach

Here's the problem with the fundamental value approach: if it really worked, then everyone would use it. And if everyone used it, they would bid up the price of companies believed to be undervalued, and then they would no longer be undervalued. This is why Dreman deserves the label "iconoclast." Now, many analysts, who make their living analyzing stocks, will argue that by uncovering certain types of information about the company that nobody else possesses, you can gain an advantage in the market. Or by analyzing past trends in prices and correlations between the movement of some assets with others, you can derive algorithms that will outperform the market as a whole. The problem is that everyone has access to the same information. So many individuals are active in the stock market that it becomes extremely unlikely that someone will gain an advantage over the other people. This inability to gain an advantage, in a nutshell, is known as the *efficient market hypothesis*, or EMH.

Formulated in the 1960s by Eugene Fama, an economist at the University of Chicago, the EMH says that financial markets are informationally efficient. This means that the price of any asset represents the collective wisdom and knowledge of all the people trading in the market. As a direct result, the EMH says that it is impossible to consistently outperform the market. You may do so transiently by luck, but not for long. The flip-flopping of mutual fund rankings is broadly consistent with the efficient market hypothesis. But even here, a slight discrepancy remains. A very small group of funds and fund managers do tend to do better than others on a consistent basis.

Bill Miller, the manager of the Legg Mason Value Trust, with $20 billion in assets, beat the S&P 500 fifteen years in a row, a streak that finally came to an end in 2006. By that statistic alone, Miller qualifies as either the luckiest of all fund managers or the most iconoclastic. Believers in the EMH say that Miller was the beneficiary of a lucky streak, and in the grand scheme of the market, he will eventually be subsumed by the law of averages. A less literal interpretation of the EMH allows for the broad efficiency of the market, but certain assumptions make it possible to exploit advantages.

Like Dreman, Miller has always adhered to the value approach to investing. He, too, points to Benjamin Graham as an early influence. But Miller goes beyond the P/E ratio. While the P/E ratio is derived from the current price and most recent earnings, Miller says that the more important metric is future earnings. This is where Miller goes beyond Graham. "The only reasonable way to compare [companies] is between the returns you expect to earn from them." To do that, you have to look to the future, not the past. It is for precisely this reason that Miller was heavily invested in Google, which, even at the time he bought it, had a P/E ratio of 50. To Miller, the distinction between value and growth investing is arbitrary. "Growth is an input to the calculation of value."[8]

Unlike Dreman, however, Miller does not believe in the utility of simple-minded stock screening based on P/E ratios and the like. He doesn't believe they say much about value. Such a screener would pass over Google because it appears overpriced according to past earnings. But many high-P/E stocks are a bargain when viewed from the perspective of *future* earnings. Again, like all iconoclasts, Miller is often able to maintain a different perception of value. While much of the market focuses on past earnings, he focuses on future earnings.

The problem, however, is that calculating future earnings is more art than science, something akin to looking into a crystal ball of the future. In contrast, P/E ratios are computed from known quantities and events that have already happened, and consequently there is no uncertainty about the actual P/E figure. P/E ratios are comforting. Computing a valuation based on the future involves quite a lot more due diligence into what a company is planning and a bit of prognostication as well. But the real issue with estimating future value, as Miller does, is the uncertainty inherent to the process. The future will always be unknowable to a degree, and it is the fear of this uncertainty that prevents many, if not most, investors from using this method. Like the other iconoclasts, Miller does not let the fear of the unknown cloud his perception of value.

## The Biology of the Fear of Failure

If fear of the unknown prevents most people from taking chances, you can sure bet the fear of failure does too. Any activity in which there is a possibility of failure is, by definition, risky, and it is this fear of failure that makes so many people risk averse. Like the fear of uncertainty and the fear of public ridicule, the fear of failure wends it way through the brain, distorting perception and inhibiting action. Thanks to several recent experiments, we are now beginning to figure out how this happens.

Although no experiment has directly examined the question of what is inside an iconoclast's brain, there are studies that have identified neural links between brain differences and behaviors such as risk taking and fear avoidance. The ability to deal with bad news and maintain one's perception, as we have seen, is a key attribute of the successful iconoclast. Dreman did not change his perception of stock valuation during the Internet bubble. And although he suffered through the loss of clients, he didn't panic. Similarly, Miller did not change his perception of value according to commonsense, if simplistic, judgments based on P/E ratios. It seems obvious that there should be something different in the brains of people like Dreman and Miller, but because these individuals are rare, it is difficult to pin down what these differences might be. In 2005, my research group found one such difference in the brains of people who reacted strongly to potentially negative information, which has direct implications for the iconoclastic brain.

While many of the early researchers in neuroeconomics focused on the brain's response to financial incentives, my group turned to the equally important dark side of decision making: loss. And where loss looms, fear follows. Every decision that a person makes involves a weighing of upsides and downsides. Some people focus entirely on the possibility of a good outcome, while others fixate on the negative. Sound decision making walks a fine line between these two extremes. From a scientific point of view, it has been surprisingly difficult to study the fear of loss on decision making. Nobody will volunteer for an experiment in which they could lose money. Moreover, ethical rules governing human experimentation prohibit experiments in which volunteers have to pay to participate.

For these reasons, we designed an experiment to examine the effect of a potentially painful outcome on decision making. Understanding how the brain processes pain is of great medical importance, but pain is also crucial to deciphering the iconoclastic brain. Iconoclasts go against the herd. So like Martin Luther King Jr. and others, they inevitably will suffer at some point from fear and the pain of social isolation, if not outright hostility. For most people, the fear of pain or loss is enough to deter them from action.

The experiment went like this.[9] The volunteer was told that the experiment was designed to understand how the brain processes pain. But there was more to it than that. In actuality, we were really interested in the brain's response to the anticipation of pain. Because unpleasant and potentially painful outcomes in life are unavoidable, how people deal with the anticipation is critical for understanding the decision-making process that distinguishes successful iconoclasts from those who simply give in to their fears. We used the prospect of physical pain in this experiment because it is scientifically expedient to deliver and controllable. The subject was shown an electrical stimulating device that is commonly used in studies of nerve function. In our experiment, however, the electrodes were attached to the top of the subject's left foot. Through these electrodes, we sent very brief electrical shocks. Although not unbearably painful, the shocks were designed to be unpleasant enough that the individual would prefer to avoid them altogether. The kicker was that they had to wait for the shocks. Every trial began with a statement of how big a shock they were going to receive and how long they had to wait for it, which ranged from one second to almost thirty seconds. For many people, the waiting was worse than the shock. How bad was it? Given a choice, almost every individual preferred to expedite the shock and not wait for it. Nearly a third of the people feared waiting so much that when given the chance, they preferred to receive a bigger shock sooner rather than waiting for a smaller shock later. This was exactly the type of impulsive behavior that we were interested in and that gets in the way of sound financial decision making. We dubbed them "extreme dreaders."

When we examined the brain responses of the different individuals, we found a neural fingerprint that differentiated the cool cucumbers from the extreme dreaders. A part of the brain associated with processing physical stimuli, called the *secondary somatosensory cortex*, had a rise in activity in the extreme dreaders when they were shown the information about how long they would have to wait. The brains of their more patient counterparts did not show this early response. Instead, their brains reacted with a gradual rise in activity up to the point of the shock. We found similar differences in other parts of the cortical pain network, including the *anterior cingulate cortex*, which lies in the midline of the brain and straddles the bundle of fibers connecting the left and right hemispheres, and is frequently activated during stressful events. Considering these findings from the other direction of causality, you could say that hyperactivity in this network of brain regions might actually be the cause of impulsive, irrational behavior, at least when it comes to the fear of something unpleasant.

## How Fear Clouds Financial Judgment

Identifying differences in brain activation in the laboratory is one thing, but demonstrating that these differences have any practical application in the real world is an entirely different matter. Andrew Lo, a professor of finance at the MIT Sloan School of Management, has been examining the link between biology and financial decision making. Lo's work is at the cutting edge of neuroeconomics and represents some of the most intriguing directions in which both neuroscience and biological information are being applied in the business world. Lo believes in the general principle of the efficient market, but because some individuals seem to do better than others, he has explored the possibility that biological differences underlie the performance inequities between winners and losers seen in any market. Although markets might be broadly efficient, Lo's work suggests that differences between individuals in the market create small, but transiently leverageable opportunities for profit. The key lies in the emotional brain, especially fear circuits.

In 2001, Lo teamed up with a young Russian physicist/cognitive neuroscientist, Dmitry Repin, to measure physiological responses in professional traders.[10] Lo and Repin recruited a small group of traders who worked in the foreign-exchange and interest-rate derivatives unit of a major global financial institution based in Boston. On a typical day, this unit engaged in 1,000–1,200 trades and averaged $3 million to $5 million per trade. Lo and Repin wired up ten traders to measure a range of physiological responses that included blood pressure, body temperature, respiration rate, skin conductance responses (sweating), and measurements of muscle contractions in the face and arm. These measurements were collected for a period ranging from forty-nine to eighty-three minutes during live trading hours. After the session, Lo and Repin examined the correlation between these physiological parameters and specific volatility events in the market. Lo and Repin used a computer algorithm to extract these events in markets that traded foreign currencies, including the euro, the Japanese yen, and the British pound. The volatility events included price deviations, spread deviations, price-trend reversals, and both price and return volatility. Lo and Repin also divided the traders into inexperienced and seasoned categories to see whether experience affects an individual's autonomic reactions to market events.

Although this was a small sample of subjects, Lo and Repin found surprising correlations between physiological responses and market trends. The most strongly correlated parameter, blood pressure, rose in both novice and experienced traders when an asset's maximum volatility went up. Volatility was measured as the difference between the maximum and minimum price over a short time interval and calculated as a fraction of the average price. It was related to the short-term variance of the asset. In a more detailed analysis, they found that this rise in blood pressure occurred well in advance of the key volatility event. This suggested that the traders' bodies responded to cues in the market that preceded the large-scale event that subsequently showed up as a price change. This observation raises the intriguing possibility that the brain (and the body) picks up subtle cues in the market that are not apparent from trend analyses.

As exciting as these findings were, Lo and Repin were not able to prove a causal link between physiological reactions and individual performance in the market. In a later experiment on eighty day traders who were participating in an online training program, they did find the first hint of a link between emotional reactivity and performance.[11] Although they were unable to use physiological measurements, Lo's team examined the link between trading results and emotional state. They also wanted to know whether a specific personality was particularly good at trading. Using standard personality inventories, Lo found no correlation between personality and trading performance. From this, he concluded that there was no ideal "stock market personality." In contrast, Lo did find correlations of positive and negative mood states with daily performance, which, by itself, is really not very surprising. People are happy when they make money, and unhappy when they lose it. The key finding was that these correlations were the *strongest for the worst traders*. The worst traders let their emotions color their perception of valuation and cloud their decision making.

## Henry Ford and the Freedom from Fear

Henry Ford was an iconoclast on so many levels, ranging from his views on capitalism and world peace to his development of the assembly line, but he had clearly articulated views about the damaging effects of fear in business and how to deal with it. Born in 1863 on a farm in Dearborn, Michigan, Ford recalls that he grew up witnessing too much hard labor on the farm. He started building steam engines first, with the goal in mind of alleviating the sweat-and-blood drudgery of farm work. And then he read of the gas engine. Built in England, these early engines couldn't develop anything near the power of a steam engine, and Ford's interest was more out of engineering curiosity than anything else. These single-cylinder jobs were hugely inefficient, requiring four cycles to develop one power stroke. And it wasn't until 1890 that Ford took a serious interest in double-cylinder engines.

At that time, Ford was working for the Edison company, and, not too surprisingly, there was little interest in gas-powered forms of transportation. The focus was on electricity. The prevailing opinion was that electricity, not gasoline, would be the power of the future. Ford bucked this trend and became an iconoclast when he quit his job in 1899 to go into the automobile business. He spent the next three years developing a two-cylinder engine that was powerful enough to move a "horseless carriage." The result was the famous Model A. It sold for $750 (about $17,000 in 2008 dollars) and could reach a speed of 45 mph. The Model

A wasn't a best seller—more of an oddity—but Ford did well enough to plow the profits into the development of what really made the Ford Motor Company: the Model T.

The Model T became possible only when Ford heard about a new type of steel that was being smelted in France. French steel contained a secret ingredient, vanadium, which made it three times stronger than regular steel. This changed everything for Ford. As with other iconoclasts, his perception of the automobile instantly changed when he saw what could be done with a vehicle that weighed a third less. Now, little gas engines that struggled to pull a heavy car suddenly weren't so anemic anymore. A little engine could do a lot with a car that didn't weigh very much. The Model T was released in 1908, and within the first year, Ford had sold 10,607 of them, more than any other manufacturer.

None of this was luck. Ford believed steadfastly in the value of work: "Freedom is the right to work a decent length of time and to get a decent living for doing so."[12] At the core of his philosophy lay the belief that he had an obligation to face the uncertainty of the future and not fear failure (two of the three basic fears that distort perception). Ford wrote: "One who fears the future, who fears failure, limits his activities. Failure is only the opportunity more intelligently to begin again. There is no disgrace in honest failure; there is disgrace in fearing to fail."[13]

With time, Ford came to believe that money was at the root of these fears: "Thinking first of money instead of work brings on fear of failure and this fear blocks every avenue of business—it makes a man afraid of competition, of changing his methods, or of doing anything which might change his condition."[14]

Ford sets a good example of how successful iconoclasts deal with fear. The first step, indeed the most important step, is the recognition that fear permeates any business. Fear is to be taken as a warning sign, not as guide for action or inaction. Once fear is recognized, it can be deconstructed and reappraised. Ford also points out that when fear is deconstructed, you will often find fear of losing money to be at the root of it. Even so, the iconoclast vanquishes the fear of failure. Ford also gives a good example of how reframing fear of failure, as in the possibility of learning from one's mistakes, allows a potential negative be turned into a positive.

## Using Genetics to Diversify a Team and Mitigate the Effects of Fear

Are iconoclasts born, or are they made? Some, like Feynman, seem to fall in the first category, while others, like Ford and Dreman and Miller, seem self-made. The fact is that all brains are not created equal. The neuroimaging evidence points to dopamine as a key neurotransmitter in decision making, so it follows that there should be something different about how dopamine is released in the iconoclastic brain. Although it is not possible to measure dopamine levels directly in the human brain, the level of dopamine activity can be inferred from an entirely different source of information: an individual's genetic fingerprint. And taking a cue from the law of large numbers, there should be substantial benefit to diversifying the genetic composition of a decision-making team.

The human genome is comprised of DNA, itself composed of complementary pairs of four nucleic acids (base pairs). This DNA is broken up into twenty-four chunks that make up the chromosomes. All told, there are about 3 billion base pairs in the human genome. Most of this is so-called junk DNA because it doesn't code for genes. The rest, however, contains the code to make proteins, which are the building blocks of the body. Amazingly, the genome contains the instructions for building every one of the proteins in the body.

When dopamine is released into the synaptic space, two things happen. First, the dopamine binds to the dopamine receptor, which causes a chain of biochemical and electrical events in the postsynaptic neuron. Second, after the initial event, the dopamine molecules must be reabsorbed into the neuron that released them. The dopamine transporter, or DAT, is the protein that serves this function. The DAT is interesting in its own right because virtually all the stimulant-type drugs, such as cocaine and amphetamine, bind to the DAT and block its function. This typically results in an excess of dopamine floating around the synapse. After dopamine is reabsorbed into the releasing neuron, it might be repackaged for a subsequent release, or it might be broken down into its constituent parts. This breakdown process, or *catalysis*, is accomplished by another protein called catechol-o-methyltransferase, or COMT for short. Together, the DAT and COMT regulate the amount of dopamine available for release.

DAT and COMT are proteins; thus the human genome contains instructions to make them like every other protein in the body. It turns out that there are subtle variations between people in their gene sequences for these proteins. Both DAT and COMT are big, a little over 1,000 base pairs for COMT and 3,900 for DAT. The mutation of a single base pair within this chain means the substitution of one amino acid for another. For COMT, a single base-pair mutation changes the 158th amino acid from a valine (Val) to a methionine (Met). Because everyone has two copies of every gene, one inherited from each parent, some people have two valines (Val/Val), some people have two methionines (Met/Met), and some have one of each (Val/Met). It turns out that Val/Val individuals have four times as much COMT activity as their Met/Met counterparts. The DAT gene is similar, and, like COMT, it is found in two common forms, called 9R and 10R.[15] The 9R form has been linked to a lower amount of DAT synthesis, which, like cocaine, may have the end result of lowering the clearance of dopamine from the synapse.

In a recent neuroimaging study, Christian Büchel, a neuroscientist in Hamburg, Germany, measured the relationship between fMRI activity in the striatal dopamine system during a gambling task similar to the one used to study the Ellsberg paradox.[16] Büchel genotyped all of the 105 people who participated in his study. He then looked for differences in brain activation that were linked to the different genotypes for COMT and DAT. Büchel found greater activity in the dopamine-rich areas of the brain when winning was more likely. How much greater depended on the particular combination of genes the individual had. Büchel found that people with the Val/Val form of COMT *and* the 10R form of the DAT showed no relationship between brain activity and probability of winning. In other words, these people were insensitive to the level of risk. On a standard measure of personality type, these people also scored high in sensation seeking.

The implications are striking for decision making, especially group decision making. These particular genetic variants are associated with lower dopamine activity, which is borne out at the level of brain activation. If a relative insensitivity to dopamine means that these individuals exhibit risky behavior when the potential rewards do not offset the level of risk, they might be driven to goose their brains with dopamine by ever-higher levels of risk taking. They thrive on risk and are comparatively immune to the damaging effects of fear on decision making. We don't know whether these forms of the genes are more common in iconoclasts. Nobody has done such a study. But given the rate of advance in both imaging and genomics, it may not be such a bad idea to find out which you are. And if you are assembling a team of individuals, it might make sense to take a cue from modern finance theory by diversifying the genetic portfolio of your team.

# SIX

# Brain Circuits for Social Networking

How you suffered for your sanity . . .
But still your love was true.
—"Vincent," Don McLean

Girls could not resist his stare:
Pablo Picasso never got called an asshole.
—"Pablo Picasso," The Modern Lovers

HOWARD ARMSTRONG was an iconoclast because he invented things, such as FM radio, that others thought could not be done, but when he killed himself, he died an unsuccessful iconoclast. His failure was not in perception or a lack of courage to stand up for what he believed. His failure was one of social intelligence: he couldn't sell his idea. To be clear, social intelligence is not strictly necessary to be an iconoclast, but it is necessary to be a successful one.

The issue comes down to the iconoclast's ability to connect with other people. As we shall see in this chapter, connecting with noniconoclasts depends on two key aspects of social intelligence: *familiarity* and *reputation*. Both functions can be understood through the circuits in the brain that implement them.

Consider two of the most iconoclastic artists of modern times: Vincent van Gogh and Pablo Picasso. Paintings by both have fetched over $100 million.[1] And both of them are responsible for some of the most iconic images in the art world: Van Gogh's *Self-Portait* (the one sans earlobe) and *Starry Night*, and Picasso's *The Old Guitarist* and *Guernica*. But there is an important difference between Van Gogh and Picasso. Van Gogh died penniless, while Picasso's estate was estimated at $750 million when he died in 1973. Although both were iconoclasts, it was Picasso who was the successful one, at least during his lifetime.

For the iconoclast, two aspects of social intelligence figure prominently in success or failure: familiarity and reputation. The two go hand in hand. In order to sell one's ideas, one must create a positive reputation that will draw people toward something that is initially unfamiliar and potentially scary. Familiarity helps build one's reputation. Picasso was a master at both. He became familiar to the art world through his massive productivity. While Van Gogh produced about nine hundred paintings in his lifetime, Picasso produced over thirteen thousand paintings and about three hundred sculptures, making him the most prolific artist ever. And everyone loved Picasso. People were drawn to him because of his charisma. That many were lovers illustrates the correlation between the charisma he displayed in peddling his art and the charisma that attracted people to his bed. Since he was five foot three, physical stature had little to do with Picasso's appeal. Van Gogh, on the other hand, while equally brilliant in his art, repelled people. The whole earlobe incident was provoked by an argument with Paul Gaugin—the recipient of Van Gogh's "gift." Where Picasso smoothly navigated multiple social circles, Van Gogh struggled to maintain connections with even those closest to him. Van Gogh inhabited an alien world. Picasso, on the other hand, was a social magnet. And because he knew so many people, the world was at his fingertips. From his perspective, the world was smaller.

Picasso was a *node*. He possessed a rare combination of social skills that allowed him to function both as what Malcolm Gladwell called a "connector" and as a "persuader."[2] Picasso's unique position illustrates a key point that differentiates successful iconoclasts from obscure ones (and Van Gogh and Armstrong fall in this category, at least during their lifetimes). Successful iconoclasts connect with other people and, in the process, shrink their worlds.

The most meaningful way to measure the size of the world today is the ease by which one person can find another. Geography no longer matters. When you can instant message, text, or Skype someone anywhere in the world, physical distance loses all relationship to the cost of communication. For someone like Van Gogh, who painted in a tortured world in which only a few people knew him, the distance to people who had money to buy his paintings was huge. Van Gogh's primary connection to the art world was through his brother, and this connection did not feed directly into the money that could have turned him into a living success. Picasso's world could not have been more different. His wide-ranging social network, which included artists, writers, and politicians, meant that he was never more than a few people away from anyone of importance in the world.

Picasso offers pointed lessons on how to shrink the world. Increase the world's familiarity with you through productivity and exposure. And develop a reputation so that people are drawn to you and not repelled. Easier said than done. But neuroscience tells us about the biological underpinnings of these two functions—familiarity and reputation—and potential ways to make the most of what you have.

## Stanley Milgram and the Six Degrees of Separation

What does it mean to connect to people? Some might think of an emotional bond. Others think of shared interests. The problem for the iconoclast is that, by definition, he will begin his journey alone and nobody will share his point of view. To be successful, then, he must foster networks, even if initially superficial, with other people. The science of networking goes back to another social psychologist of the 1950s, Stanley Milgram.

Solomon Asch didn't just mastermind classic social psychology experiments such as the one on conformity described in chapter 4. Asch was responsible for influencing the career path of Stanley Milgram, another iconoclast of social psychology. A few years after Asch's conformity experiment, Milgram arrived at Harvard as a naive graduate student. He was assigned to be Asch's research assistant. Although Milgram was thrilled to be working with someone as famous as Asch, the relationship was not entirely a pleasant one. Ideally, the mentor takes the young graduate student protégé under his wing and molds him into an independent investigator through both nurturance and tough love. Asch, however, was preoccupied with his conformity research. And Milgram, temperamentally predisposed to moodiness and sarcasm, tended to chafe at what he perceived as menial tasks dictated by Asch and the Harvard bureaucracy.[3] When Asch invited Milgram to help edit his book on conformity, Milgram accepted, in part, to finance his graduate education while being afforded time to work on his dissertation. It didn't work out as expected. Milgram spent more time on Asch's book than he had planned, and not only that, Milgram never received the acknowledgment in the book that he had hoped for.

Although Milgram was intensely unhappy during this period, it was, nevertheless, his formative moment. It was a period of time that ultimately would determine his career direction toward creating a science of social networking. As Milgram wrote in a letter in 1959, "I'm listless, uneasy, dissatisfied, bored and fed up. I'm the little man looking around for some totalitarian movement I can join."[4] Since he was looking out at the world from a vantage point of anonymity, it is no wonder that Milgram sought to figure out how he came to be in such a position.

With the Nuremburg trials still fresh in his mind, Milgram hit upon the idea of adapting Asch's experiment to a life-or-death situation, to see whether not only group pressure but also authority figures could induce conformity. Milgram came up with the most famous social psychology experiment ever performed: the shock-obedience experiment. The premise was simple. Subjects were recruited in pairs, one of whom was designated the "teacher" and the other the "learner." Whenever he gave an incorrect answer, the teacher applied an electric shock to "facilitate the learning process." It was all a ruse. The learner was Milgram's confederate, and the shock machine was a fake. The only real subject was the teacher. The true purpose of the experiment was to see how far people would go in shocking strangers under the inducement of an authority figure like Milgram. And they went far indeed, with 65 percent of the subjects maxing out the voltage into the lethal zone of the machine, despite screams and eventual silence from the learner.

Milgram became famous for this experiment, or perhaps infamous. The magnitude of the deception imparted to the subjects caused an outcry among the public and other psychologists. In the end, Milgram had achieved what he longed for as a graduate student—a killer experiment, brilliant in its conception and undeniable in its conclusions—but he still found himself on the fringe of academia. He became an iconoclast after the fact. Perhaps for this reason, he embarked on a somewhat tamer series of investigations on the nature of social networks.

To study the fabric of societal connectedness, Milgram devised an experiment to answer what he called the *small-world problem*. One way to phrase the problem is, what is the probability that any two people know each other? But this misses the more interesting aspect of *how* people are connected to each other. To approach this aspect,

Milgram formulated the question as, how many mutual acquaintances separate two randomly selected people? Although he didn't coin the phrase, it is popularly known as *six degrees of separation*.[5]

First, Milgram identified a "target person," who was a stockbroker living in Boston. Next, Milgram selected three groups of individuals to be "starting persons." One group was randomly picked from the Boston area by soliciting participants through a Boston newspaper ad. The other two groups were selected to be geographically distant from the target— in this case, people who lived in Nebraska. One of the Nebraskan groups was selected like the Bostonians, and the others were chosen from a pool of Nebraskans who owned blue-chip stocks. Each of the groups represented a different clique of people, some connected through geography, and others through a common interest in stocks. Each of the starting persons received a folder with instructions to get the letter to the target in Boston. If they personally knew the target, then they should send the packet to him. But if the recipient did not know the target personally, then they were to send the packet on to someone who they thought would be more likely to know him.[6]

Most of the packets never reached their target, but of the 29 percent that did, each passed through four to six people (average of five). What is even more interesting than the number of people each packet passed through is Milgram's observation that as the packets approached Boston, they tended to fall into common channels. Almost half of the letters reached their target through one of two people, whom Milgram called *common channels*.[7]

Who were these common channels? The first was a clothing merchant in the target's hometown of Sharon, Massachusetts. So even though the target was a stockbroker in Boston, a big chunk of the letters reached him through the geographic proximity of a local business owner where he lived, as opposed to where he worked. The clothing merchant, while having nothing to do with the stock market, played the role of a connector. By virtue of his business, the clothes merchant knew people from many different social circles. It makes sense that as the packets reached the vicinity of Boston, they should funnel to people who are viewed by the local community as well connected. These people are not iconoclasts. They couldn't be. As well-respected, upstanding citizens, connectors form the glue of local society. Iconoclasts, by their very nature, upset this delicate web of connectedness. But iconoclasts need connectors. Without them, the iconoclast stands no chance of achieving success. Sometimes iconoclasts have to create the connectors themselves.

## Ray Kroc: The Iconoclast Who Sold Hamburgers to Children

Ray Kroc, the iconoclastic salesman who took McDonald's from a sleepy burger joint in southern California to a multinational corporation with more than $20 billion in annual revenues, knew the value of connectors. Born in 1902 in a suburb of Chicago, Kroc learned early on the power of social connectedness. While working at his uncle's soda shop, "I learned you could influence people with a smile and enthusiasm."[8] He later sold coffee beans and paper products, and in 1954, when he met the McDonald brothers, he was selling milk-shake mixers. Kroc bought the right to franchise the restaurant nationwide, but it was Kroc's connection to another great iconoclast, Walt Disney, that was the source of Kroc's brilliance. Kroc and Disney had reportedly met briefly as fellow ambulance drivers in World War I. After Kroc acquired the franchise rights to McDonald's, he sent a letter to Disney, inquiring about the opportunity to open a restaurant in his Disneyland development. Unfortunately, it didn't work out right away. In fact, McDonald's and Disney didn't work out a deal until 1996, long after both Walt Disney and Ray Kroc were dead.

Kroc, however, didn't give up. He knew the value of connecting to potential customers. And if it wasn't Disney, then he would create his own "connector." Kroc realized that his customers weren't just adults. He wanted families in his restaurants, and that meant children. Taking a cue from Disney's Mickey Mouse, Kroc created Ronald McDonald to connect to children.[9] It seemed crazy at the time. Children didn't have the wherewithal to go to a McDonald's by themselves, and so conventional wisdom said that advertising to children was a waste of money. But Kroc persisted, and that is why he is an iconoclast. And he was right. Eventually, Happy Meals and movie tie-ins followed. More than anything else, Kroc was an iconoclast for single-handedly creating the concept of marketing to children through the creation of kid-friendly connectors.

## The Road to Familiarity: Face and Name Recognition in the Brain

Apart from creating connectors to children, vis-à-vis Ronald McDonald, Kroc also perfected the art of ubiquity. Although Kroc was an iconoclast himself, he built McDonald's on the notion of familiarity to the consumer and had no tolerance for nonconformity within his organization. Everything about the McDonald's experience was geared toward uniformity and familiarity. Kroc wrapped his brand in a cloak of familiarity that appealed to deep-seated needs for predictability in most people's brains.

Early work in network science focused on the egalitarian nature of social connections. In the real world, however, connections between people are rarely equal. Everyone knows the president. At least it can seem like that. Public figures, in particular, benefit from the lopsidedness of their social network. Many more people know them than they, themselves, know. The successful iconoclast cultivates this type of asymmetry in his social network.

One way to cultivate a surfeit of incoming connections is to create an aura of familiarity. Iconoclasts such as Chihuly, Picasso, and Kroc excelled at this. The type of familiarity that the iconoclast wants to cultivate comes down to face and name recognition. It is easy to see why facial recognition evolved to a level of such importance. The face is the most variable aspect of human appearance, containing more bones and muscles per square inch than any other part of the body. We use a person's face to gauge her beauty, and we value symmetry above all else.[10] The face is also a window into our emotional states. Even without language, our faces say something about what type of person we are and how we feel.

Once humans acquired language, they no longer needed to rely solely on visual cues to identify a person. Now, in addition to their face, we mentally tag the identity of an individual with their name. In online communities, identities may be flagged in other ways, such as computer-generated avatars. Although faces and names are two very different ways to categorize an individual, both are necessary to trigger a feeling of familiarity. Recognizing a face, such as that of an actor in a movie, does no good unless you can link the face with its name. The inability to make this link leads to a tip-of-the-tongue feeling of frustration, which is not a mental state the iconoclast wants to foster when they are tying to sell their ideas. Solid familiarity imparts a visual image to a person's name and nearly instantaneous recall of a person's name when seeing his face.

For many years, psychologists thought that these two aspects of familiarity, visual and mnemonic recognition, were mediated by separate processes in the brain. But recent fMRI experiments suggest that the emotional response to an individual also colors our judgments of familiarity. All primates have evolved brains that contain specialized regions devoted to the processing of faces. The most prominent of these face-responsive areas is in a fold of brain, just off the midline toward the back of the head, called the *fusiform gyrus*. Neurons in this region fire most strongly when we see a human face. The more familiar the face, the stronger these neurons fire. The psychologists Ida Gobbini and James Haxby pointed out that the relationship between fusiform activity and familiarity is influenced by several factors.[11] For example, the faces of strangers elicit more activity than famous familiar faces, but the faces of friends and family members evoke as much activity as strangers' faces. These results suggest that fusiform activity reflects the depth of facial processing. Both strangers and friends trigger more processing than famous people, but for different reasons. Whereas a stranger's face might represent a potential threat, a friend's face evokes deeper processing because it triggers a wealth of memories.

Although the fusiform area is critical for the initial processing of faces, Gobbini and Haxby found that a different set of brain regions tracked familiarity. This network implemented cognitive functions more general than just face processing. These areas included the *cingulate cortex* and a region on the side of the brain just above the ear, called the *superior temporal sulcus* (STS). The cingulate cortex is thought to represent personal traits and even the mental states of others, while the STS seems to play a critical role in the evaluation of their intentions.[12] The STS neurons are exquisitely sensitive to physical configurations of the face, aspects such as in which direction the face was pointed, what the rest of the body was doing, and, most strongly, where the eyes were looking. The Scottish psychologist David Perrett, who has studied monkey STS neurons for decades, provided one of the most concise explanations for the function of these neurons: they signal the direction of another person's attention.[13] And from attention, we extract intention. Looking to the side, for example, may signal deception, and STS neurons pick this up.

The STS neurons provide a biological bookmark for a person's character. A key element of Gobbini and Haxby's theory of familiarity depends on the emotional response that we associate with a person's face. In the simplest sense, one has either a positive or a negative emotional response to a person. Both types of emotions foster familiarity, but for opposite reasons. Positive feelings generate a desire to approach the person, while negative feelings make you want to run away. Obviously, the successful iconoclast should be in the former category. An individual who doesn't look straight into someone's eyes runs the risk of the viewer's STS neurons tagging him as a person of suspect intentions.

The amygdala seems to play the gatekeeper role in flagging the emotional response to faces. As we saw earlier, the amygdala solidifies primitive forms of learning like the association between cues and unpleasant events, especially physical ones. The amygdala also plays a critical role in social judgment. In a study of three patients who suffered complete destruction of their amygdalae, the neuropsychologists Ralph Adolphs, Daniel Tranel, and Antonio Damasio reported a dramatic impairment in judging trustworthiness. These patients were shown pictures of strangers and asked to judge their approachability and trustworthiness. All three patients judged these strangers as more trustworthy than normal, healthy control subjects did.[14] Similarly, when neuroscientists burned out monkeys' amygdalae almost a century ago, the monkeys exhibited socially bizarre behavior such as using their mouths instead of their eyes to examine objects, and they became hypersexual.[15]

David Amaral, a neuroscientist at the University of California, Davis, has reexamined the role the amygdala plays in social behavior. Through more precise lesion methods in monkeys, he has found that the amygdala's role in social function hinges on its processing of environmental dangers.[16] Amaral has suggested that the amygdala acts as a break on social interactions when it perceives a potential adversary. Such a role is consistent with the wealth of data indicating the amygdala's central function in fear conditioning and the development of specific phobias. It also explains why human patients with damage to their amygdala become impaired in their ability to evaluate trustworthiness and why monkeys with no temporal lobes try to have sex with almost any other monkey or object.

If facial appearance is so important to judging a person's character, it follows that racial biases may originate in these same face circuits. Potential iconoclasts need to be aware of how this happens so that they can take measures to calm the amygdalae of audiences. Elizabeth Phelps, a social psychologist at NYU, has been studying the neurobiology of racial prejudice. In one brain imaging experiment, Phelps presented Caucasian participants with photographs of African American and Caucasian male faces. All the men had short haircuts, no facial hair, and no distinctive clothing. Phelps found that the Caucasian participants consistently displayed more amygdala activation to the African American faces than the Caucasian ones. Moreover, the level of amygdala activation correlated with two subconscious measures of racial bias.[17] In a follow-up experiment, Phelps found the relationship also holds for African Americans viewing pictures of Caucasians, although others have recently found increased amygdala activation in African Americans viewing pictures of African Americans, too.[18] Regardless of how these racial biases are learned, their manifestation in the amygdala at the subconscious level means that they are effectively hardwired. Because the amygdala signals danger, the iconoclast needs to minimize the chance of triggering its activation in his intended audience. Things and people that look different set the amygdala on edge, while familiarity soothes it.

Arnold Schwarzenegger is a good example of an individual who has banked on his aura of familiarity to effect legislative change in California. A self-described iconoclast, he was born in 1947 in Austria. Schwarzenegger has traced his nonconformist tendencies to his childhood rebellion against a strict Austrian upbringing. "It was all about conforming. I was one who did not conform and whose will could not be broken. Therefore I became a rebel. Every time I got hit, and every time someone said, 'you can't do this,' I said, 'this is not going to be for much longer, because I'm going to move out of here. I want to be rich. I want to be somebody.'" Schwarzenegger also knows the power of appearance. "The bigger you are and the more impressive you look physically, the more people listen and the better you can sell yourself or anything else."[19]

On the surface, Schwarzenegger would appear to be an unlikely candidate for governor, especially a Republican one. But his aura of familiarity, coupled with the invincibility of the Terminator, made him an easy winner in California politics. Certainly, his legislative policies have gone far to the left of Republican ideology. From stem cell research to children's health insurance, Schwarzenegger has taken stances that are nonconformist with party politics but resonate deeply with the masses. Were it not for Article II of the Constitution, which requires the president to be born in the United States, it is almost a sure bet that Schwarzenegger would be president.

## Why the Brain Likes Familiarity

In November 2004, *Rolling Stone* magazine published its list of the five hundred greatest songs of all time. Although the editors gave the nod to Bob Dylan's "Like a Rolling Stone," it is the second song on their list that contains the most recognizable five notes in all of rock and roll history. For any fan of rock and roll, hearing Keith Richards's fuzzed-out riff that opens "Satisfaction" can't help but bring a smile to the face. It really is quite an impressive feat that the human brain can take five notes and instantly identify where they come from. In fact, two suffice for most people. Sure, the song is vastly overplayed, but it continues to show up on every list of top rock and roll songs of the past fifty years. One might debate endlessly the merits of the song and what accounts for its popularity, whether it's the disaffected lyrics or the catchy riff itself. Regardless, the fact that it has become so familiar guarantees it a permanent place in the pantheon of popular music. The human brain comes to like that with which it is familiar. And it is this sort of familiarity that the successful iconoclast must strive for. Rightly or wrongly, people put their money into things that they are familiar with.

In the 1960s, the University of Michigan psychologist Robert Zajonc further refined our notion of how familiarity defines what we like. Using pictures instead of music, Zajonc showed pictures of irregularly shaped octagons to his subjects. The pictures, however, were flashed so briefly on the screen that the subjects had insufficient time to process them. Later, Zajonc showed the pictures again and asked the subjects two questions. The first question asked how confident they were that they had seen a particular picture. The second question asked how much they liked it. Zajonc found that people liked pictures that they had seen previously, even though the pictures had been flashed so briefly that they were effectively unaware of having seen them. He termed this phenomenon "the mere exposure effect."[20]

Does familiarity with someone increase the likelihood of doing business with him? A wealth of economic data suggests that the answer is yes. Gur Huberman, a professor of finance at Columbia University, has examined where investors place their money as a result of familiarity. People who own stock in Regional Bell Operating Companies (RBOCs) tend to invest in the companies that provide their service. For example, whether someone invests in BellSouth or NYNEX is determined primarily by whether they live in the South or the Northeast. Huberman found that the fraction of people investing in local RBOCs was 82 percent higher than that of the next RBOC. From an economic point of view, this is irrational. One should not expect a local company to be a superior investment to any of the other national companies that provide essentially the same service. All of the RBOCs are listed on the NYSE, so there is no barrier to investment in any of these companies. Yet the local bias remains.

People root for the home team, and they feel comfortable investing their money in a business that is familiar to them. Familiarity bias is not limited to telephone companies. U.S. equity managers tend to prefer domestic stocks, and their portfolios reflect this bias. This home-country bias extends to other countries as well. German business students, when compared with their American counterparts, view German stocks more favorably than American ones.[21]

While familiarity increases the chances that people will like something, it also makes them feel comfortable. To bridge the gap between the mere exposure effect and the closing of a business deal, the iconoclast eventually needs to make his audience feel comfortable with his idea. From the perspective of the brain, familiar items are not necessarily more pleasurable or rewarding; it is simply that unfamiliar things tend to be alarming and potentially dangerous. *Familiarity quiets the amygdala.*

The iconoclast has several means at his disposal for increasing the familiarity of his idea with his intended audience. Publicity exposure and liberal use of mass media outlets certainly create an aura of familiarity. Schwarzenegger is proof of the benefits of good PR. Being prolific, like Picasso and Chihuly, also helps create an omnipresence of work and increases the chance that people will run into the iconoclast's ideas. Exposure creates inroads to tamp down the amygdala, but neuroeconomic evidence suggests that something else is required to elicit actual investment decisions. There is the issue of reputation.

## Shadow Networks and Why Who Knows Whom Matters

Milgram's lost-letter technique seems quaint, almost antiquated in today's world of digital communication. Apart from the occasional holiday card, written mail has ceased to be a useful form of correspondence. And while grammarians and future historians may bemoan the death of letter writing, snail mail has suffered the fate of all technologies—obsolescence. Every technology, even one that has been around for millennia, such as written correspondence, will eventually be replaced by something that is more efficient. So one might wonder in today's networked world whether people are really just six e-mail hops away from anyone in the digital domain as they are in the physical world.

In 2003, Duncan Watts, a professor at Columbia University who studies social networks, conducted a digital version of the Milgram experiment.[22] Watts set up a Web site where people could register to participate. Each of the 98,847 people who registered was randomly assigned to get an e-mail message to one of 18 targets. There was a huge attrition rate. Even though almost 100,000 people registered, data was recorded on 24,163 chains, and of these, only 384 reached their targets, for a 1.6 percent completion rate. Nevertheless, these 384 chains allowed Watts to estimate the average degrees of separation to be 4.05. But this estimate reflected the level of connectedness for successful chains only. Incomplete chains might have failed because some people were more distant and required more steps. Because each step incurred a probability of the person dropping the ball, the incomplete chains provided important data for the true degrees of separation. Taking this into account, Watts found the average degrees of separation to be closer to 7. This was a somewhat larger number than Milgram found, but then again these were international targets. Watts also found no evidence of funneling. He concluded that "social search appears to be largely an egalitarian exercise" and not dependent on a small minority of connectors.

On the surface, this may seem to be good news for iconoclasts. If there are many routes to reach any individual, then it might not really matter which route a person uses. This conclusion, however, ignores the issue of provenance. A message originating from a good friend or trusted business associate carries more weight than one coming from the high school acquaintance to whom you haven't spoken in twenty years. And a message originating from a stranger carries almost no value at all. Watts's study also underscored the high attrition rate of digital messages. Even in 2003, before spam really started to choke inboxes, recipients tended to ignore these e-mail messages and effectively terminated a chain. If we make the rather optimistic assumption that the odds are fifty-fifty that a random recipient will pass along a message, after six steps, only 1.5 percent of the messages will remain— a percentage that is almost identical to the rate Watts found.

Perhaps the world really is bigger than we would like to think. Jon Kleinberg, a computer scientist at Cornell University, proved mathematically that small-world networks don't arise from random connections.[23] Messages won't reach their intended recipient by bouncing randomly between people, in the hopes that someone will serve as a connector to another small world. People in a network need to know something about the other members, such as who they are likely to be connected to. You need a sort of shadow network, what Kleinberg called an *underlying lattice*, that serves as a black book of who knows whom.

Both kinds of networks, whom-you-know and who-knows-whom, played critical roles in the development of Linux, the first computer operating system created using the open-source model of software development. In 1991, Linus Torvalds, a Finnish computer science student, famously posted this query on the USENET list comp.os.minix:

Hello everybody out there using minix -

I'm doing a (free) operating system (just a hobby, won't be big
and professional like gnu) for 386(486) AT clones. This has been
brewing since april, and is starting to get ready. I'd like any feed-
back on things people like/dislike in minix, as my OS resembles it
somewhat (same physical layout of the file-system (due to practical reasons) among other things).[24]

Minix was a miniature version of the common, and bulky, operating system known as UNIX. It had the advantage of using very little memory, which meant it could fit within the paltry confines an IBM PC, which had less than 1 MB of RAM. Torvalds received a smattering of replies to his open call, but he also knew enough about what others were doing to not reinvent everything from scratch. Here is where Kleinberg's shadow lattice came in handy. The USENET groups made such a network possible, providing a map of who was doing what and, most importantly, how to find people who could contribute chunks of computer code.

The interesting thing about the Linux story is how USENET provided the lattice for the early hackers to communicate with each other. Because Linux was created in an open environment, everyone could see what everyone else was contributing. Code was tagged by who wrote it. And so not only did the network bootstrap itself; people began to develop a history. And this leads to the next critical element of social intelligence: reputation.

## Building Reputations for a Fair Deal

Although our brains make snap judgments about the trustworthiness and familiarity of faces, these reactions are not the only determinants of building a social network. The strength of connections between people in a network depends on the history of their behavior. Both the Milgram and Watts small-worlds experiments illustrated that successful networking is not simply a matter of who knows whom. The high rate of dropped messages, especially the digital kind, means that strong connections in a social network may be more important than degrees of separation.

A core attribute of integrity that is deeply wired in all primates is the ability to assess, and respond to, fairness. Individuals who make decisions that consider equitable outcomes for all participants possess a high degree of integrity. Those who do not, get labeled as selfish. The balance between self-interest and fairness shifts back and forth for everyone, but the importance for social networking lies in how other people perceive you. Given the choice, would you prefer to do business with a greedy person who you know will try to milk you for everything he can, or would you rather make a deal with someone who takes into consideration your needs? Some have called this the "win-win" approach to negotiation, but there is good biological reason for considering the fairness of business deals.

In a remarkable experiment, the Emory University primatologists Sarah Brosnan and Frans de Waal found that even capuchin monkeys dislike unfairness. Brosnan and de Waal taught the monkeys to perform a simple token-exchange task. A token, in the form of a small granite rock, was placed in each monkey's cage, and Brosnan simply stood in front of the cage with her hand stretched out, palm up. If the monkey gave her the token within sixty seconds, she uncovered a bowl with a piece of food in it, which was either a low-value food (a slice of cucumber) or a high-value one (a grape). The bowl was transparent, so the monkey could see its contents before deciding to exchange the token. In an interesting twist to this setup, Brosnan paired up the monkeys so that one could watch the other. Sometimes, while its partner was watching, Brosnan simply handed one monkey a grape without requiring any exchange. Brosnan then measured the rate at which the jilted monkey refused to exchange its token on the next round. After the partner witnessed an unfair exchange, its rate of participation plummeted. Like humans, Brosnan wrote, "monkeys, too, seem to measure reward in relative terms, comparing their own rewards with those available, and their own efforts with those of others."[25]

If monkeys have such strong reactions to unfairness, it is a sure bet that these responses are deeply wired in the brain. Although there may be a time and a place for the exploitation of inequities, the iconoclast who is building a social network is best served by fostering a perception of fairness and integrity. Recent neuroimaging experiments have revealed how the brain reacts to fairness and how these responses affect people's subsequent decisions to trust a person.

The classic economic game for studying fairness is called *ultimatum*. In this game, two participants who don't know each other are given a pot of money—say, $100— to split. The first player offers to split the pot in any ratio he wants. If the second player accepts this offer, both players take home their share of the pot. But if the second player rejects the offer, nobody gets anything. Despite the apparent simplicity of the instructions, the decisions of what the first player offers and whether the second player accepts are wrapped in the essence of fairness. No matter the amount of money at stake, the second player will almost always reject offers less than about 15 percent of the pot.[26] Apparently irrational from the perspective of giving up free money, it makes sense when one considers the value that we place on fairness. When individuals are faced with such an unfair split, the *anterior insula*—a part of the brain closely associated with disgusting tastes—becomes more active. The more active this part of the brain, the more likely a person will reject an offer.[27]

It is significant that people forego free money, in effect paying to punish the other person for bad behavior. In these one-shot ultimatum games, the participants don't know each other. Given our evolutionary heritage from small communities, however, we possess a reciprocity assumption—a biological golden rule. Our brains are wired to be sensitive to fairness because it might just come back to haunt us (and in the small communities of yore, it probably would). An efficient strategy for any social interaction is to assume that you will meet up again someday and the other person will remember how you behaved. Humans, in particular, have good memories and long lives, so behaving equitably toward others may well have evolved as a more adaptive strategy than short-term self-interest.

## Warren Buffett and the Evolution of Reputation

In his efforts to bring his idea to the masses, the iconoclast runs the risk of being labeled a snake oil salesman. Our brains pick up anything that is unexpected. The amygdala, in particular, serves as radar for potential threats. Its biological xenophobia serves as a hair trigger on our bs detectors. The amygdala is good at what it does, but it is not an innate response. Both trust and its counterpart, distrust, are learned responses based on an individual's past experience. And while the amygdalectomized patients appeared more trustworthy on some psychological tests, the iconoclast cannot count on putting potential investors' amygdalae to sleep with hollow promises of security. The key to trust is through reputation.

As Warren Buffett famously said, "It takes 20 years to build a reputation and five minutes to ruin it. If you think about that, you'll do things differently." Buffett's reputation runs so deeply that it commands a premium unto itself. When word gets out that Buffett is adding a company to Berkshire Hathaway's holdings, the company's value immediately shoots up. Buffet adheres, more or less, to the value approach to investing that Benjamin Graham formulated and other contrarians like David Dreman and Bill Miller continue to use, and it is hard to argue with Buffett's success. But what is unique about Buffett is his reputation for straight talk. His letters to shareholders are lessons in clarity. After Berkshire Hathaway suffered $3.4 billion in insurance losses from the 2005 hurricane season, Buffett answered the question on every investor's mind about staying in the catastrophic insurance business. "I don't know the answer to these all-important questions. What we do know is that our ignorance means we must follow the course prescribed by Pascal in his famous wager about the existence of God. As you may recall, he concluded that since he didn't know the answer, his personal gain/loss ratio dictated an affirmative conclusion."[28] It was Buffett's way of saying, assume the worst and only write catastrophic policies at higher prices.

Buffett commands a reputation premium because people trust him. It is easy to see from a Darwinian perspective why reputation and trust may have evolved to be highly valued traits. Imagine a world of creatures that are completely self-interested. These creatures are the perfect embodiment of Adam Smith's selfish individual. Each of these animals, in accordance with both Darwinian principles of natural selection and sexual selection, is primarily concerned with finding food to eat and someone with whom to mate. In the case of foraging for food, self-interest may serve the animal quite well, especially if it must compete with other animals. But imagine what would happen if two of these animals got together and somehow agreed to share the food that they found. As long as they trust each other, these cooperating creatures stand to do substantially better in the race for survival. In fact, evolution pretty much guarantees that such cooperative relationships will be discovered by animals because they are superior to completely self-interested strategies of survival. But there is a wrinkle in this story. Imagine an entire colony of these friendly creatures, which willingly cooperate with each other, sharing food and shelter. Such a lovefest creates the opportunity for more sinister operatives to take advantage of their trusting counterparts. In a culture of complete and absolute trust, evolution begins to favor creatures that can deceive other members of the species. The final balance between cooperation and deception is called an *evolutionarily stable strategy*. It means that in any society there will always be a mix of cooperation and deception. It is only the possibility of deception that confers value to cooperation.

How does such a society deal with bad apples? It punishes them. But punishment is costly, and it calls upon individual members of the society to perform essentially altruistic acts for the benefit of the common good. Recent neuroeconomic experiments have demonstrated why the mere possibility of punishment is both necessary and desirable to form cooperative relationships in a society. It is important for the iconoclast to be aware of the biological mechanisms that exist in our brains that monitor socially acceptable and unacceptable behavior, because they act as filters for potential deception.

Bettina Rockenbach, an economist at the London School of Economics, performed a critical experiment on what determines whether people trust each other. She had individuals play a public goods game. This game required each participant to contribute money to a common pool. The money in the pool accrued earnings and was then redistributed to all the participants. The more money in the pool, the more money that everyone made. But there was a selfish incentive to take a free ride. Even if a person didn't contribute anything, they still reaped the benefits of the distribution of the common pool of money. In each round of Rockenbach's experiment, participants had the choice of playing the game with, or without, the possibility of punishing free riders. Initially, most participants chose to play the game without the possibility of punishment—a sort of utopian view of the world. But after just a few rounds, more than 70 percent of the participants were playing the game that allowed punishment, whether the punishment was actually exercised or not. On closer examination, Rockenbach found that only a few individuals formed the glue of the society and punished people, but they established and enforced a cooperative culture that attracted even previously noncooperative individuals.[29] Rockenbach's experiment takes Buffett's remark about reputation one step further. The experiment demonstrates on yet another level the importance of knowing who makes up the "shadow network"—which people form the glue of the community. Initial efforts should be targeted to these people or the people immediately connected to them. This is where Armstrong ultimately failed. His onetime friend, David Sarnoff, was president of RCA and probably the single most important person in the radio community. When Armstrong had a falling out with Sarnoff, Armstrong lost his connection and damaged his reputation with the one person who could have made the difference for him.

## Building Networks

As we have seen in this chapter, the transition from solitary iconoclast to a successful one requires the masses of noniconoclasts to buy into an idea. Iconoclasts such as Ray Kroc and Arnold Schwarzenegger were successful as much for their novel ideas as their ability to connect to other people. The successful iconoclast cannot wait for the world to see things the way he does. He must reach out and connect with people who initially will not share his views. Every iconoclast encounters resistance, but it is only the successful ones who are able, through social intelligence, to persuade other people.

*Persuasion* is perhaps too strong a word, because it implies a conscious, rational process. But as we've seen in this chapter, selling an idea appeals only partly to rational thought. The successful iconoclasts have an uncommon ability to connect on a social level that transcends the idea itself. The key to doing this is through social networks. In order to be successful, the iconoclast builds a network through two fundamental approaches: familiarity and reputation.

Drawing on recent advances in network science, the iconoclast can shrink the six degrees of separation between any two individuals. The goal of the iconoclast is to decrease the number of jumps between himself and connectors in the community that he is selling to. There are no shortcuts. The biggest impediment to creating new connections is the anonymity of electronic communications. E-mail is so cheap that it might as well be worthless as a medium for creating new contacts. Although e-mail is valuable for maintaining existing networks, the iconoclast must use more expensive means of communications to create meaningful social connections.

The goal is keep people's amygdalae from firing. In addition to responding to fearful situations, the amygdala has a hair trigger for anything unfamiliar. Iconoclasts, by definition, are foreign to most people, and anything that seems new or different will tend to set off the amygdala in most people. This is not a good situation. When the amygdala fires, it activates the arousal system of the body. The end result is that people will avoid the unfamiliar.

The key to taming other people's amygdalae lies in familiarity. The successful iconoclast creates an aura of familiarity to keep the amygdalae of his target audience in check. When Ray Kroc created Ronald McDonald as a connector to children, he banked on the familiarity of clowns to kids. Without this familiarity, it would have been absurd to market hamburgers to children with no disposable income. Arnold Schwarzenegger accomplished the same feat. Having already created connections with millions of people through movie roles, he banked on his familiarity to become governor of California.

In building social networks, the iconoclast strives to achieve a sense of familiarity, but he also must pay attention to the second key element of social intelligence by maintaining a positive reputation. The human brain has evolved over the last million years in small-world environments. The iconoclast must realize that even though we live in a global economy, our brains evolved for social interactions on much smaller scales. The human brain is wired under the assumption of reciprocity. Every social interaction is undertaken under the assumption of tit for tat. This biological golden rule means that the iconoclast must approach every interaction as if the roles will be reversed someday. Burn no bridges (at least while you're an anonymous iconoclast). As Warren Buffett remarked, a reputation, which can take years to establish, can be destroyed in minutes.

Finally, would-be iconoclasts should take notice about the black book of who knows whom. Even if you don't know Donald Trump, you need to have a playbook of the routes to him. Given the high attrition rate of messages, the shorter the route, the more likely you will be able to get a message through. But distance is not always the most important factor. Messages sometimes can take a more circuitous route if they have a greater chance of reaching the intended recipient. Here is where it is helpful to have a sense of the shadow network of who knows whom.

The ultimate goal, through familiarity and reputation, is for the iconoclast to shrink his world like Picasso. Don't be a Van Gogh.

# SEVEN

# Private Spaceflight— A Case Study of Iconoclasts Working Together

Well, space is there, and we're going to climb it, and the moon and the planets are there, and new hopes for knowledge and peace are there. And, therefore, as we set sail we ask God's blessing on the most hazardous and dangerous and greatest adventure on which man has ever embarked.

—John F. Kennedy Jr., September 12, 1962

THE SPACESHIPS—MORE AIRPLANE THAN rocket really— sit majestically on the New Mexico tarmac. Diminutive by NASA standards and constructed of carbon composites to save weight, these craft look nothing like what the astronauts of yore rode into space and beyond. You can walk up to these babies and run your hand over their bodies. You have no trouble standing on tiptoes and stroking the top of the fuselage, but duck down to inspect the wings because they hover about four feet from the ground. No massive wingspan here. These spaceships are as light and compact as a Cessna. But they possess a great deal more power than a light aircraft, and they do, of course, have a somewhat higher altitude rating—something beyond 300,000 feet. That's 100 kilometers. Sixty-two miles. The edge of space.

The spacecraft, however, are not yet fully functional. They are on display at the second annual exposition of the X PRIZE Cup. A modern version of the space exposition, the X PRIZE Cup has evolved into a strange mix of participants. It is a place where venture capitalists and angel investors mingle with the engineers of hybrid air/spacecraft. The presidents of these companies hunt for infusions of cash to fuel their nascent enterprises. Hopeful passengers browse the mockups, while the spokespeople hype their craft as the safest and most efficient means to get into space. The passengers run the spectrum from middle-aged Trekkies to successful businessmen. Most are old enough to have watched Neil Armstrong and Buzz Aldrin walk on the moon, but a few were born well after the golden era of spaceflight. Everyone from the average guy checking out propulsion systems up to the CEO of the biggest company at the expo shares the dream of someday reaching outer space. The creation of private manned space travel is a case study in iconoclasm.

Putting ordinary citizens into space strikes most people as crazy. The notion of flying on a privately built rocket ship tends to elicit polar responses. Some say, "When can I sign up?" and others think, "Not a chance." Most people are in the latter category. Which makes the first group (the iconoclasts) all the more interesting. And the people who are building these spaceships are iconoclasts in the most rugged sense. They share a vision of pushing into a new frontier. It is a frontier that the vast majority of humanity currently has no access to, no interest in, and wonders why anyone should spend exorbitant sums of money to go into space when there are so many vexing problems here on Earth. It is a question as old as the space program itself. To even consider such a venture flies in the face of conventional wisdom.

Apart from being interesting in its own right, the privatization of spaceflight represents a unique case study in iconoclasm. The key players are all iconoclasts, but in different ways. Each of them, however, exemplifies at least one of the three characteristics that have already been described: (1) seeing differently, (2) dealing with fear, and (3) social intelligence.

## The Challenge

The big boys and girls want to get into orbit. And with the market price currently set at $20 million, you need a big bank account to go along with the *cojones* to ride that candle. Robert Bigelow, an iconoclast who made his fortune through Budget Suites, formed Bigelow Aerospace in 1999 to promote the commercialization of low-Earth-orbit businesses. In part of its mission statement, Bigelow summarizes a sentiment that Henry Ford voiced a century earlier, that only by conquering fear of failure is success possible: "Our goal is to get humanity into space so we can experiment, toy with ideas, try new and different things, and eventually make that miraculous mistake leading to a discovery that will change life forever."[1] But getting there is not going to be easy.

Why is it so difficult to get into orbit? In a word, energy. The force of gravity pulls all objects toward the center of the Earth. If you are standing on the surface, then the ground gets in the way and pushes back, but in space there is nothing to prevent you from falling inward. The way around the problem is to circle the planet at a high speed. To maintain this speed, the object must be outside the atmosphere, or else the air friction would slow the craft down or burn it up. The atmosphere thins out enough at an altitude of about 150 km (93 miles). In order to counteract the pull of gravity at that height, an object must be moving at 17,500 miles per hour. To get an object moving from a standstill up to that velocity requires a large amount of energy. The heavier the object, the more energy it takes.

A rocket is nothing more than a tube that shoots something out one end, and because of Newton's third law, the rocket moves in the opposite direction. In 1887, exactly two hundred years after Newton published his famous laws, a Russian teacher, Konstantin Tsiolkovsky, figured out how to use them to get into space. Starting with the third law, Tsiolkovsky reasoned that in order to achieve the critical velocity, you had to carry a propellant that could be expelled from the rocket in the direction opposite to which you wanted to go. The propellant would not have to weigh very much as long as it was shot out at a very high speed. Tsiolkovsky showed that there are only three elements of rocket design that determine how fast it goes: (1) the speed at which fuel is ejected, (2) how much the fuel weighs, and (3) how much the rocket weighs. The first two, which address the nature of fuel, are dealt with by basic chemistry that hasn't changed since Tsiolkovsky's time. It is the third factor, rocket weight, where the iconoclast comes in.

The holy grail of orbital spaceflight has been the single-stage-to-orbit (SSTO) vehicle. But as the Tsiolkovsky equation shows, you need an exceptionally light vehicle that can hold roughly ten times its weight in fuel. The added acceleration and g-forces during launch, however, mean that the vehicle actually has to withstand twice that much force, if not more. Although the space shuttle is constructed primarily from aluminum and titanium alloys, it still has a launch weight ratio of six, which is too low for an SSTO, so its engineers adopted a multistage propulsion system. The two solid rocket boosters strapped to the sides of the shuttle, each developing 2.5 million pounds of thrust, provide most of the power to get the shuttle going. The complexity of the shuttle propulsion system makes it vulnerable to failure from a number of causes, and such an approach is not commercially feasible for the private sector. The key is to make the rockets as simple as possible, and for the propulsion system, that means a single-stage vehicle.

# Burt Rutan: The Iconoclast
# Engineer Who Sees Differently

You need a different approach to rocketry. You need someone who can approach the design from a different perspective and see rockets differently than NASA. His name is Burt Rutan. Rutan has revolutionized the aerospace industry more than any other person. For forty years, Rutan has known that the key to more efficient aircraft and, ultimately, spacecraft is through materials engineering. Build them strong but light, and you can do a lot. This is a very different perception of the problem that NASA struggled with for decades. The conventional—NASA's—approach was to build bigger and more powerful engines. But Rutan has taken rocket design in the other direction, and this is what makes him an iconoclast.

Keeping it simple is an understatement for Rutan. Rutan is a hero in the aerospace industry and has achieved what no engineer since perhaps Thomas Edison has done: celebrity status. First, there are the sideburns—Elvis style, circa 1970. Retro, yes, but they seem to fit with Rutan's unusual approach to aircraft design. But then there are the accomplishments. His company, Scaled Composites, has posted a profit in over ninety consecutive quarters, which is an achievement unheard of in the aerospace industry. It has rolled out thirty-four new types of aircraft in thirty years, and in the process of testing them, has never suffered a fatal crash.[2] In the 1980s Rutan designed and built *Voyager*, the first aircraft to fly around the world without stopping or refueling on a trip that took nine days.

Within the aerospace community, Rutan is known as an iconoclast because of his unconventional aircraft designs. It was with characteristic flair that Rutan unveiled his secret spaceship in 2003. The project, known only as "Tier One" within the company, was so secret that almost nobody outside Scaled knew of its existence, even though Rutan had started conceptual designs in 1997. Considering that Rutan had never built a supersonic aircraft, and that he then began contemplating a vehicle that would need to reach Mach 3 in under a minute, even those within Scaled thought he might have gone too far. But for Rutan, space represented a stepping-stone to even more exciting possibilities, such as the moon or even other planets. He perceived an opportunity where others were afraid.

Rutan grew up in the sleepy farming town of Dinuba, California, a community in the Central Valley known primarily for its raisin production. The son of a dentist, Rutan was obsessed with airplanes and flying, and even soloed before getting his driver's license. He studied aeronautical engineering in college and then cut his teeth as a test engineer at Edwards Air Force Base in Mojave. After seven years, he left to design his own aircraft, mainly small two-seater kits for airplane hobbyists. He sold these plans under the auspices of the Rutan Aircraft Factory, or RAF. Too poor to test his designs in a wind tunnel, Rutan developed what would become a lifelong philosophy to field-testing his designs. He could be seen barreling down desert roads in his station wagon with a fuselage strapped to its roof. Echoing Henry Ford's philosophy, Rutan once said, "Testing leads to failure, and failure leads to understanding."[3] His big breakthrough came in the late '70s, when Rutan figured out an easy way to make structural components out of fiberglass strips. In a classic example of how one thing changes the perception of another, Rutan's inspiration came from the most unlikely of places: surfing. Surfboard makers of the '60s abandoned wood for fiberglass-covered foam, and Rutan adopted the same techniques for airplanes. He carved smoother, more aerodynamic shapes out of foam than could be manufactured with wood or aluminum. By laying fiberglass over the foam blanks, Rutan created wings and fuselages that were light, yet strong. In 1982, he founded Scaled Composites to design and build prototypes for the air force and NASA.

Although nobody knew it at the time, Scaled was to become Rutan's launching platform for space. In 1986, Rutan's brother, Dick, piloted a

Burt-designed aircraft called *Voyager* around the world without stopping or refueling—a feat never accomplished before. With such high-profile success, Scaled grew to more than one hundred employees by the mid 1990s with loads of corporate and government contracts. But Rutan continued to think about loftier goals. Unwilling to divert Scaled resources into such a risky venture, the Tier One project remained little more than sketches on Rutan's drawing pad.

The Tier One design was all Rutan. Reflecting his preternatural ability to perceive engineering problems differently, Rutan came up with an unconventional solution based on an old airplane flying trick. The trick involved reconfiguring the tail assembly at the apex of the craft's trajectory. Rutan designed pneumatic actuators to pop up tail booms that would change the tail surface from a low-drag supersonic configuration to a high-drag feather shape. In this configuration, the aircraft would float to the ground like a shuttlecock with its nose pointed almost straight down. Because the feather configuration resulted in a more leisurely descent, Rutan's design solved the problem of both high g-forces and high temperatures during reentry.

The rocket itself would be carried up to 50,000 feet by an equally strange Rutan-vehicle. Dubbed the *White Knight*, the transport aircraft was a spindly thing with a fuselage dangling from a delicate wing. The rocket and its pilot would hang from the underside of the center fuselage, and a wing runner to each side gave the craft the appearance of a crab. When dropped from the *White Knight*, the rocket pilot would arm the engine with one switch and fire it with another. There was no throttle.

Rutan kept the project secret until April 2003, when Rutan shocked the aerospace community by unveiling both the rocket and the *White Knight*. Having notified the Federal Aviation Administration (FAA) and the Pentagon only two weeks earlier, Rutan made a point of the absence of government involvement. "I believe the government is the reason it's unaffordable to fly into space," he said in his press conference. "We didn't want them to know. Their help causes problems."[4] Paul Allen, formerly of Microsoft, finally revealed himself as Tier One's financial backer in December 2003, after the rocket, now called *SpaceShipOne*, had passed several test milestones. At that point, Richard Branson's group struck a deal to license the technology to Virgin for the development of a spaceliner.

*SpaceShipOne* reached an altitude of 212,000 feet in May 2004, but it was the flight on June 21, 2004, that made history by reaching the edge of space. On September 29, *SpaceShipOne* completed the first of three trips into space. But about thirty seconds after rocket ignition, the vehicle entered a harrowing series of rolls, throwing both the spaceship and its pilot into a dizzying upward spiral. A spiraling reentry could well have exceeded the g-force limit of the feather configuration and resulted in a total breakup. Fortunately, the pilot was able to gain control before reentry. Even with Rutan's intuition for safe designs, at Mach 3.5 the slightest deviation of forces can result in unexpected results, fortunately none fatal in this case. But they are a reminder of the risks that will always be lurking in mankind's quest to get into space. It is not a quest for the squeamish. It is a quest for only the most iconoclastic.

## Principle 2: The Iconoclasts Who Face Down Fear of Failure

An endeavor as risky and daunting as the commercialization of personal spaceflight requires a wide cast of characters that includes not just the engineers building the rockets but iconoclasts who play a different role. These are the catalysts—the people who, by virtue of their passion, rally others to stay the course, overcome the risks of failure, and basically devote their lives to putting people into space. More than a cheerleader, the catalyst marshals financial and political resources to bring about the solution to problems that people are typically afraid of. The creation of an industry with substantial risks—risks of financial failure as well as the possibility of loss of life—demands individuals who can bring together the multiple companies to speak as one voice so that the regulatory agencies, such as NASA and the FAA, realize that private spaceflight is more than a pipe dream. This type of person confronts the great limiter to iconoclasm: fear.

For private spaceflight, Peter Diamandis, forty-five years old, is that iconoclast. A graduate of MIT and a medical doctor from Harvard, Diamandis created the X PRIZE Foundation in 1994 to foster the privatization of spaceflight. His inspiration was a $25,000 prize offered in 1919 by the real estate magnate Raymond Orteig to the first person to fly nonstop between New York and Paris, which Charles Lindbergh won in 1927. Diamandis realized that the prize was primarily symbolic. At least nine teams vied for the Orteig prize and collectively spent $400,000. The rewards came later as the competition spawned the modern aerospace industry and ultimately passenger air travel. As Diamandis states, the number of U.S. air passengers increased from 5,782 in 1926 to 173,405 in 1929, which he attributes more to the public perception of the feasibility of air travel than to any technological breakthrough.[5] This is an amazing example of how individual iconoclasts, like Lindbergh, became immediate icons simply by achieving a goal that most people thought impossible at the time, and in the process changed the public's perception, removing the first roadblock to action.

So it was with the *Spirit of St. Louis* in mind that Diamandis created the X PRIZE for the first privately built spacecraft to carry a person into space and back (*space* being defined as 100 km in altitude). Although similar in spirit, the X PRIZE suffered from a lack of visibility. In 1927, nobody had flown nonstop across the Atlantic, so the Orteig prize threw down the gauntlet for a goal that was previously unattainable. The X PRIZE was not quite the same, because in 1994, everyone knew that people could get into space. The prize, though, was about getting citizens into space. Although the prize was widely known in aerospace circles, it took Diamandis a decade to achieve real public visibility for the prize. In 2004, the Iranian-born entrepreneurs Amir and Anousheh Ansari made a multimillion-dollar donation that was also matched by several corporations, and the purse jumped to $10 million.

For Diamandis, it was the motivation to do what everyone thought couldn't be done and to reward risk taking through competition. Speaking about the fear of failure, he says, "We are killing ourselves in this country by how risk averse we have gotten. It is destroying our ability to make breakthroughs." Speaking to entrepreneurs and CEOs and venture capitalists, Diamandis exhorts, "You have to take risks, because the governments can't, and the large corporations cannot. The governments can't withstand the Congressional investigations every time something goes wrong. The large corporations can't stand the plummeting stock prices."[6]

Diamandis is not blind to the risks of spaceflight, but he implores the rocketeers and would-be passengers not to be paralyzed by risk: "There is only one group left. It is the individual who says, 'I can't afford not to! This is my dream! If I won't do it, no one else will.' That's what this program [the X PRIZE] is about. That's who you are. It's the dreamers. It's the doers. It's about those furry mammals who are evolved to take the risks, or die."

So who are these iconoclasts who are wresting away the wings from NASA? The companies have names that evoke a sense of infinite possibilities, such as Space Adventures, SpaceX, Rocketplane, Starchaser Industries, Dreamspace, and Virgin Galactic. Although not known widely outside the aerospace industry, the people backing and running these companies are cut from the same cloth that gave rise to the biggest Internet success stories. In fact, many are the same people. John Carmack, the video game guru who founded id Software and who wrote *Wolfenstein 3D*, *Doom*, and *Quake*, formed a company called Armadillo Aerospace, which is developing vertical takeoff and landing vehicles for landing on the moon. Elon Musk formed an online financial services company called X.com in 1999 that ultimately acquired the technology to become PayPal. When PayPal was sold to eBay for $1.5 billion in 2002, Musk rolled the money into SpaceX, with the initial goal of developing conventional two-stage vehicles for lifting heavy payloads into orbit. His ultimate goal, however, is the SpaceX Dragon, which is a reusable container for carrying a crew into space. Richard Branson, CEO of the Virgin empire, teamed up with Burt Rutan to build the first commercial passenger space vehicle, dubbed *SpaceShipTwo*. Branson plans to fly groups of four passengers up to 100 km in altitude under the brand Virgin Galactic. And Jeff Bezos, CEO of Amazon.com, has thrown his hat into the spaceflight ring with the formation of Blue Origin.

It is, of course, no coincidence that the private space industry reads like a who's who of Internet success stories. On a practical level, only the CEOs of companies that were successful have the capital to invest in space. Many, like Musk and Bezos, were trained as engineers or physicists and have a gut sense of what will work and what won't. But they have also navigated commercial environments with significant unknowns. Each of them has already conquered fears of the unknown in their own domains. So it is natural that these iconoclasts should look to space for the next big thing. Shepherding a start-up Internet company to a multibillion-dollar, multinational enterprise requires exactly the skills needed to get people into space safely and, just as importantly, make a profit. It only makes sense to send people into space if, as Diamandis says, there is money to be made. Only governments can do it without a profit imperative.

Potential for profit is everything. Safety will follow profit, because every one of these CEOs knows that if anyone dies, all bets are off. Because of the profit incentive, it is likely that these privately built vehicles may become more reliable and safer than anything NASA has ever built. They have to be. Volunteering to be an astronaut in a federal space program is one thing. As Mike Mullane, a space shuttle astronaut, wrote, "If [it had been] explained exactly what we had just signed up to do—to be some of the first humans to ride uncontrollable solid-fueled rocket boosters . . . without an in-flight escape system . . . on a schedule that would stretch manpower and resources to their limits—it wouldn't have diminished our enthusiasm one iota."[7] But this will not be the general sentiment of the ten thousand or so citizens who pay big money to ride a private rocket. They will expect safety and reliability on a scale never achieved before in rocketry.

## The Iconoclast as Passenger

Who would want to go into space, and what would they hope to accomplish? But most importantly, how much would they be willing to pay? These were the questions posed by the Futron Corporation in a 2002 marketing study of the commercial potential for space tourism.[8] The answers to these questions determine whether personal spaceflight makes for a viable business model. As NASA demonstrated, with both Apollo and the space shuttle, the fixed costs of mounting a space program are enormous. It is not enough to be an iconoclast and think that with the proper technology, spaceflight could become routine. There is tremendous financial risk, not to mention the potential for a catastrophic failure and the loss of life. Framing these questions from an economic perspective can provide a guide for the development of the technology, which from a business standpoint, must be reasonably assured of providing a profit.

The Futron study was critical for two reasons. First, it remains the only systematic analysis of the commercial potential of space tourism. As such, it continues to form the basis of most business models in the industry.[9] Second, the conclusion of the report was surprisingly optimistic. Futron projected total revenues of $1 billion through 2021. Like the shot heard 'round the world, the Futron study provided the economic incentive for the rocket men to press forward with their dreams. The study also provided the grease to get the necessary political machinery moving that would ultimately have to green-light any spaceflights. More than any other entrepreneurial industry, personal spaceflight requires the cooperation of a wide cast of characters. As we shall see, social intelligence becomes as important as technological wizardry.

Futron reasoned that the first space tourists would be wealthy. At the time of the study, only one private citizen had made it into space. In 2001, the American businessman Dennis Tito paid $20 million to ride a Russian Soyuz rocket and dock with the International Space Station (ISS). He spent a total of eight days in space, including six aboard the ISS. More recently, in 2006, the Iranian Anousheh Ansari became the first female citizen to make the journey (for a similar price). Because of the steep costs associated with space tourism, Futron contracted Zogby International to conduct a telephone survey of 450 people who might have the financial means to pay for a trip into space. The respondents were restricted to people with an annual household income of $250,000 or a minimum net worth of $1 million.

Futron examined the likelihood and the amount of money these people would be willing to pay for two types of spaceflights. The first type, an orbital trip, is the kind that Tito and Ansari made. Thirty-five percent of the respondents said that they would be interested in an orbital trip, and the most common reason for doing so was the chance to be a pioneer, which was followed closely by the chance to see Earth from space and to fulfill a lifelong dream.

But achieving orbit is technologically complicated and expensive, so Futron examined the appeal of a second type of space trip called a *suborbital flight*. This is simply an up-and-down trip to the edge of Earth's atmosphere. At an altitude of 100 km, you are high enough to see the curvature of the Earth and experience a sense of weightlessness. These are short trips, with perhaps two minutes at this altitude. The advantage, however, is that the energy required to reach this height is only one-tenth that of reaching orbit. The rockets can be smaller, more efficient, and technologically simpler than an orbital craft. And the cost of such a trip could be a fraction of an orbital flight. Despite the rather short duration, 28 percent of the Futron respondents said they were either "definitely likely" or "very likely" to make such a trip were it available. On the basis of its survey, Futron concluded that $100,000 was the ticket price the market would bear, although there was clearly a demand at even higher prices.

One such person is Reda Anderson, a sixty-nine-year-old woman from Los Angeles and a natural-born iconoclast. Posing in front of Rocketplane Global's prototype spaceship and wearing a flight suit, Anderson looks more like an astronaut than a space tourist. Eschewing the moniker "space tourist" in favor of "explorer," Anderson embodies the can-do spirit of what will be the first wave of citizens who reach space. Her natural gregariousness, coupled with a shrewd mind for business, served Anderson well in real estate, and because of her success, landed her in the care of George French, CEO and president of Rocketplane Global, one of the companies racing to get citizens into space. With a twinkle in her eye and looking a fair bit younger than her age, Anderson has made the most of her post–real estate life. Calling Anderson an explorer may be the most accurate description, since she has trekked through Machu Picchu, journeyed to Antarctica, led four-wheel-drive trips to Mongolia, and been one of only twelve women to have dived to the *Titanic*. For the record, the *Titanic* lies 12,500 feet beneath the surface of the Atlantic, and to make the ten-hour dive, a pilot and two divers must squeeze into the MIR, a 6-foot-wide Russian submersible. Given her résumé of exploration, space was the next logical goal.

"When I heard about the X-Prize flights and what Burt Rutan was doing at Mojave, I had to see it for myself," says Anderson.[10] After witnessing the historic flight of *SpaceShipOne* and the winning of the $10 million Ansari X-PRIZE, Anderson struck up a conversation with Chuck Lauer, the business director of Rocketplane.

"After the Rutan flight," says Anderson, "I wrote on the back of Chuck Lauer's business card 'Reda Anderson to be Rocketplane's 1st customer.' I signed it, wrapped a dollar bill around it, and handed it back to Chuck." Lauer, with a shocked expression, examined the offering, and said, "This looks like it has all the elements of a business contract." And with a handshake, he had signed up Rocketplane's first passenger, making Anderson the first person to sign a contract to go into space on a commercial vehicle.

Anderson's motivations are complex but generally mirror what Futron predicted. Above all, Anderson values the experience of doing things that other people say can't be done. "I like world-class events," she says. Since she has already taken the ride on the Vomit Comet, it's not the weightlessness that draws her to space. "I am mad that I am born with this short time frame. That irritates the hell out of me. My first question to God when I get to Heaven if there is such a place, I will ask he, she or it, 'What is this 70-year life span? There is so much to do and only 70 years to do it.'" Anderson points out, "And I have to sleep one third of the time and bathe. What a waste of time!"[11]

As two of the first space explorers of the twenty-first century, Anderson and Ansari are iconoclasts by virtue of their willingness to challenge conventional notions of what people can do. They see challenges differently than most people and do not let the fear of uncertainty (or failure) prevent them from taking risks. That they are women—and in Ansari's case, a woman from an Islamic country— underscores the uniqueness of what they are doing. Anderson, however, does not wear the feminist badge. For her, life is too short and the universe too large to waste a minute worrying about cultural or religious hang-ups. But she is not blind to the risks of this endeavor. When pushed on the issue of the possibility of death, she said, "I can't really think of it that way. I don't want to die. I want to come back in better shape than when I left." Referring to the relativistic time dilatation of spaceflight, she says, "At the speed I'll be going, I will pick up a few nanoseconds of time relative to the folks on the ground." But what if the odds of crashing were fifty-fifty? "I wouldn't do it, but I don't think the odds will be that bad."

## A Reality Check: The Risk Manager

Not everyone involved in private spaceflight is an iconoclast. This is a good thing, too. Although Anderson was probably correct in her assessment of the odds, you need someone to keep an objective eye on the actual risks. The odds are in her favor that her maiden voyage will be fine. But as David Dreman and Bill Miller illustrated in chapter 5, the perception of risk may be very different from the actual risks. This is where an objective third party comes in. With private spaceflight, the looming prospect of catastrophic failure casts a shadow over the rocketeers' enthusiasm. The risk of death, however, is very real, and is part and parcel of space exploration. Even Rutan's perfect safety record was tragically shattered on July 26, 2007. While engineers at Scaled were performing a static test of the engine that was to power Branson's spaceship, the engine exploded, overturning cars and killing three people.

You cannot escape the fact that the romanticism of spaceflight is due, in large part, to the fact that astronauts put their lives on the line with every mission. The private spaceflight industry must walk a fine line between making it safe enough for citizens and maintaining the image of frontier explorer. The most common motivation, according to the Futron study, was the opportunity to become a pioneer (i.e., an iconoclast).

Enough people have been into space that we have a pretty good sense of the risk. For U.S. launches of all types of rockets (manned and unmanned), there has been about a 9 percent failure rate. The most common cause of failure is a propulsion malfunction, which typically results in the destruction of the rocket and its payload. For manned spacecraft, the numbers are better, although whether they are good enough is a matter of personal opinion. The space shuttles have flown 115 missions, and two have had catastrophic malfunctions, for a failure rate of about 2 percent. Exact figures are not available for the Soviet program. Of the 450 or so people who have made it into space, approximately 25 have died in space-related accidents, giving a risk of death closer to 5 percent. For comparison with a similarly risky activity, climbing Mount Everest, 1,496 people had made the summit through 2001. During that same period, 172 people died in their attempts, for a death-to-summit ratio of 11.5 percent.

Ray Duffy, a senior vice president of Willis Inspace, insurance broker for the aerospace industry, knows these facts well. He is not an iconoclast. He places insurance programs for them. The absence of data and test flights in this new generation of private vehicles makes evaluating a risk an actuarial nightmare. "You can't do it," he says. That doesn't mean that insurance policies won't be written. "I believe there will be third-party liability coverage, but because the risks are unknown, the premium will be set by what the market will pay. Since these companies are small, and there aren't many of them, this means that there won't be enough premiums booked to pay the limits of liability in the event of a loss. In fact the global annual premium collected for all launch liability coverage is less than $10 million. The losses will then be paid by premiums collected for other aerospace risks."

It's more complicated than that. In the event of a failure, Duffy says, "lawyers will be lining up to sue everyone down the line from the prime to the guy who makes some widget used on the rocket. Will the part suppliers ask for indemnification from the prime? They should."[12]

Rockets are a bit like automobile models and computer software in the sense that early versions have the highest risk of failure. Most rocket failures occur during the first three launches, and after that, bugs tend to get worked out, resulting in more reliable rockets. As a result of this failure pattern, launch liability insurance is highest for the maiden voyages. Compared with the situation just ten years ago, however, rockets have become more reliable, and the growing database of launches has allowed underwriters to more accurately assess the risks of a given vehicle. But most relevant for the issue of personal spaceflight, says Duffy, is that the underwriters have not yet written any policies for passengers.

Shooting people into space is inherently risky, and while there is no track record in the personal spaceflight industry, it is simply a matter of time before a catastrophic failure. Nobody knows whether the risk of death is 1 in 10, 1 in 100, or 1 in 1,000 but in the end, it doesn't seem to matter to the passengers. Anderson is typical in this sense. She has placed her faith in George French and company. French says that he is risk averse, and this is precisely the attribute you would like for someone who has your life in his hands. Although it may seem crass, the CEOs and presidents of the companies that are competing to put people into space have a great deal more to lose than the passengers signing up for the ride. A catastrophic failure would rain down a series of investigations and lawsuits that not only would tank the offending company but could send officers to prison. And yet, these iconoclasts press on with their vision. Cognizant of the risk, but not paralyzed by fear of failure, they have begun to work together to define what will become the standards for safety in this industry. As in any business, there will be financial pressures to come up with the most cost-effective solution. Will safety be compromised? It's too soon to say, but a growing cast of characters that includes people like Ray Duffy will keep an eye on it. And the companies that succeed will be the ones that don't try to go it alone.

## Rick Homans: The G-man with Social Intelligence

Spaceflight is not going to be like climbing Mount Everest. There is no federally mandated organization to certify a mountain climber's ability and training to take novices to the top of the world. Safety will come because there are profits to be made for being safe. Foremost, there will be government oversight—not just because that is the role of government (to ensure public welfare), but because it is in the best interests of the private ventures to have government oversight.

Shoot a rocket to any reasonable altitude—let alone a rocket with a person inside—and a flurry of federal agencies will rain down a world of hurt on you. Airspace, especially in the United States, is crowded. Up to about 40,000 feet, the air is filled with aircraft, and launching a rocket into this soup could have disastrous consequences. The FAA and the Department of Transportation (DOT) control the airspace, while NASA monitors outer space. The departments of Defense and Homeland Security monitor the airspace for missiles and hostile aircraft, and the Bureau of Alcohol, Tobacco, Firearms and Explosives (ATF) is tasked with controlling explosives, which are the same substances used to propel rockets. Moreover, the Environmental Protection Agency (EPA) makes sure that the operation of rocket vehicles complies with rules to protect the public from potentially hazardous substances. The rocketeers, by and large, bemoan the alphabet soup of regulations with which they must comply, but they grudgingly acknowledge that government oversight is necessary to instill public confidence. It is also a lesson in how to sell a strange idea to the public through familiarity and reputation building.

Although a paying passenger on a rocket might assume a reasonable level of risk for dying, the same cannot be said of people on the ground. When the space shuttle *Columbia* disintegrated on reentry, debris was scattered from eastern Texas to Louisiana and covered an area of 28,000 square miles. Although nobody on the ground was injured, the risks of spaceflight were not limited to astronauts. Clearly, it is not possible to launch even a suborbital vehicle near a populated area, which rules out the coastal regions. All the companies with plans to send people into space will do so in the sparsely populated areas of the Southwest. And ground zero for these launch sites is where rocketry began in the United States: in the deserts of southeastern New Mexico. Nestled between the Old West town of Las Cruces, New Mexico, and the border mayhem of El Paso, Texas, lies White Sands Missile Range. Named for its bleached white sand dunes, White Sands has witnessed the key developments in rocketry history. Over 100 miles long and 40 miles wide, White Sands is the only fully protected airspace over ground in the United States, which means that commercial aircraft never fly over this area. The first atomic bomb was detonated here on July 16, 1945. Werner von Braun came here after WWII to continue development of the V2 rockets he had created for Nazi Germany, and his work eventually led to the rockets that would carry men into space and to the moon.

White Sands, however, is a military facility and has not been available for public use. At least until the commercialization of spaceflight began to look like a reality. The Organ Mountains, which look like a series of bloated organ pipes thrusting up from the desert floor, run in a north-south line. White Sands lies mostly to the east of the ridge, and to the west there are only a few small towns. Hatch (pop. 1,673) is best known, relatively speaking, for its annual chili festival. A little farther north on I-25 is Truth or Consequences (pop. 7,289), which was originally called Hot Springs but changed its name in 1950 when the host of the popular radio show announced he would broadcast his program from the first town to rename itself after the show. Las Cruces (pop. 74,267) is the closest city of moderate size, and that is 75 miles to the south. But along the corridor between Hatch and Truth or Consequences, the future of private spaceflight will rise from the desert sands. It is a lesson in social networking.

The ever-popular governor of New Mexico, Bill Richardson, struck a remarkable deal with Richard Branson in 2005. Branson agreed to locate the base of operations for Virgin Galactic in this corner of New Mexico if the state would build a spaceport. Because of its proximity to White Sands and the abundance of sunny, dry weather, the Hatch region was selected as the ideal site. And although Branson and Richardson made a great public fanfare out of the deal, the real credit goes to a person who excels at bringing together iconoclasts in a tour de force of networking.

Rick Homans, whose official title is cabinet secretary of the New Mexico Economic Development Department, is not your typical government bureaucrat. Homans has become the biggest booster in New Mexico government for the placement of Spaceport America in his state. His job was to bring new industries and jobs to New Mexico. No stranger to business, Homans had founded Starlight Media Group, a publisher of visitor's guides, which he eventually grew to include the *New Mexico Business Weekly* in 1994. With political aspirations, Homans sold the newspaper in 2000 and began a run for mayor of Albuquerque the next year. Although he lost the mayoral bid, Homans's campaign was notable for his lawsuit against Albuquerque's campaign spending limit. At the time, the city limited campaign spending to double the mayor's annual salary. Homans argued that such limits violated the First and Fourteenth Amendments to the Constitution. The district court agreed, and Homans went on to spend a record amount during the election. Although he received only 10 percent of the vote in a seven-way race, Homans's gutsiness caught the attention of Bill Richardson, who hired him as deputy campaign director for his 2002 gubernatorial bid. Although Richardson didn't realize it at the time, Homans was about to become the "connector" to space.

Like Richardson, Homans pushes big ideas, and the idea of a spaceport in New Mexico fit the bill. The weather was hard to beat. The open spaces meant relatively little chance of incidental injury to people on the ground. And the proximity of White Sands, with its protected airspace, made for a compelling case. Homans, though, is first and foremost a businessman, and his title reflects the mission of economic development, not economic folly. The time wasn't right in 2002. As Homans says, "Don't follow the, 'Build it and they will come philosophy.' Wait until technology calls."[13]

The call came in October 2004. After Burt Rutan won the X PRIZE competition and joined forces with Richard Branson, Homans and Richardson starting pushing hard to woo Virgin Galactic to New Mexico.

They were not the only ones. The state of California already had a spaceport of sorts—Vandenberg Air Force Base—and Rutan was based in Mojave, California. Oklahoma also had a spaceport built on the site of a decommissioned B-52 base, and, as the state is proud to point out, it already had FAA approval to launch suborbital rockets, a fact that has drawn George French and Rocketplane Global to base their operation in Oklahoma. New Mexico carried the day with Branson, but the price was steep. Branson agreed to locate Virgin Galactic's operations there if the state of New Mexico financed the building of the spaceport itself.

A spaceport needn't be as complex as an airport. Passengers take no luggage, for example. But a spaceport must have launch facilities, a passenger preparation area, a runway for landing, and capacity to handle explosives and potentially hazardous waste materials. The price tag of Spaceport America was pegged at $250 million. Although not a huge sum of money for many state governments, it was a significant outlay for New Mexico, whose annual budget in 2006 was only $5.1 billion. Richardson and Homans believe that the expenditure will return a significant piece of the economic pie for commercial spaceflight. Pushing a $250 million item on the New Mexicans may be a different story. Although the state's official nickname is the "land of enchantment," the locals still refer to New Mexico as the "land of mañana." Citing the fact that New Mexico has had a long history with the space program, Homans is banking on New Mexicans' familiarity with space. It is a great example of using familiarity to sell an idea to the public, and it wouldn't be possible in most other states.

## A Team of Iconoclasts

The privatization of spaceflight is a great example of how a group of iconoclasts can work together. Normally, we think of iconoclasts as rugged individuals who have bucked conventional wisdom to walk their own paths. Of course, this is true, but ultimately, for the iconoclast to become successful, he has to work with others, including other iconoclasts. This is not always an easy proposition for people not known for playing nice with others. But as we've seen in the spaceflight industry, it can be done with the help of other people who smooth over the rough spots.

You still need iconoclasts who exemplify the three principles of perception, freedom from fear, and social intelligence. Fortunately, you don't need iconoclasts who exemplify all three traits if you have a team of people who can exemplify some of them. The implications for management are clear. You need iconoclasts on a team, and if one iconoclast is good at seeing things differently than other people but is socially inept, then you also need a person who has the right social skills. For example, Burt Rutan is widely known as an iconoclastic engineer. His emphasis on materials engineering, which was inspired by surfboards, is legendary in aeronautics. He is not known, however, for his love affair with the media. But his newfound business partner, Richard Branson, is another story. Although Branson is no engineer, it is hard to argue with his charisma and public appeal. He is a master of the media. Of all the players in the spaceflight industry, he is perhaps the one most likely to pull off private launches.

If we take a view of iconoclasm that extends beyond the individual, we can see how to assemble a team that collectively exemplifies iconoclastic traits. In the case of the spaceflight industry, the individuals found each other. Certainly, catalysts help. People like Peter Diamandis serve as connectors for iconoclasts. They help rally support and temper the inevitable fear of the unknown. And then there are people like Rick Homans, who can grease the wheels of government and help connect people with each other so they can actually make complex endeavors happen. You need all these people. Few people possess all three traits, but through diversification, teams can.

# EIGHT

# When Iconoclast Becomes Icon

Every idea is an incitement.
—Oliver Wendell Holmes Jr., 1925

**W**HETHER NATURALLY BORN OR MADE, iconoclasts pride themselves on their nonconformity and ability to see things differently than other people. Some, however, go beyond mere iconoclasm. Through either luck or hard work, a select few go on to make the transition from iconoclast to icon. They, or their ideas, become objects of worship. Although it is not a strict requirement for success, the transformation from an outsider with crazy ideas to an object of worship is a lesson in how to get ideas that are initially strange to most people accepted by the masses.

## Arthur Jones and the Nautilus Machine

In chapter 6, the example of Arnold Schwarzenegger becoming governor of California provided a lesson in the use of familiarity to gain public acceptance. But even before his movie stardom, Schwarzenegger was a superstar of bodybuilding. Like all bodybuilders of the 1970s, Schwarzenegger relied upon free weights to build up muscle mass. Interestingly, another, far lesser-known iconoclast, named Arthur Jones, would revolutionize the exercise industry through a different approach. Jones invented the Nautilus machine. Even by iconoclast standards, Jones was odd, and so it is particularly interesting how his invention became an icon of the modern gym.

Born in Oklahoma in 1929, Jones had little patience for formal education and playing by the rules. After dropping out of high school, Jones traveled for several years throughout North and South America before serving in the U.S. Navy during World War II. After the war, he returned to the United States and started a business hunting big game for zoos and private collectors. He became known for his wild adventures and ended up producing a series of television shows for ABC in the 1950s with titles like *Wild Cargo* and *Professional Hunter*. His personal motto was "Younger women, faster airplanes, and bigger crocodiles," a credo that he unabashedly lived (Jones was married and divorced six times, all to women under age twenty-one). Always suspicious of competitors, he frequently packed a Colt .45, telling reporters, "I've shot 630 elephants and 63 men, and I regret the elephants more."[1]

Jones's main interest besides big game hunting was exercise. While working out at a YMCA in Tulsa in 1948, Jones became increasingly frustrated with his inability to develop big muscles. Gyms of that era were dreary rooms filled with archaic equipment: dumbbells, free weights, jump ropes, and medicine balls. Rather than continuing to work out with heavier and heavier weights, which was the conventional wisdom of bodybuilding, Jones decided to cut his regimen in half, giving his muscles time to recover between workouts. In his downtime he began to experiment with contraptions that would give his muscles a more even workout. Presciently, Jones realized that muscles cannot develop the same amount of force throughout their range of motion. In order to efficiently strengthen muscles, he reasoned that you needed a device that varied its resistance as a muscle went through its range of motion. It took thirty years of tinkering, but the end result was the Nautilus machine. Using a series of cams and levers, the machine was named for its resemblance to the nautilus seashell. As Jones stated in Nautilus's promotional materials, "Instead of trying to fit human muscles to an imperfect tool, the barbell—Nautilus was an attempt to design perfect tools that would exactly fit the requirements of muscles."

As we all know, just because something is a superior technology, doesn't mean that it will be readily adopted. Jones unveiled the proto-type for Nautilus, dubbed "The Blue Monster," at the Mr. America contest in 1970, where he sold his first machine. But it was Casey Viator, who came in in third place, who caught Jones's attention. Impressed with his bodybuilding potential, Jones hired Viator to work for his new company and promote the Nautilus machine. Viator won the next year, and sales of Nautilus took off.

The story of Arthur Jones and Nautilus show how even the most iconoclastic and socially gruff individual can change from an outsider to an icon. It is not even conceivable today to imagine a gym without exercise equipment based on Nautilus. Several elements go into the transition from iconoclast to icon, including luck and timing, but one element is well defined, and that is how new ideas spread through society. Ideas and products that iconoclasts bring to market follow well-defined patterns of adoption. An entire field has grown up around the study of how new ideas diffuse through society. Although it was previously thought that the method depended primarily on social factors, new evidence suggests that the underlying way in which new ideas are adopted may have as much to do with biology as sociology.

## Birds Do It, Too

The verdant hills around Southampton creep toward the sea in great undulations that, on foggy days, lap at the southernmost edges of England. A small stream, later known as Monks Brook, flows through the tiny village of Swaythling and joins up with the River Itchen on its way to Southampton. By the turn of the twentieth century, Swaythling had grown up from a quiet village whose inhabitants had farmed the hills and sold their dairy products to their neighbors in the bustling port city of Southampton. The Industrial Revolution had transformed much of England, especially London to the north. The locals, however, remained largely wedded to an agricultural life. The climate was perfect for dairy farming. Thanks to milk bottles, another product of the Industrial Revolution, farmers no longer needed to cart around gigantic vats of milk to dispense to their customers. Instead, they simply filled the bottles at the dairy. A small piece of tin foil capped each bottle. The bottles were loaded onto the delivery carts every morning, and the milkmen distributed their cargo, either by horse-drawn carriage or by motorized truck. The Swaythling residents had long taken it for granted that their daily milk would be sitting securely by their door every morning.

We don't know who the first victim was or exactly when the villagers realized that a serial criminal was living among them. But by late 1921, most people had been victimized, some repeatedly. It was always the same. The victim, still rubbing the sleep from his eyes, would open his door in the morning to pick up the bottles filled with fresh milk. Then he would see it: the foil caps opened with surgical precision. And to make matters even worse, the most prized part—the sweet cream—had been skimmed off.

Nothing was more sacred than the morning milk. Except, of course, afternoon tea. And you needed cream for that. Even though the sealed milk bottle had been a great technological advance that allowed for centralized filling and pasteurization of the milk, the spate of thefts led some to call for a return to the old ways when the milkman filled the bottles right there on the porch.

The constable was stumped. No eyewitnesses, and, to make matters worse, the thefts had begun to spread outside the village. Reports from neighboring towns began filtering in. The milk bandit had even struck in the heart of Southampton.

Of course, such widespread thievery could not remain secret forever. It was probably one of the milkmen who first laid eyes on the perpetrator. It was none other than the common English bird known as the tit. Blue tits, actually. About the size of a chickadee, blue tits are easily identified by their yellow breast feathers and blue head cap. They have a white face with a distinctive black mask running across their eyes, which gives them the somewhat beguiling appearance of a raccoon. Late in 1921, someone had finally noticed the birds following the milkmen on their rounds every morning. Within minutes of the bottles' being left on a doorstep, the birds would swoop in and pry open the foil tops. The whole process took but a few seconds, and since the milkman's attention was focused on his next delivery, he rarely turned back to see what was happening.

Under normal circumstances, this episode of bird behavior might be relegated to the annals of ornithology, but what makes it particularly interesting is that the behavior spread throughout England. Birds, of course, had not evolved to open milk bottles, but they had somehow learned this neat trick of pilfering. The ethologists James Fisher and Robert Hinde documented this remarkable spread in a landmark paper in 1949.[2] Like modern forensic scientists, Fisher and Hinde tracked the reports of milk bottle opening back to Swaythling in 1921. It was like the spread of a virus, and Swaythling was the site of the initial outbreak.

Why care about the birds? Because Fisher and Hinde's analysis pointed to something astounding about how new ideas diffuse through groups. Fisher and Hinde called it *cultural learning*. This was surprising because birds were not generally given much credit for having culture. But there it was—birds had taught each other how to skim milk. A learning mechanism that even birds use means that the way in which new ideas are adopted in humans has a very deep-seated biological mechanism behind it.

## Innovation Diffusion

Iconoclasts deal in new ideas. They innovate and, ultimately, tear down existing institutions. When Jones introduced the Nautilus, he tore down the clubby bodybuilding world and opened up fitness to a much larger audience. But the process does not happen overnight. Like the opening of milk bottles, ideas that are ultimately accepted follow a well-described trajectory of adoption in society.

According to Everett Rogers, the first scientist to empirically study innovations and the originator of the field of study, there are five attributes of innovations.[3] Bear in mind that these attributes are not objective qualities but perceptions of potential users. First, the innovation must offer an *advantage* over existing products or ideas. Second, the innovation, although potentially novel, must still be *compatible* with existing value systems and social norms. Third, the *complexity* of the innovation will determine the rate at which it is adopted by other people. The more complex the innovation is, the lower the rate of adoption. Fourth, innovations should be *triable*. This allows potential users to try out the idea without much cost to themselves. Fifth, the results of the innovation must be *visible* to other people. Again, this allows potential users to judge the relative advantages of the innovation without having to try it out themselves. Although all five attributes are important, it is really the first two—advantageousness and compatibility—that determine whether other people will adopt a particular innovation. These two attributes are also in tension with each other. The more advantageous an idea, the more it is potentially incompatible diluted form, provoked an immune response that gave lasting protection against the real thing.

It wasn't exactly rocket science, but Salk inadvertently benefited from the way in which ideas diffuse. Instead of waiting to publish his findings in a medical journal, which would have involved lengthy peer review from his competitors, he went straight to the public. On March 26, 1953, Salk appeared on CBS's national radio program and announced his results. He would be vilified for this move by fellow scientists for the rest of his life. But the public, scared by polio outbreaks, was urgently ready to adopt a vaccine. Salk's vaccine was particularly compatible with the existing social expectations. The public did not need to do anything different other than lining up for a shot, and they were already used to that. Salk became an icon overnight. And although he never won a Nobel Prize, he will always be indelibly linked to the cure for polio.

The key lesson from Salk's vaccine is the power of compatibility. Timing is important, but the iconoclast cannot control the timing of discovery. He can, however, make his ideas as compatible with existing frameworks of thought as possible. Iconoclasts are used to seeing things differently than other people, but most of the public sees things in ways that are familiar to them. Thus, the transition from iconoclast to icon means that the iconoclast must present his ideas in a way that is familiar, even if they are not.

## The Brains of Early Adopters

The birds' discovery that they could skim the cream from milk bottles by opening the tops is an amazing story of animal adaptation. There is an even deeper question behind the story, however. Why was it that the blue tits discovered this and not some other bird? Why didn't a pigeon figure this out? The fact that it was a tit and not some other bird yields an important clue about the biological basis of innovative behavior and how new ideas diffuse through societies.

Fisher and Hinde opened the door to the study of bird behavior, especially the study of how they innovate. Over the next few decades, ecologists began to systematically measure the relationship between exploratory behavior, environment, and biology. In one such setup, a wild bird is captured and then given the choice between a familiar and a novel object. The degree of novelty seeking is measured by how long it takes the bird to approach the unfamiliar object relative to the familiar one. Birds that don't like new things display characteristic signs of fear. Their feathers start to stand on end. Some species do jumping jacks, where they gingerly approach the new object and quickly make backward hops.

Unless you are an ornithologist or a bird aficionado, you probably don't give much thought to bird brains. But like people, some birds are smarter than others, and the difference has much to do with their brains. For birds, the bigger the brain, the more likely a species will assimilate new ideas. But when it comes to human brain size, there are two schools of thought. One possibility is that humans evolved large brains to solve complex problems related to survival. A big brain, for example, let an early human discover that tools could be used to kill other animals. A big brain also has more memory capacity and would let its owner use the results of past events to predict the future. Compelling arguments, but there is another side to the story.

The other school says that big brains evolved as a result of the increasing complexity of social interactions. According to this theory, as primates began living in groups, the brain expanded to deal with the complicated social relationships inherent in any community. It almost goes without saying that a major source of complexity in such a community is mate selection. The more important the social fabric, the more time members spend strategizing over politics than survival. As with existing frameworks. The Nautilus offered a huge advantage in time and efficiency over barbells, and that immediately put it into conflict with the status quo. It is here, at the extreme end of incompatibility, that we find the iconoclasts like Jones.

Iconoclasts are also innovators because they create something new, and so there is much to be gleaned from the study of how innovations are accepted or rejected. When Everett Rogers wrote his groundbreaking book, *Diffusion of Innovations*, in 1962, social scientists had been using a wide range of terms to describe innovators. Terms such as *progressist*, *experimental*, *lighthouse*, and *advance scout* were thrown around. At the other end of the spectrum, people were often spoken of as *drones*, *sheep*, and *diehards*. Colorful terms to which you could relate, but they weren't very precise. Rogers's breakthrough came when he realized that all innovations, regardless of the technology, followed a characteristic pattern of adoption, called the *S-curve* (see figure 8-1). The S-curve describes the cumulative rate of adoption of a particular idea or technology as a function of time. Early in the life of an innovation, very few people use it. With time, however, the number of adopters

**FIGURE 8-1**

**S-shaped curve of the rate of diffusion of new ideas**

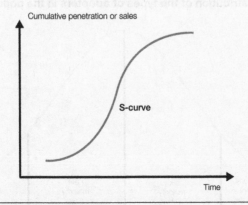

Cumulative penetration or sales

S-curve

Time

grows. For a time, the rate of growth itself increases so that the percentage of people adopting the idea accelerates. Eventually, the innovation becomes so widespread that accelerated growth is no longer sustainable, and the rate at which people adopt the idea slows down, eventually reaching zero.

Rogers eschewed the use of imprecise descriptive labels for the different categories of adopters. Instead, he simply took a cue from standard statistical descriptions of personality traits. Any human attribute, whether it is physical height or IQ, is distributed to varying degrees in the population at large. When you plot the number of people possessing each value of the attribute, you come up with a normal distribution, commonly known as the bell curve because of its shape. The bell shape comes from the fact that most people possess the average value, and extreme values are relatively rare. Rogers realized that the trait of innovativeness also followed this distribution. Most people fell into what he called the *early majority* and *late majority* categories of adopters. Only the most extreme, which he defined as two standard deviations from the average and accounting for only 2.5 percent of the population, would fall into the category of true innovators (see figure 8-2).

**FIGURE 8-2**

**Bell-curve distribution of the types of adopters in the population**

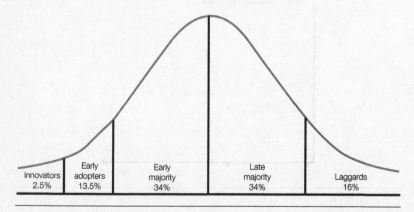

| Innovators 2.5% | Early adopters 13.5% | Early majority 34% | Late majority 34% | Laggards 16% |

Rogers did a neat trick. He realized that the S-curve resulted from integrating the bell curve of innovativeness. Integrating means adding up, in a cumulative fashion, the number of people in each category. Because the distribution of innovativeness describes *when* an individual adopts an idea, the integral of this distribution gives the S-curve of innovation diffusion, which is a graph of the number of adopters as a function of time.

This idea was given further mathematical precision by the Purdue finance professor Frank Bass. Bass said that there are really only two types of people: *innovators* and *imitators*: "Imitators, unlike innovators, are influenced in the timing of adoption by the decisions of other members of the social system."[4] This is a subtle, but important, distinction from Rogers's theory. Rogers offered a statistical argument for the rate at which innovations are adopted, but Bass offered a behavioral one. Bass said, "Innovators are not influenced in the timing of their initial purchase by the number of people who have already bought the product, while imitators are influenced by the number of previous buyers. Imitators *learn* from those who have already bought." This means that the importance of innovators will be greater at first and diminish over time.

## Jonas Salk and the Compatibility Factor

For rapid diffusion of ideas to occur, nothing beats compatibility. The first blue tit in Swaythling that discovered that he could skim the cream from the milk by piercing the foil top of the bottle was an innovator. This behavior, although novel, was completely compatible with his fellow birds' behaviors. In fact, some have argued that the milk bottle opening wasn't even an innovation, because it was simply an extension of the common motoric act of pecking at shiny things. But this is an unfair criticism. The behavior did not exist before the bottles, and so someone had to discover it. The reason it spread so quickly was because the behavior was completely compatible with what birds normally do. It is the same for human innovations.

When Jonas Salk came on the scene to tackle polio in the 1950s, he entered a fierce competition. Polio, in more ways than one, had shaped the course of history in the United States. Polio is a highly infectious virus and enters the body through the mouth, either by eating contaminated food or incidentally on the hands. Once inside the body, the virus begins multiplying in the gastrointestinal tract, after which it spreads throughout the body. Most people experience polio as a flulike illness, and that's the end of it, but about 1 percent of individuals experience much more severe symptoms. For these people, the virus enters the central nervous system and, for unknown reasons, attacks the nerves. The end result is paralysis.

In 1952, Salk decided to build on his experience with developing flu vaccines to tackle the holy grail of immunology and go for polio. Ever since Edward Jenner developed the smallpox vaccine, most immunologists believed that using a live virus was the most effective way to vaccinate an individual. The key to live vaccines depended on developing an attenuated version of the virus that actually caused the illness. Jenner used cowpox in place of smallpox. But there wasn't any such thing for polio when Salk came on the scene. Instead, he took the other route and developed a vaccine made up of killed polio viruses. It wasn't a particularly novel approach, but it was effective. Salk's major rival, Albert Sabin, who was developing a live vaccine, derided Salk, famously remarking, "Salk was strictly a kitchen chemist. He never had an original idea in his life."[5]

Salk was an opportunist. He figured that the simplest approach would win the race, and this meant a killed virus vaccine. When he found out about a new technique that allowed him to grow large quantities of polio virus in a test tube, it was a simple matter to inactivate it by dunking the virus in formalin. The killed viruses, when injected in diluted form, provoked an immune response that gave lasting protection against the real thing.

It wasn't exactly rocket science, but Salk inadvertently benefited from the way in which ideas diffuse. Instead of waiting to publish his findings in a medical journal, which would have involved lengthy peer review from his competitors, he went straight to the public. On March 26, 1953, Salk appeared on CBS's national radio program and announced his results. He would be vilified for this move by fellow scientists for the rest of his life. But the public, scared by polio outbreaks, was urgently ready to adopt a vaccine. Salk's vaccine was particularly compatible with the existing social expectations. The public did not need to do anything different other than lining up for a shot, and they were already used to that. Salk became an icon overnight. And although he never won a Nobel Prize, he will always be indelibly linked to the cure for polio.

The key lesson from Salk's vaccine is the power of compatibility. Timing is important, but the iconoclast cannot control the timing of discovery. He can, however, make his ideas as compatible with existing frameworks of thought as possible. Iconoclasts are used to seeing things differently than other people, but most of the public sees things in ways that are familiar to them. Thus, the transition from iconoclast to icon means that the iconoclast must present his ideas in a way that is familiar, even if they are not.

## The Brains of Early Adopters

The birds' discovery that they could skim the cream from milk bottles by opening the tops is an amazing story of animal adaptation. There is an even deeper question behind the story, however. Why was it that the blue tits discovered this and not some other bird? Why didn't a pigeon figure this out? The fact that it was a tit and not some other bird yields an important clue about the biological basis of innovative behavior and how new ideas diffuse through societies.

Fisher and Hinde opened the door to the study of bird behavior, especially the study of how they innovate. Over the next few decades, ecologists began to systematically measure the relationship between exploratory behavior, environment, and biology. In one such setup, a wild bird is captured and then given the choice between a familiar and a novel object. The degree of novelty seeking is measured by how long it takes the bird to approach the unfamiliar object relative to the familiar one. Birds that don't like new things display characteristic signs of fear. Their feathers start to stand on end. Some species do jumping jacks, where they gingerly approach the new object and quickly make backward hops.

Unless you are an ornithologist or a bird aficionado, you probably don't give much thought to bird brains. But like people, some birds are smarter than others, and the difference has much to do with their brains. For birds, the bigger the brain, the more likely a species will assimilate new ideas. But when it comes to human brain size, there are two schools of thought. One possibility is that humans evolved large brains to solve complex problems related to survival. A big brain, for example, let an early human discover that tools could be used to kill other animals. A big brain also has more memory capacity and would let its owner use the results of past events to predict the future. Compelling arguments, but there is another side to the story.

The other school says that big brains evolved as a result of the increasing complexity of social interactions. According to this theory, as primates began living in groups, the brain expanded to deal with the complicated social relationships inherent in any community. It almost goes without saying that a major source of complexity in such a community is mate selection. The more important the social fabric, the more time members spend strategizing over politics than survival. As we saw in the previous chapter, social intelligence is a critical aspect of getting iconoclastic ideas accepted. But what about the receiving end? What is it about the brains of noniconoclasts that determines whether a new idea is accepted or rejected?

Again, clues can be found in bird behavior. Birds might be more similar than different, but because of where they live, they just become accustomed to more or less novelty. The answer to this question is found by looking at birds raised in captivity. In such a setup, the environment is held constant, and the only thing that is different is the biology of the species. In these experiments, species differences tend to diminish. But what does pop out is the drive for exploration in young birds. Three to four weeks after the fledging stage, many birds display an intense drive for exploration. These are the adolescents. It doesn't always manifest in terms of food. Juvenile birds like to play with objects such as string that have no nutritive value. The best explanation for why some birds like to explore and others don't is that the birds pass through a period of plasticity during adolescence. If they happen to live in an environment that is complex and affords opportunity for exploration, they will do so. This experience gets imprinted during adolescence and remains relatively stable through adulthood.

Adolescence is a special time for humans as well. Setting aside the issues of sexual maturity, human adolescence is marked by an intense drive to explore the world. It is marked by a desire to try new things and eschew that which is perceived as old and stodgy. It is also the time when the dopamine system reaches its peak in physiological activity. Time and again the dopamine system pops up as a key player in both innovation and iconoclasm. Understanding the relationship between dopamine and novelty also explains why some people are receptive to new ideas. These are the *early adopters* that Rogers described, and these are the people whom the iconoclast must target if he is to become an icon.

Until recently, the relationship between dopamine and personality types was largely speculative. But two brain imaging studies have provided direct evidence of a link between dopamine activity and personality dimensions related to novelty seeking. As it turns out, this relationship changes throughout the human life span, which may explain the adolescent propensity for novelty seeking. It may also explain why, in many fields, the age of innovation and creativity reaches its peak sometime before thirty years old.

There is good evidence that the brain trades off risk and reward in dopamine-rich areas such as the striatum.[6] Is this a universal property of brain function, or is it more prominent in some individuals than others? In 2006, neuroscientists at the University of Ulm, Germany, conducted a brain imaging experiment to measure the relationship between brain activity and personality traits. The task was simple. Subjects were presented with a visual cue that looked like a two-color pie chart. On each trial, the chart indicated the probability with which the subject would win one euro. The probabilities ranged from 0 percent to 100 percent. After three seconds, the chart was replaced with either a square or a triangle. If it was a square, the subject had to hit a button on a keypad, and if it was a triangle, they had to hit a different button. On each trial, they had one second to respond. If they responded correctly, then a virtual coin was flipped with the appropriate probability to see whether they won the euro on that trial.

As in many studies before them, the scientists found a direct relationship of activity in the striatum (the brain region with the densest concentration of dopamine receptors) to the probability of winning, but this depended on the personality of the person. Individuals who scored high on the personality traits of novelty seeking and thrill seeking had the highest levels of striatal activation. Here, *novelty seeking* was defined as a tendency toward exploratory activity, intense excitement in response to novelty, and the active avoidance of monotony or frustration. *Thrill seeking* was defined by the pursuit of varied, novel, and intense sensations and experiences, and the willingness to take physical, social, legal, and financial risks to achieve these goals.[7]

The relationship between striatal activity and personality is not specific to money. A different study, conducted in Cambridge, England, found a similar link between novelty seeking and the brain's response to images of food. Here, subjects were presented with color photographs of foods that were either highly appetizing (chocolate cake, an ice cream sundae), disgusting (rotten meat, moldy bread), or bland (uncooked rice, potatoes). Subjects simply had to rate the degree to which each picture was pleasant, disgusting, appetizing, or nauseating. The brain imaging data showed that parts of the striatum became active when subjects viewed either appetizing or disgusting foods, but not bland ones. As in the German study, the Cambridge group found that the degree of striatal activation was linked to personality traits. The Cambridge group used a different personality scale, called the *behavioral inhibition/approach scale (BIS/BAS)*. The BAS measures how strongly a person pursues goals (e.g., "I go out of my way to get things I want"), their inclination to seek out new rewarding situations (e.g., "I'm always willing to try something new if I think it will be fun"), and excitability (e.g., "When good things happen to me, it affects me strongly"). The BIS, on the other hand, measures sensitivity to punishment (e.g., "If I think something unpleasant is going to happen, I usually get pretty worked up"). When the Cambridge group measured in striatal activation, they found that subjects who scored high on the BAS had the highest level of activation in response to appetizing foods. This was not simply a matter of being more emotional, because the relationship did not exist for the disgusting or bland foods.[8]

These two studies provide a key piece of evidence for the biological link between dopamine and novelty seeking. Individuals who exhibit more activity in their dopamine systems are much more likely to be people who seek out new experiences. These people should be the initial targets in a campaign to sell an idea. These people are likely to demonstrate a high level of motivation to pursue their goals, but they are not necessarily iconoclasts. These high-dopamine novelty seekers tend to be young (because young people have more active dopamine systems), but most importantly, they link iconoclasts with the rest of society.

An iconoclast who tries to sell a new idea to the masses needs to use an inefficient strategy. Most of the population will look to other people before adopting a new technology. To be efficient, the iconoclast should target the high-dopamine novelty seekers first. These people will provide the bridge to everyone else.

## Steve Jobs: The Iconoclastic Icon

You know the type: the Apple devotee. Ever since Steve Jobs created the Apple personal computer in the 1970s, the computing world has been divided between Apple people and everyone else. What is more amazing is that the Apple devotees have always been in the minority, maybe 10 percent at best. And yet, Steve Jobs has become a cultural icon by marketing to this group. He is a case study in how the quirky, iconoclastic computer designer has become one of the most worshipped people in information technology. And while Bill Gates has made vaster sums of money, it is Jobs who has achieved Buddha-like status.

Much has been written about Jobs's personality. He has been described as temperamental, aggressive, demanding, and worse. There is little doubt about his charisma at large-scale events such as Macworld Expo, but the reason that he is particularly interesting from the iconoclastic perspective is how he honed the art of marketing to the young, high-dopamine novelty lovers just described. This has nothing to do with the technical superiority of the Mac over the PC. This is about tapping into the dopamine systems of the 13.5 percent of the population Rogers identified as early adopters.

The first iPod was introduced in October 2001. With a list price of $399 for the 5 GB model or $499 for the 10 GB model, the iPod was not a cheap piece of technology. Apple has never been cheap; nor has Apple marketed its products for the budget minded. The Macintosh line of computers has always cost more than comparable PCs. So it is reasonable to ask why people are willing to shell out $500 for a device to play songs—songs that they still have to buy. The same question could be asked of why people would pay $400 for an iPhone when similar products could be had for half the price. The answer to these questions is found by asking a slightly different question, which is, what type of person would pay a premium for these ultracool gadgets?

The answer, of course, is the high-dopamine novelty seekers. Half of Jobs's genius is in his flair for design, but the other half lies in his talent for connecting to the pool of early adopters that ultimately link him to the rest of the population. Many of the iconoclasts described in this book have developed the ability to see things differently within their area of expertise. Some have developed the courage to face down the fear of the unknown, and a select few have gone on to success because of their social intelligence. But to make the transition from iconoclast to icon like Steve Jobs, you need something more than even these three qualities.

Many iconoclasts are so iconoclastic that they cannot recognize that most people do not see things differently and that most people are afraid of things that are unfamiliar. In order to reach the masses, either you need to make your ideas compatible with existing social frameworks, as Salk did with his vaccine; or if the idea is truly incompatible with existing institutions, then you need to reach out to the fraction of the population that can serve as a bridge between the ubericonoclast and the rest of the world. This is what Jobs has done.

## The Youthful Brain

Although Rogers took a statistical approach and arbitrarily said that 13.5 percent of the population are early adopters, he didn't say anything about who these people were or how they became that way. Some of the bird data suggests that environment drives innovative behavior. Under the right circumstances, even birds that are not particularly innovative will adopt exploratory behaviors. However, these studies also suggest that it is the juvenile birds that are primarily responsible for exploration. When it comes to humans, the situation is complicated by the difficulty in characterizing the environment. Humans navigate complex technologies and information systems that are changing on a daily basis. But even beyond technological challenges, the complexity of human social interactions exceeds that of any other species. To answer the question of whether iconoclasts are made or born, we must look at the development of the human brain.

The human brain is far more adaptable than previously thought. The old view was that humans are born with most of the neurons they will ever possess, and as they get older, the number of neurons steadily declines, but the modern picture of the human brain reveals a far more dynamic and complex picture of development. Different parts of the brain grow at different rates and reach maturity at different points in time. Moreover, the definition of maturity has become increasingly complicated as neuroscientists have come to understand that brain size is not the be-all and end-all of maturity.

At its most basic level, brain development can be understood as a tug-of-war between two processes: growth and pruning. Of the two, growth is more easily understood because it is quite visible. A newborn child, for example, has a brain about one-quarter the size of an adult's, but this reaches 80 percent by age two. Not all of this growth is in the number of neurons. Most of the growth is in the fibers that traverse the brain and connect different regions. These connecting fibers, or *white matter*, are swathed with insulating layers of fat and cholesterol, giving them a white appearance. The insulation, called *myelin*, increases the speed of information transmission through the fibers by a hundredfold. Because the growth of white matter generally exceeds the growth of neurons, or *gray matter*, the predominant time course of development in the brain is one of decreasing gray matter density. Part of the process is also due to the active elimination of synapses, called *synaptic pruning*. The pruning process appears to be dependent on how the neurons in a particular region are used. This means that experience literally shapes the structure of the brain during the pruning process. What is interesting, however, is that the rate at which this occurs varies by the region of the brain. In the visual cortex, synapses appear to reach their maximal density at about four months of age. After that, synaptic pruning kicks in and continues until preschool age. In contrast, the prefrontal cortex reaches maximal synaptic density at around three to four years and declines steadily through early adulthood. Until recently, these changes were essentially unobservable because it was impossible to study the brains of children and adolescents. By allowing the exquisite definition between gray and white matter, MRI has allowed neuroscientists to track brain development all the way from childhood to old age. The results provide tantalizing insights into the relative contributions of experience and genetics to make someone a novelty lover.[9]

There seems to be a direct correspondence between the development of specific cognitive functions and the onset of synaptic pruning in the parts of the brain that implement those functions. It may seem strange that less gray matter actually corresponds to maturity and not the other way around. The best explanation for this phenomenon is that the brain becomes more efficient at processing certain types of information as it matures. Initially, the brain has no template of what the world looks like. As the individual gains experience, the brain becomes better at predicting how the world works. One of the primary mechanisms of learning appears to be a specialization of synapses, which means getting rid of synapses that don't contribute and retaining those that do.

There is one exception to the pattern of declining gray matter density with age. The most lateral aspects of the brain, in the posterior temporal and inferior parietal lobes, show an unusual profile of gray matter change. Unlike all the other brain regions, which decrease rapidly beginning in adolescence, these parts of the temporal and parietal lobes show a subtle *increase* in gray matter density until about age thirty. Gray matter in this region remains remarkably stable for decades, only to decline precipitously at the onset of old age. These are the very same regions involved in perception that were highlighted in chapters 1 and 2. If we can take declining gray matter density as an index of maturity, then this suggests that in many ways perception may not ever be mature. Perception, in particular, may be the most plastic and adaptable of all cognitive functions. There is a catch. Although perception remains plastic far longer than other cognitive functions, this plasticity begins to peter out beginning around age thirty. This may explain why so many of the early adopters tend to be young adults. In addition to a robust dopamine system, their perceptual processes are more open to seeing the world in new ways.

So what about the genes? I have made a big deal about the role of dopamine in novelty seeking. And although there are statistically significant relationships between different variants of genes, such as COMT, the question remains as to how important genes are relative to experience. Making the picture more complex, genes are not static. So although one person may possess a particular form of the COMT gene, it is not active at the same level all the time. COMT activity changes throughout the life cycle and, to some extent, in response to environmental events. One study that examined the level of COMT activity in the prefrontal cortex found a steady doubling of activity from the infant brain to the adult brain.[10] This age-related increase in COMT is similar in magnitude to that conferred by the type of gene an individual possesses and is yet another argument for targeting young adults as a bridge to the general population.

## I Feel So Young

So, is early adoption all about youth? The biological evidence makes for a strong case that novelty seeking peaks during adolescence and early adulthood. Add to this the relative plasticity of the perceptual system before age thirty, and you have a strong argument for marketing to this demographic group.

The brain is lazy. It changes only when it has to. And the conditions that consistently force the brain to rewire itself are when it confronts something novel. Novelty equals learning, and learning means physical rewiring of the brain. It is a biological fact that youthful brains are more easily rewired than old brains. For the iconoclast to become an icon, not only must he possess an exceptionally plastic brain that can see things differently, but he must rewire the brains of a vast number of other people who are not iconoclasts. From this perspective, it makes sense to start with the people whose brains are most likely to be receptive to new experiences and are in such a state that they can be rewired.

As we have seen, one strategy is to appeal to the minority of the population who are generally more open to new ideas, while the other strategy is to make the new ideas seem more familiar. It helps to dichotomize these approaches because they tap into very different biological mechanisms in the brain. The novelty-seeking strategy appeals to young brains that are trying to get a leg up in the Darwinian struggle for mating rights. Possessing the newest piece of technology—for example, an iPhone—is like having a peacock's tail. It is costly in terms of time to learn new ideas, and new technology is expensive. So, for the youthful brain trying to impress competitors or members of the opposite sex, these items scream, "I am so fit that I can afford to take the time and money to invest in this new gadget."

But what if the target demographic is older? All is not lost. Although the youthful brain is more easily rewired, the older brain is not necessarily frozen in a state of inertia. It may be harder to change than the adolescent's brain, but it will change under the right circumstances. For a new idea to be adopted by a large percentage of an older population, factors such as familiarity and compatibility may weigh more heavily than the dopamine kick that accompanies novelty. Jonas Salk became an icon not through a newfangled vaccine, but through an approach that was familiar to millions of parents.

The iconoclast trying to reach a larger audience faces a tough decision in his marketing approach. Go for the high-dopamine novelty seekers and hope that they will serve as a bridge to the rest of the population, or go for the conservative masses, in which case the idea must be wrapped in a cloak of familiarity? In many ways, these two approaches are polar opposites. Aiming for one group will alienate the other. And there is no middle ground. Trying to strike a balance between novelty and familiarity will likely achieve neither.

The journey from iconoclast to icon goes beyond the three themes highlighted in this book. The "average" iconoclast possesses a perceptual system that can see things differently than other people. He conquers his fear of failure and fear of the unknown, and possesses enough social intelligence to sell his idea to other people. But the iconoclast who goes beyond mere success and becomes an icon, like Steve Jobs, possesses something even more elusive. He has the knack of wide appeal. For an iconoclast to become an icon, large numbers of people who are not themselves iconoclastic must come to accept an idea that is new to them. And that can only be achieved through one of the two roads: novelty or familiarity. Youth or experience.

# The Iconoclast's Pharmacopoeia

So IT COMES DOWN TO THIS: perception, courage, and social skills. The successful iconoclast learns to see things clearly for what they are and is not influenced by other people's opinions. He keeps his amygdala in check and doesn't let fear rule his decisions. And he expertly navigates the complicated waters of social networking so that other people eventually come to see things the way he does.

Sounds like hard work.

Neuroscience continues to reveal many of the secrets of the brain and how biological functions sometimes get in the way of innovative thinking. Knowing which parts of the brain perform functions related to perception, fear, and social relationships lets us understand how these functions go awry and how to correct them. If we have learned anything about the brain, it is how amazingly adaptable it is. While genes set the biological foundation, the structure of the brain is not static. Almost any function in the brain can be changed through hard work, practice, and experience.

While it is human nature to want to improve ourselves, that takes hard work. Wouldn't it be easier to swallow a pill that made you more daring or more willing to speak your mind? The brain contains all the machinery that runs the mind, and many, if not all, of the traits that make for iconoclastic thinking have their basis in how the brain functions. Because it is a biophysical organ, operating according to known biological and chemical reactions, the brain's functioning can also be altered, at least temporarily through the ingestion of drugs.

What follows is a brief summary of the known effects of certain psychoactive drugs. *In no way should this be taken as medical advice. Many of these substances are potentially harmful and may lead to death or disability.* Some are controlled substances and are illegal to possess without a prescription. Others are flat-out banned.

## Pharmacology 101

Every drug begins its journey by entering the body through some route. After that, its fate is determined by the competing processes of absorption and elimination. There are only a handful of ways to get a drug into the body. You either swallow it, inject it, or inhale it. The first is called the oral route; everything else is parenteral. Injections come in three flavors that depend on the depth of the shot. They can be in the skin (subcutaneous), in the muscle (intramuscular), or in a vein (intravenous). Finally, there is the mucosal route of administration, which includes absorption through membranes in the nose (intranasal) or under the tongue (sublingual).

Depending on the route of administration, a drug will be absorbed into the body at different rates. Intravenous administration, because it is directly into the bloodstream, is the fastest. Inhalation is almost as fast. Oral is the slowest because the drug must be absorbed through the

GI tract, which can take anywhere from fifteen minutes to an hour. During absorption, the concentration of the drug increases steadily in the bloodstream. At the same time, the body begins to eliminate the drug, mainly through the kidneys. The rate of elimination depends on how water soluble the drug is and how well the individual's kidneys function. Age takes a toll on this process. By age sixty, the kidneys filter at about 75 percent of the rate they do at age twenty. As a result, older individuals have a slower rate of elimination of most drugs. You will often hear of a drug's *half-life*. This is the time it takes the body to cut the blood concentration of the drug in half. The slower the rate of elimination, the longer the half-life, and the longer the drug will exert its effect in the body. Short-acting drugs have half-lives of an hour or two, while long-acting drugs have half-lives of many hours, or even days.

Know the half-life of what you take. It determines how long you will be experiencing its effects!

Some drugs are eliminated unchanged in the urine. Others go through a chemical transformation in the body called *metabolism*. For most drugs, metabolism occurs in the liver. Sometimes the metabolism converts the drug to an inactive form, but other times, the liver converts it into an active form. No hard-and-fast rules here, but if you take other drugs that are metabolized by the liver, they can interact with each other. There are so many drugs out there that it is impossible to know which ones will interact with each other. In 1990, the *Journal of the American Medical Association* published a case report of a thirty-nine-year-old woman who suffered a serious heart arrhythmia while taking the allergy medicine Seldane, along with an antifungal drug, ketoconazole. The latter inhibited the metabolism of Seldane, which, at high blood concentrations, can cause a fatal heart arrhythmia. Along with several other drugs that caused the same side effect, Seldane was eventually taken off the market.

Be careful with mixing drugs, including over-the-counter medications.

Once inside the body, the drug is then free to do its voodoo, but first it has to get where it needs to be. How does a drug know where to go? It doesn't. It goes everywhere but exerts its effect only on cells that have chemical receptors that the drug can bind to. Cells are little self-contained units. They are tiny bags of protoplasm with a tough skin of fatty, waxy material called the *cell membrane*. The membrane keeps the innards of the cell on the inside and the stuff on the outside out. The only way in or out is through special proteins and channels stuck in the cell membrane. This is where drugs work. They bind to a *receptor* in the cell membrane, and, as a result of this binding, cause a chain of biochemical events inside the cell.

The receptors, of course, don't exist for man-made drugs. They bind chemicals and hormones within the body. Drugs just hijack these receptors. If a drug mimics the effect of a naturally occurring chemical at the receptor, it is called an *agonist*. Some drugs block the receptor, in effect preventing its natural function. These are called *antagonists*. Because there is a limited concentration of a given receptor on a cell, it is possible to saturate all of them with a drug. This happens when the concentration of the drug exceeds the concentration of receptors. At this point, it doesn't matter how much more drug you take. No further effect is possible.

There is a subtlety here. Most drugs are not very discriminating. They will bind avidly to the receptor for which they are designed, but they will also bind, albeit weakly, to other receptors. When this happens, you get side effects.

Increasing the dose of a drug may increase its intended effect only to a point. After that, only the side effects will increase.

## Drugs That Change Perception

Iconoclasm begins with perception, so our discussion of psychotropic drugs begins with the broad class of substances known as hallucinogens.[1]

The prototype, of course, is lysergic acid diethylamide—aka LSD. But there are many, many others.[2] Discovered by the Swiss chemist Albert Hoffman in 1938, while working at the pharmaceutical company Sandoz, LSD was derived from a fungus that grew on grain. This broad class of naturally occurring chemicals, called ergot alkaloids, have been known for centuries to possess psychotropic properties. Some of the ergots are used to treat migraine headaches. What they all have in common is their resemblance to the neurotransmitter serotonin. LSD is startlingly potent. While most drugs require a dose from 1 to 100 milligrams to exert an effect, LSD needs only about 20 *micro*grams. This means that on a per-weight basis, LSD is about one thousand times more potent than most every other drug that acts on the brain. Even more interesting, there is little evidence that people become addicted to hallucinogens. Nevertheless, LSD is classified by the Food and Drug Administration (FDA) as a Schedule I drug, which means that there is no therapeutic potential, and it is illegal to possess.

Once inside the brain, LSD binds to almost all the serotonin receptor subtypes. With such small doses, however, the drug concentration is extremely low, and most of LSD's psychological effects are a result of binding to the $5\text{-HT}_{2A}$ subtype. Nobody really knows how LSD causes its effects, but there are remarkably consistent elements of the experience. Strictly speaking, LSD does not cause hallucinations. Hallucinations are the hallmark symptom of schizophrenia, and having them means hearing voices that aren't there, or, more rarely, seeing things that aren't there. A hallucination represents a break with reality. But LSD doesn't do this. LSD—and all the "hallucinogens," for that matter—causes perceptual distortions. Users often describe the appearance of radiant colors, trails left by moving objects, and the perception that inanimate objects such as trees and buildings swell and breathe. Sometimes people and objects appear to morph into each other. A sense of time dilation is common. Some people experience a loss of their sense of self and feel as if they become disembodied.

The canon of literature on psychedelic trips is vast. A recent treatise, with a slightly more scientific bent, is John Horgan's book *Rational Mysticism.*[3] Horgan describes his journey to (no surprise here) the West Coast, to ingest ayahuasca, which is a mixture of herbs whose predominant psychotropic ingredient is dimethyltryptamine—DMT—a chemical cousin of LSD. Many naturally occurring tryptamines have hallucinogenic effects and are found in peyote, mescaline, and psilocybin (mushrooms).

It is hard to deny the effect that these substances have had on many people. Clearly, there is a bit of bias here. Those who have written about their psychedelic trips, or written songs about them, or created art based on them, are the people who had positive experiences. Many have had bad trips laden with paranoia and anxiety. These are not the stories that are popularized. Many people report effects lasting years. Now what is interesting from the perspective of the iconoclast is the effect on perception. While many well-accepted drugs act to calm the anxious person, and therefore help to quell the fear that gets in the way of iconoclasm, only the hallucinogens act directly on the perceptual system.

From the beginning, we have seen the importance of perception to the iconoclast. The ability to see things differently than other people, chemically aided or not, is the first requirement of iconoclasm. In a double-blind, placebo-controlled study of psilocybin, researchers found an increase in "indirect semantic priming," which is a measure of the formation of remote associations.[4] Unlike with other drugs, the psychological effects of hallucinogens depend on the prior expectations of the user and the environment that they are taken in. Both of these factors play heavily in their use during religious ceremonies. Thus, subjects given LSD in a hospital setting and told they might experience schizophrenic-like symptoms and panic attacks, did.[5]

Since the heyday of psychedelic research waned in the 1960s and 1970s, relatively little hard science has been done on humans. We are left only with a large body of descriptive behavioral findings from the previous era and a paucity of data using modern brain imaging tools. In 1987, however, Dean Wong, a pharmacologist at Johns Hopkins, synthesized a radioactive tracer of LSD. Using positron emission tomography, Wong found that LSD bound to serotonin receptors located in the frontal, temporal, and parietal cortex. Binding was notably absent in the striatum.[6] Other imaging studies have measured the change in brain metabolism after the ingestion of hallucinogens. These studies consistently find that LSD and related compounds increase metabolism by up to 25 percent in the frontal cortex.[7] Activity in the thalamus, which is a sort of gateway for sensation coming from the body, is also affected. The location of LSD binding, because these brain regions are critically involved in perception, suggests that LSD's psychological effect does, in fact, result from a chemical alteration of perceptual processes.

As we saw in chapter 1, visual stimuli are ambiguous, and so perception is a psychological and biological process that assigns categories to the things we see. LSD acts directly on the brain hardware that performs this function. LSD breaks down the effects of past experience and preexisting categories, creating the possibility of unlikely perceptions. There are minimal effects on memory, and there is some evidence that LSD may actually improve some types of learning, so the individual remembers their experience. Some of the persistent effects, such as flashbacks, may also result from activation of the $5\text{-}HT_{2A}$ receptor. When the $5\text{-}HT_{2A}$ receptor is stimulated, a cascade of reactions occur inside the neuron that, within about an hour, result in the activation of several genes. Many of these genes cause proteins to be synthesized in the cell that change the physical structure of the neuron itself.[8]

After reviewing all of these findings, it is hard to find compelling evidence against hallucinogens (apart from the fact that they are illegal). Their safety profile is as good as any of the other drugs and better than the stimulants and sedatives. The hallucinogens are the only class of drugs known to affect perception directly. The main risk, because they are illegal, is that it is impossible to know what one is actually taking.

You might take amphetamine or ecstasy (an amphetamine derivative with some mild hallucinogenic effects), for example, thinking it was psilocybin.

## Drugs That Decrease Fear

As we saw in chapter 3, fear is a major impediment to iconoclastic thinking. You can have the greatest idea in the world, but an aversion to risk is so deeply wired into the human brain that the fear of failure or looking like a fool kills many potential iconoclasts before they even get out of the gate. The fault lies with the autonomic nervous system.

### Beta-blockers

When you get excited, whether it is from something wonderful or something awful, your body responds by releasing adrenaline. Adrenaline, which is also called epinephrine (yes, the same stuff in an EpiPen), is released by the adrenal glands into the bloodstream and circulates throughout the body. Epinephrine affects pretty much every organ in the body. It constricts blood vessels, raising blood pressure. It makes the heart beat faster and stronger. It dilates air passages in the lung, allowing more oxygen to diffuse into the blood. It shuts down the GI tract. And of course, it gets into the brain. In fact, a chemical cousin, called norepinephrine, acts as a neurotransmitter. The physiological term for this is *arousal*. All of this is good, and necessary, if you're being chased by a lion on the African savanna, or if you're in pursuit of that strikingly hot man or woman hanging out at the bar. Too much arousal, though, and you may find yourself paralyzed by anxiety. This is where beta-blockers come in.

There are two broad classes of receptors for adrenaline, which are called alpha and beta. In general, the alpha- and beta-receptors cause opposing effects. Different organs express different types of receptors, which is why adrenaline can simultaneously dilate bronchi in the lungs and constrict blood vessels. Primarily because of the effect of beta-receptors on blood vessels, drugs that block them are quite effective at lowering blood pressure. Lots of these drugs exist—for example, propranolol (Inderal), metaprolol (Lopressor, Toprol-XL), and atenolol (Tenormin). Because they block many of the effects of adrenaline, beta-blockers can eliminate many of the physical manifestations of anxiety. Beta-blockers are frequently used by performers to stop subtle shaking of the hands or warbling of the voice. Indeed, for performance anxiety, it is hard to beat beta-blockers. They do not cause addiction or physical tolerance. They are short acting, and the side effects are fairly minimal. The main things to worry about are their effects on blood pressure and heart rate, which could cause a person to faint. Several controlled studies have suggested that the optimal time to take a beta-blocker is about one hour before performance. This could be quite helpful, for example, for the would-be iconoclast who has to make a presentation. This type of situation, speaking in front of others, puts many people on edge and is truly the most common phobia, which is a shame, because many people have great ideas but are too inhibited or scared to present them to groups of other people. Ten to 40 mg of propranolol, an hour before a presentation, is often enough to take the edge off.[9]

Beta-blockers may have effects in the brain that go well beyond their actions on the body. Receptors for norepinephrine are found throughout the brain, but the amygdala has been a site of much interest for neuroscientists. Fearful, traumatic memories depend critically on the amygdala, and it has been demonstrated recently that beta-blockers might actually prevent the formation of traumatic memories by interfering with these receptors. The effect might work even after the trauma, essentially preventing the individual from reliving the event.[10] Of all the beta-blockers, propranolol is the one that most readily gets into the brain. As in the movie *Eternal Sunshine of the Spotless Mind*, soon it may be possible to selectively erase unpleasant memories through such pharmacologic manipulations. Because perception is, in part, determined by experience, the selective erasure of experiences has the potential to alter perception as well. So, in addition to their efficacy in treating performance anxiety, beta-blockers may help to blunt the unpleasant memory should your idea go down in flames. This would be a boon for helping people "get back on the horse."

## Antidepressants

The other big class of drugs that have potential for decreasing fear are the antidepressants. Although there is a long history of drugs that have been demonstrated to have mood-elevating effects, it is really only the modern versions of these that have captured the public's attention. We are, of course, referring to Prozac and all the Prozac-like drugs. Ever since Peter Kramer wrote *Listening to Prozac*, the possibility of using serotonin selective reuptake inhibitors (SSRIs) to tweak personality has been on the table.[11] Serotonin receptors are found all over the brain, and as with dopamine, there are several subtypes of receptors. In fact, there are a lot of subtypes, designated by descriptions such as $5\text{-HT}_{1A}$. In addition to the receptors, there is the serotonin transporter, which, like the dopamine transporter, mops up free-floating serotonin. The SSRIs block the serotonin transporter, presumably making more serotonin available to work its action. The most common drugs that do this are fluoxetine (Prozac), sertraline (Zoloft), and paroxetine (Paxil). As this is one of the most commercially lucrative classes of drugs, there are lots more. Some of the variants, such as venlafaxine (Effexor), also block norepinephrine reuptake.

For decades, psychiatrists thought that too little serotonin in the brain was the cause of impulsive decision making, primarily impulsive decisions such as suicide. The reason was that when the brains of suicide victims were examined, they were found to have lower levels of serotonin. However, more recent studies, in which healthy volunteers are temporarily depleted of serotonin, have not found a significant increase in impulsivity on standardized measures such as gambling tasks, although there is a suggestion that serotonin depletion causes reduced sensitivity to rewards of different magnitudes.[12] If this is true, there may be a role for SSRIs in straightening out an individual's utility curve, which would make him less risk averse. This could be a good thing for the iconoclast who is afraid to take a chance on his idea.

Apart from treating depression, the other major application of SSRIs is in the treatment of anxiety. If taken regularly for several weeks, SSRIs are effective in reducing panic attacks and generalized anxiety. They also seem to be quite good at reducing social anxiety. The precise mechanism by which this happens in the brain is not known, but because it takes several weeks of treatment, most scientists believe that the beneficial effect of these drugs does not result from the immediate blockade of serotonin reuptake. Instead, evidence points toward the turning on and off of specific genes within neurons.

Like all medications, the SSRIs have their share of side effects. Nausea and GI distress top the list. They usually go away after a week or so, but the problem of sexual side effects does not. Depending on which report you believe, the incidence of SSRI-induced sexual dysfunction may be as low as 15 percent or as high as 70 percent.

## Sedatives and Alcohol

Anxiety is the great inhibitor of iconoclasts. The beta-blockers work well for performance anxiety. And although the SSRIs work for general anxiety, they take many weeks to kick in, and the side effects may be too burdensome. Many people want a quick fix—you know, something to take the edge off. Enter the class of drugs known as sedatives and hypnotics. Back in the day—say, the 1950s—these drugs were called minor tranquilizers. They were all derived from a class of drugs known as barbiturates. Some of these drugs are still around today—classics such as amobarbital (Amytal), pentobarbital (Nembutal), and secobarbital (Seconal). These are the drugs your mom and pop took, but nobody really uses them much anymore. They're just too dangerous. They globally depress the entire central nervous system. They work great as an anticonvulsant and for inducing anesthesia, but they knock most people for a loop. Plus, you can fatally overdose on them. You can become addicted to them, and if you try to kick the habit, suffer seizures. Stay away from barbiturates.

In the 1960s a much safer alternative to the barbiturates was discovered: Valium—mother's little helper. This class of drugs is called the benzodiazepines (or benzos) and includes many of the all-time favorites such as alprazolam (Xanax), chlordiazepoxide (Librium), clonazepam (Klonopin), diazepam (Valium), lorazepam (Ativan), and triazolam (Halcion). Without a doubt, the benzodiazepines decrease anxiety—and quickly, too. They do this by binding to GABA receptors in the brain. GABA, which stands for gamma-aminobutyric acid, is an *inhibitory neurotransmitter*, which means it inhibits neurons from firing and is found all over the brain. GABA is necessary to keep the brain from firing out of control in seizures. Benzos are not too discriminating, and after ingestion, will bind all over the brain too. This is great in places such as the amygdala, where a benzo might decrease anxiety. Not so hot in the rest of the brain. They impair motor coordination, alertness, and memory. In fact, a common use of some benzodiazepines is to induce a state of amnesia during certain medical procedures, such as colonoscopy. Even so, many people find a small dose of a short-acting benzo helpful in situations of extreme anxiety. Just don't operate a motor vehicle or heavy machinery. The short-acting benzos are alprazolam (Xanax) and lorazepam (Ativan). Triazolam is short acting but is no longer available in the United States because of reports of amnesia and hallucinations in people taking it. Actually, any of the benzos can cause these effects. Apart from these cognitive side effects, it is important to know that benzos can be habit forming. People get seriously addicted to this stuff and have a very hard time getting off of them. If you have problems with alcohol (see below), stay away from benzos. They act very similarly.

Alcohol really belongs in a class of its own, but as far as its effects, it is very similar to the benzodiazepines. Alcohol, along with tobacco, is probably the most widely available legal drug that directly affects the brain. We need not go into the subjective effects of alcohol, for they are already widely known. The term *alcohol* includes a number of chemically related molecules. The type you ingest, however, is ethanol. And although the ingestion of ethanol is subjectively felt as physically stimulating, its main effect on the brain, like the benzodiazepines, is as a depressant. Ethanol acts on a wide range of receptors in the brain, including the GABA receptor as well as excitatory receptors. Apart from the anxiolytic effects of alcohol, one study found that heavy drinkers exhibited steeper temporal discount functions for money, which means that heavy drinkers are generally more impatient than teetotalers.[13] There are potential cardiac health benefits to moderate alcohol consumption. That said, many people, about one out of every thirteen adults in the United States, have serious problems controlling their alcohol usage. The health risks are severe: hepatitis, cirrhosis, GI bleeding, and a bunch of cancers. It is also true that a lot of famous iconoclasts, such as Jackson Pollock, were alcoholics.

So: alcohol may have a role in decreasing anxiety, but use it in moderation.

## Stimulants

Stimulants have an intimate relationship with the dopamine system and therefore one's relationship to novelty seeking and the fear of the unknown. Cocaine binds to the dopamine transporter (DAT) and blocks the reuptake of dopamine into the neuron. The amphetamine-related compounds, which include amphetamine and methylphenidate (Ritalin), also bind to the dopamine transporter and, to varying degrees, block the reuptake of dopamine. They also exert their effect on other neurotransmitters, especially norepinephrine, which is kind of like adrenaline for the brain. Amphetamine comes in two forms, called stereoisomers. The more potent form is d-amphetamine, which is sold under the trade name Dexedrine. Adderall, a drug prescribed for attention deficit hyperactivity disorder, is a mixture of d- and l-amphetamine (the other stereoisomer), which results in a smoother onset and offset of its effects. Speaking of onsets and offsets, the rate at which a drug gets into the brain has a lot to do with the "high" that people get out of it. The faster the onset of action, the more powerful the high. Inhaling or injecting drugs, because the onset is so fast, leads to addiction very quickly.

Once inside the brain, the stimulants release both dopamine and norepinephrine and block their reuptake into the neuron. Most of the stimulants actually decrease blood flow to many parts of the brain. The psychological effects include increased wakefulness and alertness. Many people experience an elevation in mood with more initiative, self-confidence, and ability to concentrate. Higher doses may lead to euphoria and increased sexual drive. Appetite becomes suppressed, and this category of drugs is frequently used to treat obesity (the "phen" of fen-phen infamy was phentermine—an amphetamine derivative). A recent entrant into the field of stimulants is modafinil, which is marketed under the trade name Provigil. The FDA approved modafinil for the treatment of narcolepsy, but its mechanism of action appears similar to that of amphetamine.

As for judgment, many of the stimulants, notably methamphetamine, are notorious for increasing impulsive decisions. This data originates from epidemiological studies showing a dramatic increase of high-risk behaviors in people addicted to methamphetamine. In one of the few studies that have examined financial risk taking and stimulant use, Martin Paulus, a psychiatrist at the University of California, San Diego, found that individuals addicted to stimulants, primarily of the amphetamine variety, exhibited greater risk-taking behavior on simple gambling decisions. He also found greater activity in the striatum of these individuals.[14] Interestingly, another study, by Brian Knutson at Stanford, found that a single dose of amphetamine equalized the upside and downside of striatal activation when individuals were anticipating either gains or losses.[15] The implication is that amphetamine might decrease loss aversion. Warren Bickel, a psychologist at the University of Arkansas, has also applied econometric techniques to study the effect of different drugs on financial decisions. In a 2006 study of delay discounting in cocaine addicts, Bickel found that the cocaine addicts had higher discount rates. This means that when it comes to financial decisions that span long periods of time, cocaine users behave much more impatiently than nonusers.[16] So far, the argument in favor of stimulants does not seem good: bad judgment and impulsive behavior do not make an iconoclast. A major problem with stimulants, apart from their addiction potential, is that they are "dirty" drugs. They are promiscuous with the neural receptors and are not very discriminating on where they bind.

The receptor side of the dopamine system is complicated. There are at least five different subtypes of dopamine receptor, each with a different effect on the neuron. The big differences, however, are in the D1 and D2/D3 dopamine receptor subtypes, which have almost opposite effects to each other. The end result of dopamine release depends on how many of each receptor subtype are expressed in a cell and how much dopamine is released. Better prospects for tweaking the dopamine system in a more productive way than stimulants might focus on these receptor subtypes.

A relatively new batch of drugs for Parkinson's disease targets the D2/D3 dopamine receptor subtype. Ropinirole (Requip) and pramipexole (Mirapex) are agonists for the D2/D3 receptor. They seem to alleviate some symptoms in early-stage Parkinson's disease, but they are weakly associated with an increase in impulsive behaviors such as gambling and sex addiction.[17] On the plus side, both drugs have been reported to promote the release of nerve growth factors in cultures of dopamine neurons, but in general, the D2/D3 agonists do not look promising for iconoclasm either. Caution: there have been some reports of heart valve disease in patients taking these drugs. A safer alternative, with similar behavioral effects, is to take L-DOPA, which is a precursor in the synthesis of dopamine and is the first-line drug treatment for Parkinson's disease. L-DOPA does improve reaction time in healthy people, but the effect is small.[18] A recent imaging study found that healthy subjects who were given a single dose of L-DOPA earned more money when performing a simple gambling task. Although the effect was small, earning about 10 percent more money, the brain imaging results showed an enhancement of striatal activity when subjects stood to win money.[19]

The problem with all the stimulants is that people get addicted to them and then they do stupid things. Milder stimulants, such as caffeine, exert their effects indirectly on the dopamine system, and although you build up tolerance, it doesn't cause a great deal of personal or societal harm. Caffeine blocks adenosine, which itself inhibits the dopamine system. Although subtle, caffeine's behavioral effects are widespread. It improves reaction time, slightly decreases error rates, increases alertness, and even aids in disengaging from one task and switching to another.[20] Although caffeine increases alertness slightly, there is no evidence that it changes risk attitudes, and most studies indicate that a good dose of caffeine has about the same effect as modafinil.[21] Like all the stimulants, caffeine will not make someone an iconoclast.

Nicotine occupies a special place. Depending on the dose and the individual's tolerance, nicotine can act as either a stimulant or a sedative (stimulant for someone not habituated to it; sedative for someone who is). Nicotine does not act through the dopamine system, but interestingly, a recent study found that smokers had steeper discount functions for money, which means that they are more likely to make impulsive decisions. They also had steeper probability discount functions, which means that they deviated from rational valuations more than nonsmokers.[22] Do impulsivity and irrational valuations make someone an iconoclast? Probably not. Although it is impossible to assess whether nicotine was the causal agent of these behavioral differences, or people who were inherently this way gravitated to nicotine, it's probably best to avoid nicotine. Plus, it's bad for your health.

## Antipsychotics

Although the stimulants have mood-elevating properties, their predominant effect on behavior is to make people more impatient. So, if stimulants aren't the ticket, then it's reasonable to ask whether blocking the dopamine system might have a beneficial effect. What's the opposite of amphetamine? Answer: the class of drugs known as antipsychotics.

Antipsychotics are now the frontline treatment for major psychiatric illnesses in which hallucinations and bizarre behavior are prominent symptoms. We're talking schizophrenia and manic depression here. The first antipsychotics were derived from aniline dyes in the 1930s, and when ingested, found to have sedative effects. By the 1950s, chlorpromazine (Thorazine) quickly gained acceptance as a treatment alternative to convulsive therapy and frontal lobotomy in schizophrenia. Many drugs like Thorazine have been synthesized since. The more common ones today are haloperidol (Haldol), risperidone (Risperdal), olanzapine (Zyprexa), and quetiapine (Seroquel). All these drugs have the pharmacological effect of blocking the dopamine D2 receptor. Some also block serotonin receptors. As a general rule, the main effect of these drugs is to decrease exploratory behavior, decrease vigilance, and generally impair cognitive performance. When healthy subjects were given a dose of haloperidol and scanned while performing a gambling task, they earned less money, and their striata were less active.[23] Plus, the side effects of these drugs are bad: slow movements, a risk of developing Parkinson's disease, painful muscle contractions, weight gain, and diabetes.

Nothing good here. Unless you are mentally ill, stay away from them.

## Hormones That Affect Social Intelligence

The final category may seem like an odd one for iconoclasm, but the growing availability and use of hormones warrants some comment. And it is hormones that may ultimately affect one's social intelligence. Hormones are different from any of the other neurotransmitters such as dopamine or serotonin. Neurotransmitters are released only between neurons and therefore remain in the brain. Hormones, on the other hand, are secreted by some organ in the body and released into the bloodstream. Because hormones enter the bloodstream, they exert effects all over the body. So, in this sense, they're very similar to drugs. In the old days, the only way to get hormones was to extract them from the part of the body that made them. Insulin, for example, used to be extracted from pig pancreas. Nowadays, most hormones are created in the laboratory by chemical methods.

The first class of hormones to consider is the steroids. All steroids begin with cholesterol. The adrenal glands, which sit like globs of fat on top of each kidney, convert cholesterol into several chemicals with different effects on the body. But there are really only two main types of steroid: glucocorticoids and mineralocorticoids. Aldosterone is the main mineralocorticoid, and it regulates the balance of salt and water in the body. The main glucocorticoid in humans is called cortisol, which is also known by the name hydrocortisone. This is the same stuff you can buy over the counter as an anti-itch cream. Cortisol is the front line stress hormone of the body. Whenever you encounter something stressful or frightening, cortisol is released. Cortisol affects so many parts of the body that it is hard to even begin to categorize them. Metabolically, cortisol inhibits cells from using glucose, stimulates the liver to synthesize more glucose, and accelerates the breakdown of fat and protein. Because it raises levels of glucose in the blood, cortisol—and, in fact, all steroids—worsens diabetes. Cortisol causes the heart to beat more vigorously and, as a result, raises blood pressure. Perhaps most prominently, cortisol inhibits the immune system, which means it works great as an anti-inflammatant.

Cortisol also has direct effects on the brain. Synthetic versions of steroids, such as prednisone, are an order of magnitude more potent than cortisol and sometimes result in bizarre changes in mood and thought. For many years, both synthetic and natural steroids were thought to alter moods in a negative way, but in the 1990s two different classes of steroid receptor were discovered in the brain, each with a different effect on mood. The mineralocorticoid receptor (MR) is a steroid receptor concentrated in the hippocampus, while the glucocorticoid receptor (GR) is found throughout the brain but especially in the striatum. The overall effect of steroids on mood appears linked to the ratio of activated MRs and GRs.[24] Under the right conditions, cortisol increases arousal, concentration, and mood.[25] Cortisol also acts synergistically with dopamine. As a result, many of cortisol's acute effects resemble amphetamine's. At high doses, however, steroids hit the receptors in the hippocampus and interfere with memory. Because of cortisol's wide-ranging effects on the body, chronic use of cortisol, or any steroid, will cause detrimental effects to many organ systems. Side effects of regular steroid use include hypertension, GI bleeding, diabetes, obesity, osteoporosis, and because of the redistribution of fat, "moon face" and "buffalo hump."

Another type of steroid hormone that has received a great deal of recent attention as a potential cognitive enhancer is testosterone. Like cortisol, testosterone is derived from cholesterol. In men, it is synthesized primarily in the testes, but women have testosterone too, made in the adrenal glands. Interestingly, the effect of testosterone depends on the age of the person. During puberty, testosterone causes the development of the external genitalia, grows body hair, and increases muscle mass. After about age twenty-five, however, testosterone levels decline steadily, so that it is cut in half by age eighty. As a consequence, the geriatric literature is burgeoning with anecdotal reports that testosterone, taken in late life, is some sort of fountain of youth, restoring failing memory and even staving off Alzheimer's disease. A chemical precursor to testosterone, DHEA, has received a lot of hype. DHEA was easily available over the Internet or through health stores. The FDA wants to regulate it. But in a two-year double-blind, placebo-controlled study of DHEA and testosterone in elderly men and women, no significant effects were found on either physical or mental function.[26] There weren't even any improvements in quality of life. Although neither testosterone nor DHEA has been conclusively shown to aid memory, testosterone does affect the emotional system of the brain. Neuroscientists in the Netherlands have found that giving a single, sublingual dose of testosterone to healthy women did two things. First, when the women viewed movies of actors making facial expressions of different emotions, the women didn't subconsciously mimic the actors' expressions. Normally, when people view these movies, they subconsciously mimic the expressions, implying that testosterone somehow decreased normal empathic responses. Second, testosterone decreased their startle responses by about 20 percent.[27] So, although testosterone might make you braver, or at least less prone to being startled, it might also make you a jerk. Plus, if you're a woman, you'll start growing chest hair.

Conclusion: testosterone and maybe DHEA do have effects on social and emotional processing (not necessarily in a good way), but their effects on memory are more hype than reality. These hormones don't appear to have good potential for iconoclasm, and may raise the risk of prostate cancer.

One hormone that might actually live up to the hype is oxytocin. Also secreted by the pituitary gland, oxytocin is released in massive amounts during labor. In women, it strengthens uterine contractions. In animals, oxytocin acts in the amygdala to reduce fear and aggressive behavior. Mice that have been genetically engineered to lack oxytocin show a profound deficit in social recognition behaviors for other mice. In some animals, oxytocin promotes monogamous pair-bonding. In humans, oxytocin can be injected, as when it is used to induce labor, or it can be absorbed intranasally through a small puffer device (Syntocinon).

A handful of recent experiments have unequivocally demonstrated that intranasal oxytocin enhances several aspects of social function in humans. A test called the "Reading the Mind in the Eyes Test" asks the subject to infer a mental state from a picture of someone's eyes. Most people do pretty well on this, although some pictures are a bit tricky. Interestingly, in a placebo-controlled study, healthy volunteers who received intranasal oxytocin did better on the difficult pictures.[28] Another study used an experimental economic procedure called the "trust game." In this game, two people take turns sending money back and forth. At each turn, the individual has the choice of keeping some money or returning some to the other player. The amount returned triples in value. Thus, there is a financial incentive to return all the money because it will triple, but each player must trust that the other person will do the same. Amazingly, oxytocin increased participants' willingness to trust other each other.[29] Much of this effect seems to be mediated by the amygdala. An fMRI study found that the amygdala activation in response to fear-inducing pictures was decreased by oxytocin.[30]

Summary: of all the hormones studied, oxytocin appears to have real potential for decreasing fear, especially in social situations. It may augment an individual's ability to read another person's intentions, increase empathy, and promote trusting behavior. The side effects appear to be minimal. Because of its labor-inducing properties, *oxytocin should definitely not be used by pregnant women.*

## Summary

So there you have it. The quick road to iconoclasm (well, not really).

Some of the drugs described here may have a limited role in augmenting certain iconoclastic brain functions while diminishing other mental processes that seem to get in the way. The SSRIs and beta-blockers have real potential to decrease performance-related anxiety and social phobia. They are also fairly safe to use and carry only mild side effects. Benzodiazepines may do the same, but you can get addicted to them. Stay away from the stimulants—too much addiction potential, and they just make you impatient and impulsive. The hallucinogens might have potential for creating new insights and perceptions, but they are, of course, illegal. And finally, the hormone oxytocin seems to function broadly to promote social bonding, which may be a boon for social intelligence.

## Introduction: Doing What Can't Be Done

1. Details surrounding Armstrong's life and death are from Thomas Lewis, *Empire of the Air: The Men Who Made Radio* (New York: HarperCollins, 1991).

2. Ibid., 254.

## One: Through the Eye of An Iconoclast

1. Dale Chihuly, interview with author, Seattle, WA, November 15, 2006.

2. See Sammy Davis Jr., Jane Boyar, and Burt Boyar, *Yes I Can: The Story of Sammy Davis, Jr.* (New York: Farrar, Straus and Giroux, 1965).

3. See Nancy Etcoff, *Survival of the Prettiest: The Science of Beauty* (New York: Anchor Books, 1999).

4. See Brian A. Wandell, *Foundations of Vision* (Sunderland, MA: Sinauer Associates, 1995).

5. See Kristin Koch et al., "How Much the Eye Tells the Brain," *Current Biology* 16 (2006): 1428–1434.

6. See G. Kanizsa, "Margini quasi-percettivi in campi con stimolazione omogenea," *Rivista di Psicologia* 49, no. 1 (1955): 7–30.

7. See Cindy Gill, "Magnetic Personality," *Pitt Magazine*, Fall 2004.

8. See Leila Reddy and Nancy Kanwisher, "Coding of Visual Objects in the Ventral Stream," *Current Opinion in Neurobiology* 16 (2006): 408–414.

## Two: From Perception to Imagination

1. See Gerald L. Edelman, *Neural Darwinism: The Theory of Neuronal Group Selection* (New York: Basic Books, 1987).

2. See Neal Gabler, *Walt Disney: The Triumph of the American Imagination* (New York: Alfred A. Knopf, 2006).

3.  For an excellent discussion of the evolutionary theory of perception, as well as many beautiful illustrations of optical illusions, see Dale Purves and R. Beau Lotto, *Why We See What We Do: An Empirical Theory of Vision* (Sunderland, MA: Sinauer Associates, 2003).

4.  See Xiong Jiang et al., "Categorization Training Results in Shape- and Category-Selective Human Neural Plasticity," *Neuron* 53 (2007): 891–903.

5.  See W. Schultz et al., "Neuronal Activity in Monkey Ventral Striatum Related to the Expectation of Reward," *Journal of Neuroscience* 12 (1992): 4595–4610.

6.  See Kalanit Grill-Spector, Richard Henson, and Alex Martin, "Repetition and the Brain: Neural Models of Stimulus-Specific Effects," *Trends in Cognitive Sciences* 10 (2006): 14–23.

7.  See Martha Farah, *The Cognitive Neuroscience of Vision* (Malden, MA: Blackwell Publishing, 2000).

8.  See S. M. Kosslyn et al., "Topographical Representations of Mental Images in Primary Visual Cortex," *Nature* 6556 (1995): 496–498; and Xu Cui et al., "Vividness of Mental Imagery: Individual Variability Can Be Measured Objectively," *Vision Research* 47 (2007): 474–478.

9.  See William James, *The Principles of Psychology*, vol. 1 (New York: Dover Publications, 1950).

10.  See A. C. Nobre et al., "Functional Localization of the System for Visuospatial Attention Using Positron Emission Tomography," *Brain* 120 (1997): 515–533.

11.  See Farah, *The Cognitive Neuroscience of Vision*.

12.  *Sporting News*, March 3, 1948, in Jules Tygiel, *Baseball's Great Experiment: Jackie Robinson and His Legacy* (New York: Oxford University Press, 1983).

13.  *Look*, March 19, 1946, cited in Tygiel, *Baseball's Great Experiment*.

14.  Tygiel, *Baseball's Great Experiment*, 52.

15.  See David J. Walsh, transcript of interview with Branch Rickey, 1955, ed. Manuscript Division and Branch Rickey Papers, Library of Congress.

16.  See Kary B. Mullis, "The Polymerase Chain Reaction," Nobel Lecture, 1993.

## Three: Fear—The Inhibitor of Action

1.  See Jackie Robinson and Alfred Duckett, *I Never Had It Made* (New York: G. P. Putnam's Sons, 1972).

2.  Ibid.

3.  Ibid.

4.  Ibid.

5.  For an excellent explanation of the human stress system, see Robert M. Sapolsky, *Why Zebras Don't Get Ulcers*, 3rd ed. (New York: Owl Books, 2004).

6.  Emily Robison, interview on *60 Minutes*, May 14, 2006.

7.  See Adam Sweeting, "How the Chicks Survived Their Scrap with Bush," *Telegraph*, June 15, 2006; and Christoph Dallach and Matthias Matussek, "Let Them Hate Us," *Spiegel Online*, July 11, 2006.

8.  Natalie Maines, interview on *60 Minutes*, May 14, 2006.

9.  See Whitney Pastorek, "Heart of Dixie," *EW.com*, January 2006.

10.  For an excellent review of the amygdala, see Elizabeth A. Phelps and Joseph E. LeDoux, "Contributions of the Amygdala to Emotion Processing: From Animal Models to Human Behavior," *Neuron* 48 (2005): 175–187.

11.  See Alex Berenson, "A Software Company Runs Out of Tricks; The Past May Haunt Computer Associates," *New York Times*, April, 29, 2001; and William M. Bulkeley and Charles Forelle, "Directors' Probe Ties CA Founder to Massive Fraud; Report Suggests Suing Wang for $500 Million; Evidence of Backdating," *Wall Street Journal*, April 14, 2007.

12.  See William McCracken and Renato Zambonini, *CA, Inc. Special Litigation Committee Report*, Chancery Court, Delaware, 2007, 5.

13.  Quotes in this section from Jim Lavoie and Joe Marino, interview with author, Newport, RI, June 7, 2007.

14.  See Daniel Ellsberg, "Risk, Ambiguity, and the Savage Axioms," *Quarterly Journal of Economics* 75 (1961): 643–669.

15.  See Ronald C. Kessler, Murray B. Stein, and Patricia Berglund, "Social Phobia Subtypes in the National Comorbidity Study" *American Journal of Psychiatry* 155, no. 5 (1998): 613–619.

16.  See K. N. Ochsner et al., "Rethinking Feelings: An fMRI Study of the Cognitive Regulation of Emotion," *Journal of Cognitive Neuroscience* 14 (2002): 1215–1229.

17.  See Phelps and LeDoux, "Contributions of the Amygdala," 175–187.

## Four: How Fear Distorts Perception

1.  See Presidential Commission on the Space Shuttle Challenger Accident, *Report of the Presidential Commission on the Space Shuttle Challenger Accident* (Washington, DC: Presidential Commission on the Space Shuttle Challenger Accident, 1986).

2.  Ibid.

3.  See James Gleick, *Genius: The Life and Science of Richard Feynman* (New York: Pantheon Books, 1982).

4.  Ibid.

5.  Ibid., 140.

6.  Ibid., 184.

7.  See Richard P. Feynman and Ralph Leighton, *"Surely, You're Joking, Mr. Feynman!" Adventures of a Curious Character* (New York: W.W. Norton & Company, 1985).

8.  Ibid., 134.

9.  This section was reconstructed from Asch's published observations of the experiment and his subjects' reactions. See Solomon E. Asch, "Effects of Group Pressure upon the Modification and Distortion of Judgments," in *Groups, Leadership and Men: Research in Human Relations*, ed. H. S. Guetzkow (Pittsburgh, PA: Carnegie Press, 1951); Solomon E. Asch, *Social Psychology* (New York: Prentice-Hall, 1952); and Solomon E. Asch, "Studies of Independence and Conformity: I. A Minority of One Against a Unanimous Majority," *Psychological Monographs: General and Applied* 70, no. 9 (1956): 1–70.

10.  See Gregory S. Berns et al., "Neurobiological Correlates of Social Conformity and Independence During Mental Rotation," *Biological Psychiatry* 58 (2005): 245–253.

11.  Martin Luther King, Nobel Lecture, December 11, 1964.

12.  Ibid.

13.  In actuality, the bell-shaped curve will be skewed because the left-hand side is bounded by zero, while the right-hand side is unbounded.

14.  See Scott E. Page, *The Difference: How the Power of Diversity Creates Better Groups, Firms, Schools, and Societies* (Princeton, NJ: Princeton University Press, 2007).

15.  James Surowiecki made much of this statistical law and even went as far as suggesting that individual decision making will always be worse than collective decision making, at least when the members of a group act independently of one another. See James Surowiecki, *The Wisdom of Crowds: Why the Many Are Smarter Than the Few and How Collective Wisdom Shapes Business, Economics, Societies, and Nations* (New York: Doubleday, 2004).

## Five: Why the Fear of Failure Makes People Risk Averse

1.  Standard & Poor's Mutual Fund Persistence Scorecard, midyear 2006.

2.  The game is called the St. Petersburg paradox because Bernoulli published it in the *Papers of the Imperial Academy of Sciences in Petersburg*: Daniel Bernoulli, "Exposition of a New Theory on the Measurement of Risk," *Econometrica* 22, no. 1 (1738; 1954): 23–36. The paradox was originally formulated by Bernoulli's cousin, Nicolas Bernoulli, but Daniel gets credit for proposing a solution.

3.  John von Neumann and Oskar Morgenstern, *The Theory of Games and Economic Behavior*, 2nd ed. (Princeton, NJ: Princeton University Press, 1947).

4.  Quotes in this section from David Dreman, telephone interview with author October 4, 2006.

5.  The steady-state value is 1/(cost of capital). See Michael J. Mauboussin, "M&M on Valuation," in *Mauboussin on Strategy*, ed. M. J. Mauboussin (Baltimore: Legg Mason Capital Management, 2005); and Merton H. Miller and Franco Modigliani, "Dividend Policy, Growth, and the Valuation of Shares," *Journal of Business* 34, no. 4 (1961): 411–433.

6.  See Mauboussin, "M&M on Valuation."

7.  See Kirk Kazanjian, *Value Investing with the Masters: Revealing Interviews with 20 Market-Beating Managers Who Have Stood the Test of Time* (New York: New York Institute of Finance, 2002).

8.  Quoted in Kazanjian, *Value Investing with the Masters*.

9.  See Gregory S. Berns et al., "Neurobiological Substrates of Dread," *Science* 312 (2006): 754–758.

10.  See Andrew W. Lo and Dmitry V. Repin, "The Psychophysiology of Real-Time Financial Risk Processing," *Journal of Cognitive Neuroscience* 14, no. 3 (2002): 323–339.

11.  See Andrew W. Lo, Dmitry V. Repin, and Brett N. Steenbarger, "Fear and Greed in Financial Markets: A Clinical Study of Day-Traders," *American Economic Review* 95, no. 2 (2005): 352–359.

12.  See Henry Ford, *My Life and Work* (Garden City, NY: Doubleday, Page & Company, 1923).

13.  Ibid.

14.  Ibid.

15.  The DAT gene has two common forms, with either a 9 or a 10 repeat (9R or 10R) of a 40–base pair sequence near its tail end.

16.  See Juliana Yacubian et al., "Gene-Gene Interaction Associated with Neural Reward Sensitivity," *Proceedings of the National Academy of Sciences* 104, no. 19 (2007): 8125–8130.

## Six:  Brain Circuits for Social Networking

1.  Picasso's *Garçon à la pipe* went for $104 million at Sotheby's in 2004, while Van Gogh's *Portrait of Dr. Gachet* sold for $82.5 million at Christie's in 1990 ($119 million in 2004 dollars).

2.  See Malcolm Gladwell, *The Tipping Point: How Little Things Can Make a Big Difference* (New York: Little, Brown and Company, 2000).

3.  For the definitive biography on Stanley Milgram, see Thomas Blass, *The Man Who Shocked the World: The Life and Legacy of Stanley Milgram* (New York: Basic Books, 2004).

4.  Letter to Marilyn Zeitlin, reprinted in Blass, *The Man Who Shocked the World*, 58.

5.  The term was popularized by John Guare in his play *Six Degrees of Separation* (New York: Random House, 1990).

6.  A set of stamped postcards was included in the packet, and each person who received it was instructed to put his or her name on a postcard and mail it back to Milgram. In this manner, Milgram was able to track the steps that each packet took on its way to Boston. To prevent a packet from endlessly looping between the same people, Milgram asked each recipient to add their name to a roster that was enclosed as part of the packet, with the additional instruction to send the packet to someone not already on the roster.

7.  See Stanley Milgram, "The Small World Problem," *Psychology Today* 1 (1967): 61–67; and Jeffery Travers and Stanley Milgram, "An Experimental Study of the Small World Problem," *Sociometry* 32, no. 4 (1969): 425–443.

8.  Quoted in Eric Schlosser, *Fast Food Nation: The Dark Side of the All-American Meal* (New York: Perennial, 2002).

9.  Ibid.

10.  See Nancy Etcoff, *Survival of the Prettiest: The Science of Beauty* (New York: Anchor Books, 1999).

11.  See M. Ida Gobbini and James V. Haxby, "Neural Systems for Recognition of Familiar Faces," *Neuropsychologia* 45 (2007): 32–41.

12.  See J. P. Mitchell, T. F. Heatherton, and C. N. Macrae, "Distinct Neural Systems Subserve Person and Object Knowledge," *Proceedings of the National Academy of Sciences, U.S.A.* 99 (2002): 15238–15243; Chris D. Frith and Uta Frith, "Interacting Minds–A Biological Basis," *Science* 286 (1999): 1692–1695; and Truett Allison, Aina Puce, and Gregory McCarthy, "Social Perception from Visual Cues: Role of the STS Region," *Trends in Cognitive Sciences* 4, no. 7 (200): 267–278.

13.  See D. I. Perrett et al., "Organization and Functions of Cells Responsive to Faces in the Temporal Cortex," *Philosophical Transactions of the Royal Society, London, B* 335 (1992): 23–30.

14.   See Ralph Adolphs, Daniel Tranel, and Antonio R. Damasio, "The Human Amygdala in Social Judgment," *Nature* 393 (1998): 470–474.

15.   See H. Kluver and P. C. Bucy, "Preliminary Analysis of Functions of the Temporal Lobes in Monkeys," *Archives of Neurology and Psychiatry* 42 (1939): 979–1000.

16.   See David G. Amaral, "The Amygdala, Social Behavior, and Danger Detection," *Annals of the New York Academy of Sciences* 1000 (2003): 337–347.

17.   See Elizabeth A. Phelps et al., "Performance on Indirect Measures of Race Evaluation Predicts Amygdala Activation," *Journal of Cognitive Neuroscience* 12, no. 5 (2000): 729–738.

18.   See Andreas Olsson et al., "The Role of Social Groups in the Persistence of Learned Fear," *Science* 309 (2005): 785–787; and Matthew D. Lieberman et al., "An fMRI Investigation of Race-Related Amygdala Activity in African-American and Caucasian-American Individuals," *Nature Neuroscience* 8, no. 6 (2005): 720–722.

19.   See Betsy Morris, "Arnold Power," *Fortune*, August 9, 2004.

20.   See William Raft Kunst-Wilson and R. B. Zajonc, "Affective Discrimination of Stimuli That Cannot Be Recognized," *Science* 207 (1980): 557–558.

21.   See Gur Huberman, "Familiarity Breeds Investment," *Review of Financial Studies* 14, no. 3 (2001): 680.

22.   See Peter S. Dodd, Roby Muhamad, and Duncan J. Watts, "An Experimental Study of Search in Global Social Networks," *Science* 301 (2003): 827–829; and Duncan J. Watts, *Six Degrees: The Science of a Connected Age* (New York: W. W. Norton & Company, 2003).

23.   See Jon M. Kleinberg, "Navigation in a Small World," *Nature* 406 (2000): 845; and Duncan J. Watts and Steven H. Strogatz, "Collective Dynamics of 'Small-World' Networks," *Nature* 393 (1998): 440–442.

24.   See Linus Torvalds, "What Would You Like to See Most in Minix?" 1991, http://groups.google.com/group/comp.os.minix/msg/b813d52cbc5a044b.

25.   See Sarah F. Brosnan and Frans B. M. de Waal, "Monkeys Reject Unequal Pay," *Nature* 425 (2003): 297–299.

26.   See W. Guth, R. Schmittberger, and B. Schwarze, "An Experimental Analysis of Ultimatum Bargaining," *Journal of Economic Behavior and Organization* 3, no. 4 (1982): 367–388.

27.   See Alan G. Sanfey et al., "The Neural Basis of Economic Decision-Making in the Ultimatum Game," *Science* 300 (2003): 1755–1758.

28.   Chairman's Letter to Berkshire Hathaway Shareholders, 2005, p. 7.

29.   See Ozgur Gurerk, Bernd Irlenbusch, and Bettina Rockenbach, "The Competitive Advantage of Sanctioning Institutions," *Science* 312 (2006): 108–111.

## Seven: Private Spaceflight—A Case Study of Iconoclasts Working Together

1.   www.bigelowaerospace.com (accessed December 2006).

2.   See David H. Freedman, "Entrepreneur of the Year," *Inc.*, January 2005.

3.   Ibid.

4.  See Michael A. Dornheim, "Flying in Space for Low Cost," *Aviation Week & Space Technology*, April 20, 2003.

5.  http://www.xprize.org/about/our-story.

6.  Keynote address at the International Symposium for Personal Spaceflight (ISPS), Las Cruces, NM, October 18, 2006.

7.  See Mike Mullane, *Riding Rockets: The Outrageous Tales of a Space Shuttle Astronaut* (New York: Scribner, 2006), 35.

8.  See S. Suzette Beard and Janice Starzzyk, *Space Tourism Market Study: Orbital Space Travel and Destinations with Suborbital Space Travel* (Bethesda, MD: Futron Corporation, 2002).

9.  Futron updated its projections in 2006 to account for changes in technology and assumptions about potential passenger attributes.

10.  See Sam Dinkin, "Go Granny Go!" *Space Review*, 2005, http://www.thespacereview.com/article/429/1.

11.  Unless otherwise noted, quotes in this section are from Reda Anderson, personal interview with author, October 16–20, 2006.

12.  Quotes in this section are from Ray Duffy, personal interview with author, October 16–20, 2006.

13.  ISPS, October 18, 2006.

## Eight: When Iconoclast Becomes Icon

1.  See Patricia Sullivan, "Arthur Jones: Revolutionized Exercise Industry," *Washington Post*, August 30, 2007.

2.  See J. Fisher and R. A. Hinde, "The Opening of Milk Bottles by Birds," *British Birds* 42 (1949): 347–357; and R. A. Hinde and J. Fisher, "Further Observations on the Opening of Milk Bottles by Birds," *British Birds* 44 (1951): 392–396.

3.  See Everett M. Rogers, *Diffusion of Innovations*, 5th ed. (New York: Free Press, 2003).

4.  See Frank M. Bass, "A New Product Growth for Model Consumer Durables," *Management Science* 15, no. 5 (1969): 215–227.

5.  Wilfrid Sheed, "Virologist," *Time*, March 29, 1999.

6.  See Kerstin Preuschoff, Peter Bossaerts, and Steven R. Quartz, "Neural Differentiation of Expected Reward and Risk in Human Subcortical Structures," *Neuron* 51, no. 3 (2006): 381–390.

7.  See Birgit Abler et al., "Prediction Error as a Linear Function of Reward Probability Is Coded in Human Nucleus Accumbens," *Neuroimage* 31 (2006): 790–795.

8.  See John D. Beaver et al., "Individual Differences in Reward Drive Predict Neural Responses to Images of Food," *Journal of Neuroscience* 26, no. 19 (2006): 5160–5166.

9.  See Arthur W. Toga, Paul M. Thompson, and Elizabeth R. Sowell, "Mapping Brain Maturation," *Trends in Neurosciences* 29, no. 3 (2006): 148–159.

10.  See Elizabeth M. Tunbridge et al., "Catechol-o-methyltransferase Enzyme Activity and Protein Expression in Human Prefrontal Cortex Across the Postnatal Lifespan," *Cerebral Cortex* 17, no. 5 (2006): 1206–1212.

## Appendix: The Iconoclast's Pharmacopoeia

1.   For a comprehensive modern review of the psychobiology of hallucinogens, see David E. Nichols, "Hallucinogens," *Pharmacology & Therapeutics* 101 (2004): 131–181.

2.   The most comprehensive catalog of these substances, and their subjective effects, is to be found in the pair of books by Alexander and Ann Shulgin, the husband-and-wife team of "chemical explorers." See Alexander Shulgin and Ann Shulgin, *PiHKAL: A Chemical Love Story* (Berkeley, CA: Transform Press, 1991); and Alexander Shulgin and Ann Shulgin, *TiHKAL: The Continuation* (Berkeley, CA: Transform Press, 1997). PiHKAL stands for "phenethylamines I have known and loved." TiHKAL stands for "tryptamines I have known and loved."

3.   See John Horgan, *Rational Mysticism: Dispatches from the Border Between Science and Spirituality* (New York: Houghton Mifflin Company. 2003).

4.   See M. Spitzer et al., "Increased Activation of Indirect Semantic Associations Under Psilocybin," *Biological Psychiatry* 39 (1996): 1055–1057.

5.   See Nichols, "Hallucinogens," 131–181.

6.   See D. F. Wong et al., "Localization of Serotonin 5-HT2 Receptors in Living Human Brain by Positron Emission Tomography Using N1-([11C]-methyl)-2-Br-LSD," *Synapse* 1, no. 5 (1987): 393–398.

7.   See F. X. Vollenweider et al., "Positron Emission Tomography and Fluorodeoxyglucose Studies of Metabolic Hyperfrontality and Psychopathology in the Psilocybin Model of Psychosis," *Neuropsychopharmacology* 16 (1997): 357–372.

8.   See Nichols, "Hallucinogens,"131–181.

9.   See Franklin R. Schneier, "Social Anxiety Disorder," *New England Journal of Medicine* 355 (2006): 1029–1036.

10.   See Jacek Debiec and Joseph E. LeDoux, "Noradrenergic Signaling in the Amygdala Contributes to the Reconsolidation of Fear Memory: Treatment Implications for PTSD," *Annals of the New York Academy of Sciences* 1071 (2006): 521–524; and James L. McGaugh, "Memory—a Century of Consolidation," *Science* 287 (2000): 248–251.

11.   See Peter D. Kramer, *Listening to Prozac* (New York: Viking, 1993).

12.   See Robert D. Rogers et al., "Tryptophan Depletion Alters the Decision-Making of Healthy Volunteers Through Altered Processing of Reward Cues," *Neuropsychopharmacology* 28 (2003): 153–162.

13.   See Matt Field et al., "Delay Discounting and the Alcohol Stroop in Heavy Drinking Adolescents," *Addiction* 102 (2007): 579–586.

14.   See D. S. Leland et al., "Young Adult Stimulant Users' Increased Striatal Activation During Uncertainty Is Related to Impulsivity," *Neuroimage* 33, no. 2 (2006): 725–731.

15.   See B. Knutson et al., "Amphetamine Modulates Human Incentive Processing," *Neuron* 43 (2004): 261–269.

16.   See Sarah H. Heil et al., "Delay Discounting in Currently Using and Currently Abstinent Cocaine-Dependent Outpatients and Non-Drug-Using Matched Controls," *Addictive Behaviors* 31 (2006): 1290–1294.

17.  See D. Weintraub et al., "Association of Dopamine Agonist Use with Impulse Control Disorders in Parkinson Disease," *Archives of Neurology* 63, no. 7 (2006): 969–973.

18.  See P. Rihet et al., "Dopamine and Human Information Processing: A Reaction-Time Analysis of the Effect of Levodopa in Healthy Subjects," *Psychopharmacology* 163 (2002): 62–67.

19.  See Mathias Pessiglione et al., "Dopamine-Dependent Prediction Errors Underpin Reward-Seeking Behaviour in Humans," *Nature* 442 (2006): 1042–1045.

20.  See Zoe Tieges et al., "Caffeine Improves Anticipatory Processes in Task Switching," *Biological Psychiatry* 73, no. 2 (2006): 101–113.

21.  See W. D. Killgore et al., "The Effects of Caffeine, Dextroamphetamine, and Modafinil on Humor Appreciation During Sleep Deprivation," *Sleep* 29, no. 6 (2006): 841–847.

22.  See Brady Reynolds et al., "Delay Discounting and Probability Discounting as Related to Cigarette Smoking Status in Adults," *Behavioural Processes* 65 (2004): 35–42.

23.  See Pessiglione et al., "Dopamine-Dependent Prediction Errors," 1042–1045.

24.  See E. Ron de Kloet, Melly S. Oitzl, and Marian Joëls, "Stress and Cognition: Are Corticosteroids Good or Bad Guys?" *Trends in Neurosciences* 22, no. 10 (1999): 422–426.

25.  See Werner Plihal et al., "Corticosteroid Receptor Mediated Effects on Mood in Humans," *Psychoneuroendocrinology* 21, no. 6 (1996): 515–523; Sonia J. Lupien et al., "The Modulatory Effects of Corticosteroids on Cognition: Studies in Young Human Populations," *Psychoneuroendocrinology* 27 (2002): 401–416; and Heather C. Abercrombie et al., "Cortisol Variation in Humans Affects Memory for Emotionally Laden and Neutral Information," *Behavioral Neuroscience* 117, no. 3 (2003): 505–516.

26.  See K. Sreekumaran Nair et al., "DHEA in Elderly Women and DHEA or Testosterone in Elderly Men," *New England Journal of Medicine* 355, no. 16 (2006): 1647–1659.

27.  See E. J. Hermans, P. Putman, and J. van Honk, "Testosterone Administration Reduces Empathetic Behavior: A Facial Mimicry Study," *Psychoneuroendocrinology* 31 (2006): 859–866; and E. J. Hermans et al., "A Single Administration of Testosterone Reduces Fear-Potentiated Startle in Humans," *Biological Psychiatry* 59 (2006): 872–874.

28.  See Gregor Domes et al., "Oxytocin Improves 'Mind-Reading' in Humans," *Biological Psychiatry* 61 (2007): 731–733.

29.  See M. Kosfeld et al., "Oxytocin Increases Trust in Humans," *Nature* 435 (2005): 673–676.

30.  See Peter Kirsh et al., "Oxytocin Modulates Neural Circuitry for Social Cognition and Fear in Humans," *Journal of Neuroscience* 25, no. 49 (2005): 11489–11493.

Note: Page numbers in *italics* indicate illustrations.

# ABOUT THE AUTHOR

GREGORY BERNS IS THE DISTINGUISHED Chair of Neuroeconomics at Emory University, where he directs the Center for the Biological Study of Collective Action. He is a professor in the departments of psychiatry and economics and in the Goizueta Business School. He is a founding member of the Society for Neuroeconomics. For the past fifteen years, he has used brain imaging technologies to study the neurobiology of human motivation and decision making, especially the effects of novelty and peer pressure. His work has been published in prestigious journals like *Science and Neuron*, and he is the author of *Satisfaction*, a book about the neurobiology of happiness. Professor Berns appears frequently in the media, including the *Wall Street Journal*, the *New York Times*, CNN, and *Primetime*. He received an AB in physics from Princeton University; a PhD in biomedical engineering from the University of California, Davis; and an MD from the University of California, San Diego.